ECONOMICS
FOR
NONPROFIT
MANAGERS

DENNIS R. YOUNG AND RICHARD STEINBERG

THE FOUNDATION CENTER

Library of Congress Cataloging-in-Publication Data

Young, Dennis R., 1943–
    Economics for nonprofit managers / Dennis R. Young and Richard
Steinberg.
        p.   cm.
    Includes bibliographical references and index.
    ISBN 0–87954–610–7
    1. Nonprofit organizations—Management.   2. Managerial economics.
3. Microeconomics.   I. Steinberg, Richard.   II. Title.
HD62.6.Y676   1995
658'.048—dc20   95–20119
                                                                      CIP

ECONOMICS
FOR
NONPROFIT
MANAGERS

CONTENTS

LIST OF FIGURES

LIST OF TABLES

ACKNOWLEDGMENTS

We want to express our appreciation to the Center on Philanthropy at Indiana University. Young thanks the Center for hosting him as a visiting scholar during the 1992-93 academic year, enabling him to spend time on this book. Steinberg thanks the Center for providing him with release time to work on this project. Young also wishes to thank the Mandel Center for Nonprofit Organizations at Case Western Reserve University for support of incidental expenses and for the opportunity to engage in this project. Thanks are due to the staff of the Center, especially Caroline Saslaw, for their help during various stages of preparing the manuscript.

Young wishes to thank the Mandel Center students enrolled in MAND 415 during the fall of 1992 for encouraging him to undertake and continue this project, which grew out of his lecture notes. Both authors wish to thank Dirk Holsopple for his work in preparing the figures for this textbook, and Marshall Curry for his extensive and insightful comments on draft chapters.

We would also like to thank each other for mutual encouragement and for tolerance of each other's very different working habits and schedules.

Dennis R. Young
Richard Steinberg

FOREWORD

Dennis Young and Richard Steinberg have produced the first introductory textbook intended primarily for students of nonprofit management. These organizations constitute a rapidly expanding sector of the economy, and economics has much to contribute to our understanding of the factors that shape their decisions.

Nonprofit organizations combine attributes of the private sector and government in fascinating ways. Both students and managers of nonprofit organizations need to understand the elements of the economist's "tool kit," and Young and Steinberg have provided a fine introduction to microeconomics as it applies to the nonprofit sector in a mixed economy. Amending the conventional analysis to accommodate the special characteristics of the nonprofit marketplace, they have done much more, however, than simply demonstrate that traditional economic analysis can be extended to nonprofit organizations.

By showing that nonprofit organizations typically face competition not only from other nonprofits but from private firms and sometimes governments, Young and Steinberg challenge the reader to think about differing organizational goals ("objective functions") and how they affect the outcome of the competitive process. Are nonprofits more altruistic than other organizations? Are nonprofit managers really different from their private enterprise and government counterparts—that is, less motivated to maximize their own incomes? By highlighting the "nondistribution constraint," which restricts what a nonprofit organization may do to achieve its goals—for example, paying out to managers any profit they generate—Young and Steinberg compel the reader to think about regulatory problems and the limits to competition in industries where consumers are poorly informed.

They also show how subjects examined in conventional texts can be understood through illustrations from the nonprofit world. Thus, for example, when they turn to labor markets, they focus on volunteer labor. While volunteer labor is not even counted in official labor-force statistics, and is generally unimportant for private firms, it is a significant factor in the nonprofit world, and Young and Steinberg show how even volunteers respond to economic forces despite their lack of pay. Similarly, when they discuss how revenues affect a nonprofit organization's decisions, they focus on charitable donations, demonstrating for the reader how supply and demand operate even in unconventional markets, the reasons why people donate, and how a nonprofit organization is able to affect the amount of donations it receives.

The concept of "market failure," applied to activities such as basic medical research and aid to the poor—which private firms cannot be counted on to provide at efficient levels because they benefit persons other than those who pay for them—is fundamentally important in economics. In most textbooks, such activities are said to justify a role for government. Young and Steinberg show, however, how nonprofit organizations are also active in the provision of such goods and services. In the process, they justify the need for nonprofit organizations in a predominately private-enterprise economy, and they highlight the questions of what society should expect from nonprofits relative to government.

These discussions make it clear that nonprofits are both like and unlike private firms and public-sector entities. No organization can avoid making decisions about precisely what goods and services to provide, how to allocate resources to produce them, to whom they should be made available, and how to finance these activities. Economics can help us understand how the ways in which organizations deal with these matters determine which organizations will survive, whether nonprofit organizations will displace private firms from certain markets or industries in the long run or, instead, be driven out by them, and whether taxes and subsidies have the same kinds of effects on nonprofit organizations as they do on private firms.

In chapter after chapter, problems faced by nonprofit managers are analyzed with the tools of introductory microeconomics. Young and Steinberg illustrate their lessons with lively examples involving such varied nonprofits as universities, museums, day-care centers, and Meals on Wheels programs, while touching on such practical questions as whether to raise funds through direct mail or phone solicitation and whether public subsidies to nonprofits distort those decisions. As a result, readers of this well-written introduction to economics are rewarded by learning the fundamentals of economics as they apply both to decisions faced by nonprofit managers in output and input markets and to the relationships of nonprofits with private firms and governments.

Burton A. Weisbrod

PREFACE

Only within the last decade have rigorous programs of graduate education been developed at U.S., Canadian, and British universities to prepare current and future managers and leaders of private nonprofit organizations for the special challenges they face. The new master's degree and certificate programs in nonprofit management, as well as new nonprofit management concentrations within business and public administration curricula, recognize that nonprofit organizations have become an increasingly critical component of our public service delivery system, our democratic society, and our market economy. These programs also acknowledge that nonprofit organizations have unique characteristics that require special curricular attention. No longer is it acceptable to ignore the nonprofit sector and assume that its participants will accumulate and adapt the knowledge they need from programs designed for other venues, namely business and government. The special issues that nonprofits face in managing paid and volunteer work forces, raising and managing charitable funds and other revenues, defining and pursuing public service missions, responding to particular requirements of the law, maintaining fiscal integrity, evaluating their performance in the absence of a clear bottom line, and maintaining accountability to multiple constituencies now come together in new curricula that recognize nonprofit management and leadership as an emerging field.

Despite the whirlwind of activity in developing nonprofit management curricula in recent years, one area of educational concern—that of economic analysis—has shown only slow progress. Few would argue against the importance of including this discipline in the tool kits of nonprofit managers and leaders. After all, the stewardship of scarce resources can make or break any nonprofit organization. Yet few of the new programs to date include courses in economics for nonprofit managers. There are two related reasons for this. First, many of the students entering nonprofit management programs are not well trained in quantitative analysis and may not have previously studied economics. Many of these students are wary of courses that require quantitative thinking or mathematical analysis and have avoided such courses in their educational experience to date. The typical education of a would-be nonprofit manager includes training in some of the "softer" disciplines, such as social work, education, the humanities, or the arts. As a result, students are reluctant to undertake graduate studies that emphasize quantitative and analytical reasoning, and educators, mindful of the marketplace, are reluctant to force-feed them.

The second factor slowing the introduction of economic analysis into graduate curricula for nonprofit managers and leaders is the lack of appropriate curricular materials and teaching strategies. Most texts on economics are designed for the economics major or the policy analyst and emphasize the mathematical development of theory and the quantitative analysis of problems of business and government. Few economics texts even recognize that there is a third, nonprofit sector, much less include discussion or examples relevant to it.

These two factors are related as follows: Because there are no appropriate materials, attempts to introduce economics into nonprofit curricula have suffered from the intimidating and irrelevant nature of existing texts. This has been unfortunate for two reasons. First and foremost, it is critical for nonprofit managers to be able to utilize the tools and ideas of economic analysis to make better decisions. It is no accident that business and public administration curricula generally include economics as a critical element, and nonprofit organizations have just as much need of the skills and knowledge relating to that discipline. Second, ironically, economists have been at the forefront of recent research aimed at understanding the nonprofit sector and analyzing its policy and management issues. Nonprofit managers should have access to this emerging research to inform their own decisions, but the translation of research into pedagogy has not yet occurred. An exception is Burton Weisbrod's *The Nonprofit Economy* (1988), which gives students a broad understanding of the role of nonprofits in the U.S. economy but does not attempt to teach them principles of economic analysis.

This textbook tries to address the need to introduce the ideas of economic analysis into the educational portfolios and conceptual tool kits of nonprofit managers and leaders. Its basic premise is that the concepts of microeconomic analysis, such as opportunity cost, analysis at the margin, market equilibrium, market failure, and cost-benefit analysis, are critically relevant to the management and policy issues that nonprofit managers and leaders grapple with every day. Moreover, these concepts are not terribly difficult to understand, nor does understanding them require a high level of mathematical preparation. One simply needs to translate these ideas into plain English and simple mathematical constructs and to apply them specifically to the problems of nonprofit organizations. Nonprofit managers do not have to become economists, but they ought to be able to employ economic reasoning and converse with economic analysts and consultants.

We believe that this book will also interest those who are already familiar with economics as traditionally taught and have become interested in nonprofit organizations. Readers in this category should pay special attention to the details of our presentation that apply specifically to nonprofit organizations. These include the special role of the nondistribution-of-profit constraint in creating and abating market failures, the economics of fundraising and volunteer recruitment, the differing objective functions and regulatory environments of nonprofit organizations, the special impact of competition on nonprofit performance, interactions among various sources of revenue, the role of cross-subsidization, and pricing of services with distributional objectives. Some of our results extend the findings of traditional microeconomics. For example, the rules for output determination and the effects of entry on equilibrium appear here in a slightly different form.

We have been induced to write these chapters after years of trying to use other texts in Case Western Reserve University and Indiana University/Purdue University at Indianapolis' courses on nonprofit economics. It all began with an experiment by Dennis Young to write up his lecture notes in a readable, accessible style. He found that students were hungry for such material and that it improved their motivation and their ability to learn economics. Both of us are indebted to our students for their encouragement and hope that this project will stimulate faculty in other nonprofit programs to include economics as a basic part of their curricula. We are convinced that no program in nonprofit management at the graduate level can claim to be complete without economic analysis, and that the most successful programs in this new field will be those that can present this subject to their students in an effective and accessible manner.

Dennis R. Young
Richard Steinberg
October 1994

CHAPTER **1**

Why Should a Nonprofit Manager Study Economics?

- A community agency for the elderly runs a day-care program and a Meals on Wheels program. How should it allocate its limited staff and budget between these two programs?
- A relief agency receives a grant to plan a program to help refugees. Should it add a staff member or buy a computer system with these funds?
- A private college wishes to raise money to build a new wing on its library. Should it undertake a direct-mail campaign or seek funds through personal solicitations, or both? How much money should the college invest in these fund-raising efforts?
- A church runs a popular adult-education program that is losing money. Should the church expand or contract the program?
- A museum sells art reproductions in its gift shop. How high should the quality of these items be, and at what price should they be offered for sale?
- A community foundation receives a major gift from a local benefactor. How should it invest these funds?
- A small hospital wishes to provide home health care services. Should it do so on its own or in partnership with other hospitals?
- An orchestra requires major repairs to its concert hall. Should it dip into its endowment to undertake these repairs?

- A local united fund wishes to attract a well-known youth agency into its system. What share of the proceeds should it offer to induce this potential new member to join?
- An environmental advocacy group is mounting a campaign to clean up hazardous waste in its community. Should it hire a paid public relations staff member or continue to rely exclusively on volunteer efforts?
- A community theater in a working-class neighborhood must revise its ticket prices in order to account for increased expenses. How should it design its price schedule in order to stay fiscally healthy while accommodating community members who cannot pay much to attend performances?
- A nonprofit mental health agency is considering raising money by offering its services at a profit to local businesses for their employee benefit plans, but it could lose money if donors react adversely or not enough businesses sign up. Should it go ahead with the initiative?
- A nonprofit research institute is considering a performance compensation system whereby its staff members would receive salary bonuses tied to the dollar value of the research contracts they bring in. Should it go ahead with this proposal?

What do these decisions faced by managers and leaders of various nonprofit organizations have in common? In a word, they are all decisions about the *effective use of scarce resources* to accomplish organizational goals. In each case, leaders must choose among courses of action because available resources are not sufficient for pursuing all desired possibilities, or because making one choice eliminates others. Thus, if the relief agency buys a new computer with its grant, it will not have funds to add a staff member. If the youth agency joins the united fund, it must forgo funds it would otherwise raise on its own. In all such cases, actions and decisions require *trade-offs*. The relief agency must weigh the benefits of a computer against the benefits of having another staff member. The youth agency must compare the benefits of united fund raising to the benefits of raising funds by itself. The orchestra must weigh the benefits of using its endowment for a current crisis against the benefits of saving the funds for future initiatives or security. And the advocacy group must compare the benefits of using its volunteers for public relations against the benefits the volunteers could produce in fund raising or other assignments.

These kinds of decision-making situations are a principal reason why managers and leaders in nonprofit organizations should study economics.

No less than leaders in business and government, nonprofit leaders must make decisions about allocating scarce, valuable resources, and they must make difficult choices and trade-offs. The discipline of economics is designed to help decision makers make logical decisions in circumstances of scarcity. Indeed, it can be argued that the study of economics is even more important in the nonprofit world than in the business world because some of the choices are complicated by the fact that they involve unpriced resources such as volunteer time or services provided at no charge. This makes the values of alternatives more difficult to measure and choices more difficult to make. The basic principles of economics provide a framework for thinking through such nuances of nonprofit decision making.

Operational decision making is not the only reason why nonprofit managers and leaders should study economics. These leaders operate in complex, often harsh public policy environments that are also driven by the scarcity of resources. In many cases, nonprofit organizations are in business to change that environment for the better. In all cases, they are significantly affected by the realities of the world around them. Consider, for example, a few of the ways in which nonprofit organizations in the United States are affected by public policy and governmental decision making:

- Determination by the Internal Revenue Service (IRS) of whether a commercial activity is related or unrelated to a nonprofit organization's mission affects whether the profits will be taxed and hence the degree to which the organization may decide to undertake the activity.
- Postal subsidies to nonprofit organizations affect the degree to which these organizations can mount public appeals and the choices they make between mail-based and other forms of solicitation.
- Policies specifying how donated property may be valued and its value deducted from personal income for tax purposes affect whether such property is donated to nonprofits or disposed of in other ways.
- Income-tax rates affect how much disposable income individuals and corporations have and how much of it they are willing to donate to charities.
- Interpretation of antitrust laws affects whether nonprofits choose to collaborate or compete with one another and how they determine their pricing and service policies.

These policies affect all nonprofit organizations. Nonprofits operating in particular fields (e.g., environmental conservation, housing for the poor, the fine arts, or higher education) will be familiar with a host of other policies that affect their decision making—for example, tax credits for pollution control, housing subsidies, grants for artists, or student loans. All these policies represent social trade-offs in the use of scarce resources. All nonprofits are affected by public policies, and many advocacy-oriented nonprofits are in business to seek changes in those policies. Without an appreciation of the choices and trade-offs involved in these policies, nonprofit leaders can neither react effectively to public policies already in place nor develop intelligent alternatives to those policies they wish to change.

The preceding examples provide another important reason to study economics. Government policies, by altering financial *incentives*, can influence the behavior of nonprofit organizations and their constituencies. Tax rates influence how much people give to charity, service subsidies such as scholarships and low-cost loans affect how much consumers demand and how much organizations are willing to supply of particular goods and services, and subsidies on inputs such as postal rates influence how much nonprofit organizations use particular resources such as the postal service. Thus, if nonprofit leaders are to understand, effectively utilize, and intelligently influence the formulation of policies affecting their organizations or constituents, they must understand the effects of incentives. In large measure, this is what economics is about—the study of incentives and how these incentives influence the behavior of individuals and organizations involved in choices about the use of scarce resources.

In the remainder of this chapter we take a quick tour of the conceptual framework of economics. We first define economics as a field of study and characterize it as a science. Since economics is about valuing goods and services, we discuss the basis on which value is measured and consider the various institutional mechanisms through which society allocates valuable resources. We go on to consider the two main branches of economics, microeconomics and macroeconomics, and then give attention to the essential ideas that economists use to guide their thinking. This takes us into a discussion of economic efficiency, the principal criterion by which economists judge the merit of alternative actions. Finally, we note the limitations of this criterion and juxtapose it with various notions of equity or fairness.

WHAT IS ECONOMICS?

In a general sense, economics is about the way people, through organizations and as individuals, utilize scarce resources to satisfy their wants and needs. More precisely, economics is the study of how people (individuals, organizations, industries, sectors, countries, society) generate, accumulate, allocate, distribute, and consume resources in order to create value. Integral to this definition is the notion of creating economic value. By utilizing resources in the most desirable way, by making the best choices or trade-offs, people increase the value of the goods and services at their disposal.

As with other disciplines that study society, economics is not an exact science. There are too many uncontrolled variables to account for, and measurements are often too difficult to consistently permit accurate descriptions and forecasts. Although recent progress has been made in experimental economics, segments of society cannot easily be put into a laboratory to allow precise testing and experimentation. However, economics is a science in the sense that it utilizes the scientific method to describe and analyze social phenomena. It relies largely on careful, often quantifiable formulation of theories and hypotheses and on testing of those hypotheses, where possible, against objectively collected data and observations.

Having classified economics as a science, one must ask, What kind of science is it? How, precisely, does economics become useful to those who toil in the fields of management and policy making? We can speak of economics as a science on at least three levels:

1. Economics is a *behavioral science*: it helps us describe and understand how people and institutions behave. Such understanding is an obvious prerequisite to formulating policies and strategies (incentives) for influencing such behavior in desired ways. For example, the "theory of the firm" describes how organizations set prices and make decisions about how much to produce. It thus suggests how those decisions might be influenced by such factors as taxes or changes in technology. In the nonprofit world, economics can help us understand the behavior of donors, service consumers, paid workers and volunteers, suppliers of other input resources such as equipment or real estate, and nonprofit organizations themselves, and how all these entities are influenced in their behavior by changes in government policy or internal management incentives and decisions.

2. Economics is a *decision science*: it helps us make good decisions in situations that involve resource-related choices. For example, by providing a precise definition of benefits and costs, economics helps us to evaluate the relative merits of alternative courses of action, such as whether or not to undertake a new educational program or a fund-raising initiative. (Economics might even help Alexander in the accompanying Blondie cartoon by enabling him to define realistic alternatives!)

3. Economics is also, perhaps surprisingly, a *moral science*. By defining "value" in an explicit way, and by conceptualizing a theory of social welfare, economics forces us to confront moral issues at a more rigorous level and

Reprinted with special permission of King Feature Syndicate.

gives us a way of thinking about how various courses of action affect society. For example, economic analysis can help to evaluate the benefits of a job-training program for underprivileged youth and to identify the costs to other groups required to achieve these benefits.

For leaders and managers of nonprofit organizations, all three of these aspects of economic science are important. We need to understand how our organizations and our constituents (consumers, donors, volunteers, suppliers) behave, for all of them are economic actors and influence the work and performance of nonprofit organizations. We need to know how to make difficult decisions with important resource implications; otherwise our organizations will not be efficient or effective. And we need to understand what kinds of actions are in the public interest and what kinds are not, for that is, ultimately, what justifies the existence of most nonprofit organizations.

WHAT IS THE BASIS OF VALUE IN ECONOMICS?

Underlying the scientific uses of economics—as a behavioral, decision-making, or moral science—is the concept of *scarcity* as the source of value. Economists attribute value to a unit of a good, service, or resource to the degree that it is in short supply relative to people's desire for more of it. That is, economists focus on the *incremental* value of scarce resources—how much more of something is desired relative to what is already available. Thus, ocean water at the shore, sand in the desert, and ice in Antarctica have no incremental economic value. While water is essential for the ecology and people desire a healthy ecological system, ocean water has no incremental value because more salt water at the shore does not contribute to this purpose. And, while ice is useful for preserving food, adding more ice to Antarctica does not make food preservation any easier. On the other hand, fresh water in California and clean air in Mexico City are most certainly of economic value. Again, a rare painting would have value only if people wanted it. (You may have saved only one of the many pictures you drew in the third grade, but it would have no economic value if no one else wanted it.)

In the nonprofit world, managers deal with many kinds of valuable, scarce resources. The services they produce are often not sufficient to serve all who need them, the time that volunteers can devote to organizational activities may be limited, the artworks or archival materials they tend may be rare and of intense interest to scholars and connoisseurs, and there is never enough money, staff, or time to accomplish all objectives. These are all resources in the nonprofit sector that have value because they are scarce and people want more of them.

While the concept of value based on incremental scarcity is clear, the *measurement of value* is often difficult. In principle, economists define the measure of economic value as follows:

> *The incremental economic value of a good, service, or resource is measured by what people are* intrinsically willing to pay *for another unit of it.*

The word *intrinsic* is important here. It highlights the fact that people often do not have the information they need to determine how much something is worth to them, or do not have an incentive to reveal that value to anyone else. (We will discuss both of these problems extensively in later chapters.) If they did have the information and incentive, their expressed willingness to pay would properly represent the economic value of the good or service at issue.

It is one thing to identify willingness to pay as the indicator of value and another thing to measure it in practice. How does one determine what people are really willing to pay for something? Economists often rely on the efficient operation of markets to create observable prices for goods and services. Under proper circumstances, these prices can be accurate measures of the incremental economic value of resources. However, there are many instances where markets for valued resources do not exist or where they function poorly. In such cases, prices do not accurately reflect incremental economic value. Thus, in general, we must distinguish between economic value as characterized by willingness to pay and the price at which a good or service may be selling. For example, the value of a glass of water to a severely dehydrated long-distance runner, as measured by the runner's willingness to pay, is likely to be substantially higher than the price at which the water is available. As we will discover later, people's willingness to pay is just one factor influencing the price at which a good or service may be offered for sale.

As we will discuss in subsequent chapters, the economic measure of value is not without controversy. People may be philosophically uncomfortable with associating willingness to pay with value. However, if a nonprofit manager facing a budget constraint allocates more dollars to one use than to another, he or she is implying that the first use is more highly valued. In the economist's view, such actual behavior, rather than testimony, is the real test of value.

One difficult issue connected with the economist's measure of value has to do with the existing distribution of economic resources among groups in society. In brief, if some groups have fewer resources than others, they are intrinsically more limited in what they can pay for the services they want. Does this mean that services to poorer groups are less worthy? Not necessarily, but the determination requires some sophistication in accounting for benefits accruing to more affluent groups as a result of help given to poorer groups. It also may require making social judgments on the basis of non-economic criteria such as equity or fairness. We will return to this issue later in this chapter.

HOW DOES SOCIETY ALLOCATE VALUABLE ECONOMIC RESOURCES?

We have already noted that markets are a key mechanism on which economists rely to determine the value of goods and services. But markets are just one mechanism that society uses to allocate valuable resources. How do markets do this, and what are the other mechanisms?

Markets are decentralized institutions in which independent producers (sellers) and consumers (buyers) *exchange* their goods and services voluntarily through agreement on *prices* received for quantities sold. (In a cruder form of markets, products and services are traded directly, or bartered, without reference to a common system of money and prices.)

Governments allocate goods, services, and other resources via taxation, expenditure, and regulatory policies, procedures, and rules developed through the *political process*, administered by bureaucracy, and enforced with the legitimate *coercive (police) power* of the state.

Voluntary institutions such as associations, nonprofit corporations, and foundations allow individuals and groups to *voluntarily* solicit, accumulate, and distribute economic resources as they see fit in order to address social, mutual, and individual interests.

Other non-market institutions that allocate resources include individual action (direct altruism, crime), families and informal groups, and organized crime.

Notice that while free markets may be a dominant mode for allocating valuable resources in Western industrialized countries such as the United States, they are by no means the only mode. Even in the United States, one of the most strongly market-oriented Western countries, the for-profit sector's share of national income was only 78 percent in 1990, with government and nonprofit sector institutions accounting for the rest (Hodgkinson et al., 1992). Moreover, markets themselves are influenced by other institutional mechanisms such as government taxation and regulation, and they depend on government for the enforcement of contracts and property rights.

Where markets dominate as the institutional basis for allocating valuable (scarce) resources, *prices* are the key mechanism for allocating these resources. Not surprisingly, therefore, much of economics involves the study of prices and the quantities supplied and purchased at different prices. In addition to markets, however, society uses numerous other mechanisms to allocate valuable resources. These include taxation; rules, policies, and direct orders used within organizations; planning within organizations and systems of organizations; rationing through waiting and queuing up for goods and services; lotteries; ethical norms, rules, and traditions used by families and ethnic and religious groups; and coercion and brute force. For our purposes, it is relevant to focus on certain mechanisms that are important in the nonprofit sector. These include persuasion, social pressure, and other forms of solicitation to induce people to give resources and volunteer time, as well as individually motivated initiative (voluntary giving of time and money). This is not to say that prices are unimportant as an allocation mechanism in the nonprofit sector; indeed, prices govern many, if not most, of the input and product markets in which nonprofit organizations are involved (e.g., see Hammack and Young, 1993). However, allocations of charitable resources such as donated funds and gifts in kind, volunteer time, and the provision of charitable services are not primarily governed by market prices.

The limited role that prices play, and the variety of other mechanisms in place for allocating resources in nonprofit organizations, point to the challenges of applying economic analysis to this sector. In parts of the economy that are solely market driven, prices allocate resources toward their most valued uses. What, if anything, ensures that proper allocations will be made outside the sphere of the market? Will the decentralized choices of individual donors and volunteers efficiently support the most pressing social needs, or are voluntary coordination (e.g., through United Ways) and state intervention required? Clearly, the concepts of economics that grow out of analysis of markets require careful adaptation and extension in order to be useful for understanding the nonmarket segments of the economy. Nonetheless, these concepts provide insights and a starting point for our analysis of nonmarket environments.

WHAT ARE THE MAJOR BRANCHES OF ECONOMICS?

The study of economics is normally divided into two major parts. *Micro-economics* is concerned with the study of economic processes at the level of individuals, organizations, industries, and markets. It is concerned with such topics as

- the decision-making behavior of consumers, organizations, industries, and other groups;
- prices, quantities, qualities, costs, revenues, benefits, and taxes associated with particular goods and services;
- external benefits and costs, public goods, monopolistic arrangements, information problems, and other causes of market failure that require intervention or supplementation by nonmarket institutions; and
- the *efficiency* with which resources are allocated among alternative inputs and outputs, technologies, and institutional forms (e.g., business vs. nonprofit organizations).

In this book, we will be almost exclusively concerned with microeconomics. The other main branch of economics is *macroeconomics*. This branch studies how the economy works as a whole and is concerned with *aggregate phenomena* such as

- gross domestic product and income;
- the money supply;
- inflation, unemployment, and business cycles;
- aggregate demand and supply for all goods and services at once;
- aggregate savings, investment, and economic growth; and
- the balance of payments.

This is not to say that nonprofit leaders can safely remain uneducated in macroeconomics. Many nonprofits must be prepared to raise their service level when a recession is forecast. During a time of greater need, obtaining donations may also be particularly hard. Thus, savings and endowment decisions must be planned for in advance. Moreover, nonprofits are subject to the same inflationary pressures as other organizations in society, and they must pay attention to interest rates and other macroeconomic variables that affect their economic health.

In the next chapter, we will see how the nonprofit sector fits into the economy as a whole. For example, how big a part of the economy do nonprofits represent in terms of income, employment, and other parameters, and how do they interact with the other sectors? However, this book does not cover the theory or principles of macroeconomic analysis or provide a detailed description of the macro economy. Basic macroeconomics does not require modification or elaboration for nonprofit managers; they must learn about the same macro issues—inflation, interest rates, unemployment, economic growth, and so on—as everyone else. For this purpose, we refer the reader to a standard introductory economic textbook such as Schiller (1993) or Gill (1993).

HOW DO ECONOMISTS THINK?

Economists have a particular way of looking at the world. In general, they make certain simplifying assumptions in order to render their analyses manageable and incisive. To the extent that their assumptions are close to the truth, they are able to produce insights by clearing away the brush and getting a clear view of the trees, if not the forest. To the extent that their assumptions are off base as applied to a given situation, they must adjust these assumptions in order to refine their analyses. Here are some of the key ideas and assumptions that economists use:

Economists usually assume that people are "rational." Specifically, they assume that

- People know what their alternatives are in a given situation and have good information about these alternatives. If this is not the case, economists assume that information comes at a cost and analyze the implications of costly information. For example, economists would assume that donors are aware of the different charities they may give to and that these donors will seek more detailed information about these alternatives to the extent that they feel such information will be worth the satisfaction they receive from making more informed decisions.
- People are able to make clear and consistent choices among alternatives. In particular, economists would assume that if a donor prefers charity A to charity B and charity B to charity C, then the donor will prefer charity A over charity C;
- People optimize; they choose their preferred alternative from among those available to them. Thus, if choices A, B, and C are available to the donor who prefers charity A over the others, then, economists would assume, the donor will choose to give to charity A.
- People act out of self-interest, broadly defined. Thus, economists would assume that donors derive some kind of personal

satisfaction or benefit from giving, though not necessarily a material benefit.

This last criterion is particularly interesting from the viewpoint of nonprofit organizations. It does not mean that people necessarily act to maximize their own wealth, but rather that they define their own preferences in particular, individual ways and act on those preferences. Thus, although there is no such thing as pure altruism as far as economists are concerned, people can derive self-satisfaction in a variety of ways, including doing good things for others.

Generally, economists prefer to take individuals' preferences as given and avoid the question of how people form their preferences in the first place or how these preferences may evolve over time. While this simplification is one reason why economic analysis can remain sharp and focused, it can also be a limitation. In cases where this limitation is particularly important, economists have begun to collaborate with psychologists and sociologists to formulate alternative models that are more complex but still simple enough to provide tractable insights.

Economists distinguish between positive and normative analysis. This distinction corresponds to the different kinds of science that economics encompasses. *Positive analysis* describes economic behavior based on theory, mathematical modeling, and empirical estimation techniques. This is economics as a behavioral science.

Normative analysis describes alternative courses of action and suggests which course is most desirable, assuming that the decision maker is rational and wants to make the most "efficient" decision. This is economics as a decision science and as a moral science.

Economists are primarily concerned with efficiency. It is very important, therefore, to understand what an economist means by efficiency. We can approach this question in two steps:

1. *Productive efficiency* means that goods or services of a given quality and quantity are produced at the lowest possible cost, or that the highest possible quality or quantity is attained for a given level of cost. Productive efficiency implies that the best combination of inputs and production methods (technology) is used.
2. *Allocative efficiency* means that all resources are allocated to their most highly valued uses; that is, production is efficient and the quality and quantity of goods and services produced reflects the preferences (maximum willingness to pay) of society (consumers in a broad sense).

Note that allocative efficiency is an all-encompassing criterion that reflects the full meaning of economic efficiency—that is, *the degree to which society's resources are put to their most valued uses.*

Economists have an interesting theoretical way of determining whether allocative efficiency has been achieved. They use the *Pareto criterion*, which was formulated by nineteenth-century Italian economist Vilfredo Pareto:

> *Inefficiency exists if changes in production methods or allocation of resources can be made so that no one in society is worse off and at least one person is better off.*

An important question for economists has been whether the Pareto criterion can be applied usefully in practice. In particular, this definition permits many different situations involving widely disparate allocations of resources to be called efficient. For example, suppose that a charity has received from a local company three vouchers, each of which pays for a day of housekeeping services for elderly residents of the community. If there are only two eligible clients in that community, then each of the following allocations is efficient: three vouchers to the first client and none to the second; two vouchers to the first and one to the second; one voucher to the first and two to the second; and no vouchers to the first and three to the second. It would be inefficient to distribute only two of the vouchers and throw out the third, because no matter which client got the third voucher, the act of giving that third voucher out would make somebody better off and nobody worse off.

Now suppose that initially the first client is given two vouchers and the second is given only one. The caseworker discovers that a mistake was made, demands that the first client return one voucher, and gives this voucher to the other client. Is this change inefficient because we have made one person worse off? No, we are simply moving from one efficient allocation to another. What the Pareto criterion does is define *in*efficiency. An economy is said to be efficient if it is not inefficient. Neither the initial allocation nor the redistributed allocation was inefficient, but the Pareto criterion is mute on the question of which allocation is better.

Thus, the Pareto criterion is like the preliminary round in a tournament: it eliminates some allocations from further consideration but does not select an overall winner. To choose among alternative efficient allocations, we need some other criterion, and this distributional question hinges on political and ethical notions of fairness or *equity*. Whereas pretty much everyone can agree that efficiency is good, there is considerable dispute over how to think about equity. Economists, in collaboration with philosophers and other social scientists, think about equity systematically within the following categories:

1. *Horizontal equity*: the degree to which individuals or organizations in the same category (e.g., income class, age group, family, or organization size) are treated the same way.

This criterion is relevant to the issue of property taxation and public expenditures for education. In the nonprofit world, the issue of horizontal equity arises in a number of areas. For example, in appeals for donations, donors are often asked to compare their giving efforts to those of others of similar income or wealth. Horizontal equity is also a consideration in the geographic distribution of charitable resources. For example, needy people living in prosperous suburban areas are more likely to be well served by nonprofit social agencies than are similarly needy people living in the inner city.

2. *Vertical equity*: the degree to which there is a reasonable distribution of rewards or burdens among different classes of individuals (e.g., income classes).

This criterion underlies the concept of progressive income taxation, which is based on the normative principle that taxes should be indexed according to one's ability to pay. Economists have argued for progressive taxation and the importance of vertical equity as a criterion for social decision making on several grounds, including the idea that the more money people have, the less they value each additional dollar (this phenomenon is called the diminishing marginal utility of income) and the observation that wealthier people tend to consume more than their proportional share of public-sector goods (this is called the benefit principle). In the nonprofit world, the vertical equity criterion reveals itself in the use of sliding-fee scales that accommodate lower-income service consumers. For example, students are often granted discounted rates for membership in scholarly research societies in recognition of their more limited resources and the fact that they may not benefit as fully from the society's programs as regular members do.

Several facets of horizontal and vertical equity seem especially relevant to nonprofits:

- *Equity of endowments* is the degree to which people start out in the same situation in life (i.e., have equal opportunities). This is a consideration, for example, in determining public policy on inheritance taxes, which in turn influences how people plan their estates and bequests to charity. This example involves the issue of vertical equity (whether people in different wealth categories are treated differently by tax policy) and also that of horizontal equity (whether all children get to start life with comparable advantages).

- *Equity of process* is the degree to which the rules of the game are "fair," or the same, for all participants. This is an issue, for example, in the controversy over unrelated business income tax on commercial activities of nonprofits. Should the rules be the same for businesses and nonprofits in similar circumstances (horizontal equity)? Should small businesses and nonprofits be treated differently from large ones (vertical equity)?

- *Equity of outcomes* is the degree to which differential resources are provided to different groups so that they can achieve fair final outcomes. This applies to such provisions as special tax exemptions for the blind, affirmative action policies, and day care for children of working mothers. Here we are concerned with horizontal equity (are all individuals within the target group treated the same way?) and vertical equity (is the target group as a whole given sufficiently greater benefits than other groups?).

Policy and management issues that confront nonprofit leaders and public officials often require grappling with trade-offs between efficiency and equity. For example:

- Laws mandating access to public facilities by the handicapped may be enormously costly, and resources devoted to their implementation might be more efficiently allocated in other ways. However, these laws do help assure equal treatment for handicapped individuals.

- Program-related investments by foundations (allocations of funds in the form of loans or other instruments designed both to provide the foundation with financial returns and to achieve social objectives) have the potential to sacrifice efficiency by decreasing returns on charitable endowments, but they may produce a fairer distribution of societal resources.

- Confiscatory inheritance taxes and progressive income taxes may reduce efficiency by undermining incentives to work, but they may help even out the distribution of income in society.

- Subsidies of nonprofit postal rates may be an inefficient way to allocate public resources because such subsidies may bias nonprofit organizations toward using more costly means of

communication, but they may help nonprofits carry out work to
aid the most unfortunate members of society.

These various issues are much more complex than a few sentences
can indicate. However, properly defining and clearly articulating program
or policy goals enables us to understand and sometimes reconcile the
conflicts between efficiency and equity. For example, if access for the
handicapped can be shown to produce general benefits for society, then it
may be efficient as well as equitable to implement such programs. In other
cases (e.g., deciding whether to invest in programs for children or in
programs for the elderly, in AIDS treatment programs or in preventive
education programs), economic efficiency cannot be the only decision
criterion because priorities need to be assigned to various groups. Nonetheless, the efficiency-equity framework encourages clear thinking about
these essential considerations.

SUMMARY

The study of economics is important for managers and leaders of nonprofit organizations in several ways. At the *appreciative level*, nonprofit
leaders must have a sense of how nonprofit organizations fit into the rest
of the economy, how big a part of that economy they occupy, how they
interact with other kinds of economic units, how their own organizations
behave, and how they are affected by changes in the economy as a whole.
At the *policy level*, nonprofit managers and leaders must understand how
their organizations are affected by changes in public policy, and they must
be able to analyze the impact of policies they seek to change or implement
in order to accomplish the goals of their organizations. The tools and
concepts of economic analysis are invaluable at this level. Finally, at the
managerial level, managers and leaders of nonprofit organizations continually make decisions that have important resource implications. Economics
provides the conceptual principles and methods that make the consequences of alternative decisions explicit and logically consistent and can
thus lead to better choices. In the following chapters, we will review some
of the basic ideas of economic analysis in order to inform the thinking of
nonprofit managers and leaders at all three of these levels. Our intent is
not to make economists out of our readers, but rather to enable them to
understand and utilize the work of economists more effectively and to
encourage them to use the powerful concepts of economic thinking in
their daily and long-term decision making about issues of critical concern
to nonprofit organizations.

REFERENCES

Eggert, James. *What Is Economics?* Mountain View, Calif.: Mayfield Publishing Co., 1993.

Gill, Richard T. *Economics: A Concise Micro/Macro Text.* Mountain View, Calif.: Mayfield Publishing Co., 1993.

Hammack, David C., and Dennis R. Young. *Nonprofit Organizations in a Market Economy.* San Francisco: Jossey-Bass, 1993.

Heilbrun, James, and Charles M. Gray. *The Economics of Arts and Culture.* New York: Cambridge University Press, 1993.

Hodgkinson, Virginia A., Murray S. Weitzman, Christopher M. Toppe, and Stephen M. Noga. *Nonprofit Almanac 1992-1993: Dimensions of the Independent Sector.* San Francisco: Jossey-Bass, 1992.

Levi, Maurice. *Thinking Economically.* New York: Basic Books, 1985.

Rhoads, Steven E. *The Economist's View of the World.* New York: Cambridge University Press, 1985.

Schiller, Bradley R. *Essentials of Economics.* New York: McGraw-Hill, 1993.

Weisbrod, Burton A. *The Nonprofit Economy.* Cambridge, Mass.: Harvard University Press, 1988.

EXERCISES

1. Can you think of three trade-offs that must be made in a nonprofit organization for which you have worked or volunteered? Did that organization address these trade-offs systematically? Do you think management decisions would have been different if the tools of economics had been applied to these questions?

2. Critically analyze the following imaginary quote: "Because volunteers are not paid by the employing organization, economics is irrelevant to the questions of volunteer recruitment and allocation." (William Acrimony, *The 3.5-Minute Nonprofit Manager.*)

3. Critically analyze the following imaginary quote: "If a donor has unsatisfied consumption needs, he is acting irrationally by disregarding his self-interest." (Aynt Rand, *The Bubblehead.*)

4. Imagine a world where the entire economy consists of two nonprofit fraternities, Alpha Alpha and Kappa Chino, each containing three "brothers." There is only one good in this economy—beer, and, needless to say, every brother likes more beer better than less beer. Beer is not produced, but magically appears under everyone's pillows each night, brought by the beer fairy, who is a teetotaler and not part of the economy. The beer fairy places the same number of six-packs under each brother's pillow within a fraternity but may give different amounts to each fraternity. An economy is a complete listing of the quantities of each good consumed by each individual. In this case, since there is only one good, a complete specification of the economy consists of the amount of beer consumed by each brother in Alpha Alpha and the corresponding amount consumed by each brother in Kappa Chino. Suppose that there are five feasible economies, A through E. The beer allocations in each are as follows:

	Economy				
	A	**B**	**C**	**D**	**E**
Alpha Alpha	2	2	1	3	3
Kappa Chino	2	3	5	3	1

a. Which economies (if any) are efficient?

b. What (if anything) can you say about the fairness of economy C for each of the categories of equity discussed in the text?

CHAPTER **2**

The Place of the Nonprofit Sector in the U.S. Economy

Broadly speaking, there are three organized sectors in the U.S. economy—the private for-profit business sector, the public or government sector, and the private nonprofit sector. Each of these sectors is highly diverse internally, and highly interdependent and intertwined with the other sectors. The purpose of this chapter is to describe generally how the nonprofit sector fits into the U.S. economy. In the process, we will present a number of economic concepts that are helpful for understanding the importance and functions of nonprofit organizations.

DISTINCTIVE CHARACTERISTICS OF NONPROFIT ORGANIZATIONS

What distinguishes a private nonprofit organization from a business or a government agency? In some ways, nonprofits share the characteristics of these other kinds of organizations:

- Like businesses, nonprofit organizations must break even financially. That is, over a reasonable period of time (determined in part by their ability to borrow and to secure donations and grants, and by the patience of their creditors) they must take in enough income to pay their bills.

- Like businesses, nonprofits are governed by private citizens rather than by public officials.
- Like government, nonprofits have purposes or missions that address aspects of the general public interest or the collective interests of particular groups.
- Like government, nonprofit organizations must observe the "nondistribution constraint," which stipulates that if the organization makes a profit (generates a financial surplus), it may not distribute that surplus to those who "own" or control it.

Because of this mixture of characteristics, nonprofit organizations have sometimes been called "businesses with public missions" (Bryce, 1987). This characterization identifies some ideas important to the economic analysis of nonprofits.

First, it is important to recognize the role of *profit* in the behavior of nonprofit organizations. Nonprofit organizations may indeed generate profits, but they must use those profits in ways consistent with the mission of the organization.

Second, the concept of *constraint* is important in economic analysis. Constraints are limits to the choices available to economic actors (donors, purchasers of service, nonprofit organizations). Budget limitations, government policy, and technological feasibility constrain economic choices. For example, the recent IRS ruling that, under tightly specified circumstances, nonprofit managers can receive part of their compensation in the form of a share of the organization's net financial surplus altered the nature of the "nondistribution constraint" on nonprofit organizations. It is now feasible to provide limited profit sharing, and some nonprofits may exercise this option. Economic analysis allows us to determine how the rational choices of economic actors change when technological progress, government policy, market conditions, and other factors alter constraints on their behavior.

Constraints also create *incentives*. As mentioned in Chapter 1, incentives, or inducements to behave in a certain way, are an important aspect of economic analysis. Taxes and subsidies provide incentives for consumers and taxpayers to do certain things and restrain from doing other things. In nonprofit organizations, the nondistribution constraint establishes conditions that encourage nonprofit organizations to become more "trustworthy" in their dealings with consumers. By prohibiting those in control from enriching themselves with the organization's profits, this constraint removes incentives for nonprofit managers or directors to increase those profits by exploiting consumer ineptness or ignorance. In addition to this direct incentive effect, the nondistribution constraint sends a signal to potential nonprofit managers and employees that there will be no stockholder pressure to maximize profits at any cost. Thus, nonprofits attract workers who are motivated more by altruistic or service goals than by money. This sorting effect amplifies the direct incentive provided by the nondistribution constraint and allows consumers and donors to place more trust in nonprofit than in for-profit organizations (Hansmann, 1987).

The generic concept of a nonprofit as a privately controlled organization that must observe the nondistribution constraint masks the full flavor and variety of this sector. Nonprofits carry out different kinds of services, derive their funds from various sources, and benefit various types of constituencies. As a result, different categories of nonprofits are treated differently by public policy. For example:

- *Public benefit* nonprofits (organizations classified as 501(c)3 in the federal tax code) address the needs of broad segments of the public, while *mutual benefit* organizations (e.g., clubs and trade and professional associations) provide benefits primarily to their own members. Contributions to public benefit organizations are deductible from personal income taxes while contributions to mutual benefit organizations are not.
- *Private foundations* have narrow bases of donor support (e.g., single individuals, families, and corporations), while *community foundations* have many sources of donor support. Thus, community foundations are classified as public charities and are treated more liberally in the tax code.
- So-called *social welfare organizations* (classified as 501(c)4) include civic leagues and organizations devoted to particular social causes (e.g., the National Abortion Rights Action League, the American Civil Liberties Union, and the Sierra Club), and engage substantially in political advocacy activities. Donations to these organizations are not deductible from income taxes.
- Because of constitutional considerations, *religious organizations* (e.g., churches, synagogues, mosques) are treated differently from other nonprofit organizations by public policy. In particular, contributions to these organizations are tax deductible even though the organizations need not file tax or registration forms with the government.

Note that government policy utilizes *incentives* and *constraints* to distinguish among the treatments of nonprofit organizations in various categories. Nonprofits that serve the public at large are eligible to receive tax-deductible

donations, while those serving only their own members or engaging substantially in political advocacy are not. Thus, taxpayers have a special incentive to support public benefit organizations through their contributions.
Other government policies, such as U.S. postal subsidies and exemptions
from local property taxes and state and local sales taxes, provide similar
incentives.

Private foundations are subject to payout requirements (constraints on
how they can spend or accumulate their money) as well as excise taxes to
support the regulatory system and penalty taxes to ensure compliance with
the more restrictive set of rules applying to them. These policies encourage
foundations to acquire broad sources of support in order to avoid being
classified as private foundations, and they discourage close control of a
foundation's resources by a few patrons. In part, such policies are designed
to discourage the rich from using foundations as a tax shelter while continuing to control their wealth.

All nonprofits are exempt from paying corporate income tax on their
"profits," as long as those profits derive from activity related to the mission
of the organization. Profits from commercial activities that do not directly
contribute to the organization's mission are subject to an unrelated business
income tax (UBIT) similar to the corporate income tax. Income from the
sale of computers to the general public by a university bookstore is an
example of unrelated business income. The differing tax treatment of related
and unrelated income provides an incentive to shift revenue-raising efforts
toward related ventures.

In these various ways, government policy uses incentives and constraints to encourage "appropriate" behavior by the various subcategories of
nonprofit organizations as well as by the nonprofit sector as a whole.

THE SIZE AND SCOPE OF THE NONPROFIT SECTOR

As we describe the part that nonprofits play in the overall economy, we will
encounter several additional useful economic concepts. In particular, there
are a variety of ways to measure the scope of nonprofit activity in economic
terms.[*]

One question we can ask is, How many nonprofit organizations are
there in the United States? In 1990, there were 1,375,000 such organizations,
representing 5.9 percent of all formally incorporated organizations. About
29 percent of these organizations were mutual-benefit organizations such as
clubs, unions, and trade associations. Another 26 percent were churches. The

---

[*] Most of the following statistics are taken from the *Nonprofit Almanac 1992-1993* (Hodgkinson et al, 1992).
Other sources include *The Nonprofit Economy* (Weisbrod, 1988) and *America's Nonprofit Sector* (Salamon, 1992).

rest were charities, hospitals, educational institutions, day-care providers, social service agencies, arts and cultural institutions, research organizations, advocacy groups, international relief and development agencies, foundations, united funding organizations, and a host of other charitable and public purpose nonprofit organizations.

The second question is, What is the economic importance of these organizations? This question is complicated by a special factor—assessing the value of volunteer labor. As we will discuss in later chapters, volunteer time is an unpriced but nonetheless valuable resource that contributes directly to the production of services by nonprofit organizations. Thus, it is conceptually correct to include the value of volunteer labor in the computation of national income accruing to nonprofit organizations. However, it is hard to assign a numerical value to such labor. As an approximation, researchers equate the value of an hour of volunteer time with the average hourly wage of nonagricultural workers in the U.S. economy, plus a 12 percent margin for fringe benefits (Hodgkinson et al., 1992).

In addition to the problems associated with volunteers, estimates of the nonprofit share of the economy are also hampered by the fact that the value of output services delivered at zero or low cost is underestimated in national income accounts. Given these caveats, we can report the following estimates of the size of the nonprofit sector in the United States for the year 1990:

- Including estimated volunteer contributions, private nonprofit organizations (of all types) earned $315.9 billion. This represented 6.8 percent of the total national income.
- Excluding the value of volunteer time, nonprofit organizations earned $193.7 billion, representing 3.8 percent of the national income.
- Approximately 91 percent of the national income earned by nonprofits was accounted for by public benefit–type (501(c)3 tax deductible) and social welfare advocacy (501(c)4) nonprofit organizations, including churches.

Another way of appreciating the size of the nonprofit sector is to focus on employment:

- In 1990, an estimated 9.3 million paid (full-time-equivalent) workers were employed in the nonprofit sector, representing 6.7 percent of all paid workers.

- 93 percent of these workers were employed by public benefit and social welfare nonprofit organizations.
- Nonprofit workers earned $169.9 billion, representing 5.2 percent of earnings from work in the economy as a whole.
- Approximately 92 percent of these earnings went to employees of public benefit and social welfare nonprofit organizations.
- 6.4 million full-time-equivalent volunteers were employed by nonprofit organizations.
- This volunteer time was equivalent to $109.1 billion in earnings from work.
- Nonprofits employed 68 percent of all volunteer time in formal organizations in the United States; the remaining volunteer time was spent in public schools, for-profit day-care centers, hospitals and nursing homes, and other government and business settings.
- Approximately 90 percent of volunteer time in nonprofits was employed by public benefit and social welfare nonprofits.

It is clear from these numbers that nonprofit organizations attract the bulk of volunteer labor in the economy. Why is this so? What special advantage do nonprofits have in attracting volunteers? We will deal with this question in Chapters 3 and 9 when we discuss economic theories of nonprofit organizations.

Interestingly, although public benefit organizations make up only 71 percent of the organizations in the sector (only 46 percent if we exclude churches), they account for more than 90 percent of the income, earnings, and employment of the sector. Thus, many key functions of the nonprofit sector, such as advocacy and trade and professional representation, are underemphasized by these foregoing measures.

Finally, it is worth observing that, overall, the nonprofit sector is small—only 5 to 10 percent of the economy by various economic measures—compared to business and government. If, however, we think of nonprofits as an "industry" commensurate with, say, public utilities, steel making, or food retailing, it is large in terms of the number of people employed and the dollars it receives and spends.

THE COMPOSITION OF THE NONPROFIT SECTOR

Like the business sector, the nonprofit sector is quite diverse, consisting of many different "industries." However, because the nonprofit sector cuts across industries, this is too simple a characterization: while it wholly contains certain "pure" nonprofit industries, it also contains a share of "mixed" industries. Pure nonprofit industries include churches, trade and professional associations, foundations, and advocacy organizations. Virtually all organizations in these industries are nonprofit organizations. "Mixed" industries include health care, day care, education, nursing homes, mental health services, and arts and culture. In some of these mixed industries, such as the arts, nonprofit organizations share the stage primarily with the for-profit sector, while in others, such as higher education, they primarily complement government provision. In still other mixed industries, such as hospitals and nursing homes, all three sectors are well represented.

One puzzle for economists is the question of why certain industries are "mixed." If the nonprofit form presents certain advantages in a given industry, why aren't all organizations in that industry nonprofit? And if in another industry the form does not offer such advantages, why aren't all organizations in that industry of some other form? A related question is why the proportion of nonprofit organizations varies so widely from one mixed industry to the next. This is another issue for economic theory, and another way of posing the question, What "competitive advantage" do nonprofit organizations have in some situations that they do not have in others? We will discuss these questions more fully in Chapters 3 and 9. Here, we begin by asking, How big is the nonprofit share of different industries, and how can this share be measured?

Lester Salamon (1992) has done a lot of this work for us. His book uses a variety of measures, including shares of the number of organizations, the number of beds or clients, and industry expenditure or revenues. Here are some of the figures for the United States:

- In 1989, nonprofits represented 51 percent of hospitals, 56 percent of hospital beds, and 65 percent of hospital expenditures.
- In 1987, nonprofits represented 32 percent of clinics and other health-care organizations, 45 percent of employees of these organizations, and 43 percent of their revenues.
- In 1987, nonprofits represented 20 percent of nursing homes, 22 percent of nursing home beds, 26 percent of nursing home employees, and 27 percent of nursing home revenues.
- In 1990, nonprofit institutions represented 49 percent of colleges and universities, 34 percent of higher education expenditures, and 20 percent of enrollments.
- In 1990, nonprofits represented 24 percent of elementary and secondary schools, 8 percent of expenditures, and 11 percent of enrollments.
- In 1987, nonprofits represented 23 percent of vocational schools,

25 percent of employees of those schools, and 22 percent of revenues.

- In 1987, nonprofits represented 59 percent of social service organizations, 58 percent of their employees, and 74 percent of their revenues.
- In 1987, nonprofits represented 95 percent of orchestras and 97 percent of orchestra employees.
- In 1987, nonprofits represented 40 percent of theaters and 51 percent of theater employees.
- In 1987, nonprofits represented 71 percent of museums and 95 percent of museum employees.

These numbers yield some interesting observations. For one thing, it is puzzling that the nonprofit share varies so widely among industries, even industries that seem closely related to one another. Why, for example, is the nonprofit share so different between higher education and elementary and secondary education, between hospitals and nursing homes, and between orchestras and theaters? Successful economic theory of the nonprofit sector must explain not only why certain industries are nonprofit and others are not, but why there is so much variation within industries and among closely related industries.

Another interesting observation is the extent to which nonprofits differ from other organizations in a given industry. For example, in both higher and lower education, the proportions of nonprofit organizations are higher than the proportions of enrollments and expenditures, indicating that nonprofit organizations are smaller, on average, than other schools. However, nonprofit museums and hospitals are larger, on average, than their counterparts in other sectors. This, too, is a puzzle that we would like to understand.

HOW NONPROFITS INTERACT WITH OTHER SECTORS

The presence of mixed industries suggests that nonprofit organizations either complement or compete with other kinds of organizations in the provision of particular kinds of goods and services. In fact, the question of whether they compete head-on by providing the same kinds of services to the same kinds of clients or occupy a different niche within a given industry is key to understanding the role of nonprofits in the economy. Although competition between for-profits and nonprofits has been a controversial public policy issue in recent years, economists believe that nonprofits and for-profits often occupy different market segments within industries. While nonprofits derive about half their income, on average, from fees and service charges (excluding government reimbursements), relatively little of this revenue comes from commercially competitive ventures that are not directly related to their missions. Within their mainline or "related" service activities, many nonprofits address market segments having a strong public benefit component and holding little interest for for-profit business, such as legal services for the poor, social services for the disadvantaged, and fine or performing arts such as opera, symphony orchestras, and art museums. In other industries, including the hospital, nursing home, and day-care industries, nonprofits appear to provide essentially the same services and compete for the same paying customers as for-profit organizations. In these cases, however, there is evidence that nonprofits offer subtly different varieties of service than do for-profits (see Weisbrod, 1988).

In addition to competition, there are many other ways in which nonprofit organizations interact with other entities in the economy. For example:

- Nonprofits often serve as contractual agents for government, delivering public services that government pays for. Salamon (1987) estimates that in the fields of social services, employment/training, health, and arts/culture, for example, nonprofits delivered more than 40 percent of government-funded services in 1982.
- Nonprofits contract with business to provide services such as mental health care for corporate employees.
- Nonprofits form partnerships with business and government in areas such as urban development and biotechnology research.
- Nonprofits form for-profit subsidiaries to separate commercial activity from mission-related activity.
- Businesses establish corporate foundations and nonprofit trade associations.
- Governments regulate the behavior of nonprofit organizations in various ways.
- Nonprofits operate fund-raising campaigns and payroll deduction plans within government agencies and corporations.
- Corporate and government executives are involved as volunteers and board members of nonprofit organizations. Indeed, governments appoint board members to some nonprofit organizations in which they have a major interest. For example, the board of the Indiana University Foundation, a private nonprofit that supports a public university, includes designated governmental representatives and private citizens appointed by the board.

While it is helpful to view the nonprofit sector as a separate and distinct part of the economy with its own unique characteristics, nonprofit organizations clearly do not operate in isolation from the rest of the economy. They do not comprise an *independent* sector in an economic sense, but rather an *interdependent* sector that derives its support from a variety of sources and interacts with other sectors in many other ways. Nonprofits' financial dependence on various sources of income in 1989, as documented by Salamon (1992), is shown in Table 2.1.

Again, economists are interested in why there is such wide variation in the sources of funds across nonprofit industries.

- Is the diversification of revenues practiced by many nonprofits a good thing? Does it provide protection against the risks of relying on a single source of support, or does it simply complicate the process of managing and accounting for multiple types of funds?
- Does heavy reliance on government funds imply a loss of autonomy and independence? That is, as government supplies more of the funding, do nonprofits lose their ability to decide for themselves what services to produce and how to produce them?
- Does heavy reliance on fees make nonprofits too sensitive to market considerations and less able to focus on mission? As sales become a more important revenue source, do nonprofits gear their services more to paying customers at the expense of those who may need their services but are limited in their ability to pay?

TABLE 2.1
Sources of Income for Nonprofit Organizations

Industry	% Fees*	% Government	% Private Giving
Health	55	36	9
Education	63	17	19
Social/Legal	23	42	35
Civic	27	41	32
Arts/Culture	26	11	63
ALL	51	31	18

*Excludes government reimbursements.
Note: Percentages in each industry may not total 100% due to rounding.
Source: *Salamon (1992).*

These are questions that economists try to address when they model the operations of nonprofit organizations as economic agents and ask what changes in policy (incentives and constraints) may be desirable.

HOW NONPROFITS ALLOCATE THEIR FUNDS

Economic analysis can also help assess whether nonprofits are dividing their limited funds among input resources (e.g., labor, equipment, supplies) efficiently. By far the largest share is spent on labor. Overall, nonprofits spend almost half their current expenditures on personnel, while they spend less than 5 percent on construction and capital expenses. The emphasis on personnel costs varies by industry. Excluding volunteer time, Hodgkinson et al (1992) estimate the percentages of annual operating expenses devoted to personnel costs in 1987 as follows:

48 percent in health care
52 percent in education
40 percent in arts and culture
43 percent in environment
51 percent in human services

The very substantial labor contribution to nonprofit organizations raises several important economic considerations for nonprofit managers:

- Productivity is a serious concern as wages and salaries rise, and the ability to substitute capital (computers, answering machines, etc.) for labor in the nonprofit sector must be continually explored.
- The productivity of paid labor must itself be continually enhanced through appropriate education and training.
- Volunteer labor can sometimes substitute for paid employees. However, productive volunteers are scarce and must be trained. Nonprofit managers must decide how much to invest in volunteer recruitment and training and must also determine the combination of paid and volunteer labor that is best for their organization.

GROWTH OF THE NONPROFIT SECTOR

One reason that nonprofit organizations have received increasing attention in recent years is that their share of the economy is growing rapidly. From

1977 to 1990, the nonprofit sector (including the value of volunteer time) increased its share of national income from 5.5 percent to 6.8 percent, its share of employment from 9.3 percent to 11.4 percent, and its share of earnings from work from 7.1 percent to 8.5 percent.

During this period, the number of nonprofit organizations increased by 22 percent. Moreover, nonprofit employment rose 44 percent from 1977 to 1987, compared to a 25 percent rise in nonagricultural employment in the economy as a whole. The pattern within industries varied. For example, in the same period, nonprofit employment in health care rose 37 percent, in education it rose 30 percent, in religion it dropped 4 percent, in social services it rose 68 percent, and in the arts and culture it rose 85 percent.

The relatively fast growth of the nonprofit sector in recent years again raises the question of what special advantages can be attributed to nonprofit organizations. Why are these organizations growing faster than government or business? We have some ideas about why this is happening.

First, nonprofit organizations reside primarily in the service side of the economy rather than in the production of material goods. The service sector of the U.S. economy has been growing rapidly, and the growth of the nonprofit sector is comparable to the growth of the service sector as a whole. For example, between 1981 and 1987, employment in the for-profit and nonprofit service sectors in New York State both grew by 17 percent (Ben-Ner and Van Hoomissen, 1990).

Second, government has grown in recent years principally by increasing its expenditures, not by expanding public-sector employment. Increasingly, government services are delivered through private agencies. Employment by government increased 27 percent between 1977 and 1990, compared to a 63 percent rise in employment by nonprofits. Government now prefers to deliver much of its services through contracts with nonprofit organizations, rather than delivering services itself or contracting primarily with for-profit businesses (see Smith and Lipsky, 1993).

SUMMARY

The nonprofit sector is the smallest of the U.S. economy's three sectors, but it is an extremely critical sector in terms of the kinds of services it produces and the functions it serves. It is also the most rapidly growing sector, as the U.S. economy becomes more and more a service economy and as government privatizes the delivery (if not the financing) of its services. The nonprofit sector is highly diverse in its composition and its reliance on different sources of funds, and it interacts closely with government and business in many important ways. Economics helps us to understand the special advantages of nonprofit organizations in different parts of the economy and why the sector is positioned as it is.

REFERENCES

Ben-Ner, Avner, and Theresa Van Hoomissen. "The Growth of the Nonprofit Sector in the 1980s." *Nonprofit Management and Leadership.* Winter 1990, pp. 99-116.

Bryce, Herrington J. *Financial and Strategic Management for Nonprofit Organizations.* Englewood Cliffs, N.J.: Prentice Hall, 1987.

Hansmann, Henry. "Economic Theories of Nonprofit Organization." Chapter 2 in Walter W. Powell (ed.), *The Nonprofit Sector: A Research Handbook.* New Haven: Yale University Press, 1987.

Hodgkinson, Virginia A., Murray S. Weitzman, Christopher M. Toppe, and Stephen M. Noga. *Nonprofit Almanac 1992-1993: Dimensions of the Nonprofit Sector.* San Francisco: Jossey-Bass, 1992.

Salamon, Lester M. *America's Nonprofit Sector: A Primer.* New York: The Foundation Center, 1992.

Salamon, Lester M. "Partners in Public Service: The Scope and Theory of Government–Nonprofit Relations." Chapter 6 in Walter W. Powell (ed.), *The Nonprofit Sector: A Research Handbook.* New Haven: Yale University Press, 1987.

Simon, John G. "The Tax Treatment of Nonprofit Organizations: A Review of Federal and State Policies." Chapter 5 in Walter W. Powell (ed.), *The Nonprofit Sector: A Research Handbook.* New Haven: Yale University Press, 1987.

Smith, Stephen Rathgeb, and Michael Lipsky. *Nonprofits for Hire.* Cambridge, Mass.: Harvard University Press, 1993.

Weisbrod, Burton A. *The Nonprofit Economy.* Cambridge, Mass.: Harvard University Press, 1988.

EXERCISES

1. Identify four industries in the U.S. economy as follows:

   a. an industry in which all service-providing organizations are private and nonprofit;

   b. an industry in which none or very few participating service providers are private and nonprofit;

   c. an industry in which private nonprofit providers co-exist with for-profit and governmental providers; and

   d. an industry in which private nonprofit and for-profit providers co-exist but government does not participate as a provider of service.

For each industry, offer an economic explanation of that industry's distribution of nonprofit versus other providers.

2. How would you classify the United Way of Cleveland according to the various taxonomies offered in the text? The American Cancer Society? The Sierra Club?

CHAPTER 3

Policy and Management Issues

In this chapter, we examine some of the policy and management issues affecting today's nonprofit organizations and ask how economic analysis can contribute to the understanding and solution of some of these issues. As we have learned, the central concern of economic analysis is efficiency—that is, *how resources can be put to their most highly valued uses*. While we will encounter a number of other useful ideas and concepts from economics along the way, our focus here will be on efficiency.

POLICY ISSUES

In this section, we will briefly discuss three areas of public policy affecting nonprofit organizations: the choice of nonprofits over other institutional forms for the provision of particular services; issues of competition; and tax policy issues. These broad policy areas are among the most important ones affecting the future of nonprofit organizations, and they nicely illustrate how the ideas of economic analysis can help policy makers and managers conceptualize the issues and think them through.

Institutional Choice

In Chapter 2, a question that arose repeatedly was, What is the competitive advantage of the nonprofit organizational form? That is, when are nonprofits more efficient than for-profit or governmental organizations, and when are they not? Why are nonprofits found in some areas of the economy and not in others? Why are they found in greater numbers in some industries than in others? And why are they growing faster than other organizational forms? We also observed that nonprofit organizations are shaped by governmental policy, which can encourage or discourage the flow of resources to particular nonprofit organizations. Because government sets the rules of the game, the question of competitive advantage is closely related to the public policy issue we call *institutional choice*—that is, the determination of which parts of the economy government should encourage nonprofits to participate in and which parts it should not.

Recent studies of the nonprofit sector around the world show that governments make different choices regarding this issue (Gidron, et al., 1992). These choices are largely determined by historical developments and by political and social traditions, but there are economic factors as well. In the following section, we discuss two of these factors—information asymmetry and heterogeneity.

Information Asymmetry and the Inefficiencies of For-Profit Enterprises

Economists have identified three types of goods and services about which consumers are less well informed than sellers. The resulting *information asymmetry* is one economic factor underlying institutional choice. Several possible reasons for information asymmetry exist.

First, a good or service may be so complex that the purchaser must rely on the provider's expertise to make decisions. A good example is medical care, where the consumer must rely on the expertise and goodwill of care providers, trusting them to supply the appropriate quantity and quality of service. The pricing of medical services is also complex, and the consumer (or the consumer's insurance company) must rely, to some extent, on the provider's assertion that an appropriate amount is being charged for the level of care supplied.

A second category of information asymmetry involves situations where a donor contributes toward a collective good, such as aid for the impoverished, food for the hungry overseas, or cancer research. In such cases, the donor must rely on the skill and dedication of recipient agencies, trusting that they will use donations efficiently to support the type of service intended by the donor. Even when the promised quality of service is delivered, individual donors cannot discern whether the service has been paid for by their donations or those of others, and they cannot ascertain whether their donations have been used as intended or diverted for private uses. Thus, donors require assurance that their contributions have been well spent.

A third category of information asymmetry includes cases in which those who purchase services do so on behalf of others. For example, many adults may find themselves choosing among day-care centers for their children or nursing homes for their parents. In these cases, purchasers often have trouble ascertaining that the quality of service experienced by the client matches the quality agreed upon between the purchaser and the provider. Moreover, a "lock-in effect" often makes it difficult or medically risky to move a client to another facility if the purchaser or the client later discovers that the promised quality of service has not been delivered.

In situations involving information asymmetry, sellers may intentionally mislead consumers. Doctors who recommend unnecessary tests (or, more egregiously, unnecessary surgery) can pocket additional profits. Nursing homes that sedate their residents excessively do not need as large a staff to care for their customers, and this cost reduction adds to their profits. The temptation for organizations to mislead consumers in order to maximize profits is called *contract failure* (Hansmann, 1987). Nonprofit organizations are believed to be less prone to contract failure than for-profit organizations because they cannot gain from misleading customers. Any surplus resulting from sales, donations, or cost cutting cannot be distributed to "owners," and so there is more reason for donors and consumers to trust nonprofit organizations.

How does contract failure lead to inefficiency? Clearly, if there is contract failure, consumers will not be able to make choices that maximize the value of their purchases. In a world where all enterprises operated for profit, donors would not be able to contribute confidently toward the supply of goods and services because information asymmetry would prevail and donors would know that their contributions were likely to be ineffective. Hence, socially valuable enterprises would be hampered. Consumers would pay too much for health care and would have less income to devote to more highly valued purchases. Nursing home residents would be treated less compassionately, and the children of elderly parents would be denied the opportunity to purchase a higher level of service.

Information asymmetries also lead to subtler inefficiencies. For example, some providers may offer services with attractive, easily discernible characteristics (e.g., nice lobbies and grounds in nursing homes), while cutting back on the qualities that are harder to evaluate (e.g., nursing care). Such providers eventually drive out more scrupulous providers, who find it too expensive to compete by offering both tangible and intangible quality features. Weisbrod (1988) calls these service characteristics "type 1" and "type 2," respectively. Inefficiency results when, because of information asymmetry, type 2 attributes are underproduced relative to what consumers actually desire, while type 1 attributes are overproduced.

One theory argues that nonprofit organizations have a competitive advantage and are more trustworthy in situations of information asymmetry because the nondistribution constraint eliminates any incentive for non-profit providers to cheat consumers and pocket the difference as profits. Thus, it is argued, government should encourage the participation of non-profits under such conditions.

This is not the whole story, however. As Weisbrod (1988) argues, the nondistribution constraint comes at a price. In particular, if providers are motivated largely by the promise of wealth, prohibiting the distribution of profits may put a damper on the development of needed services. For example, the expansion of the nursing home industry in the 1960s and 1970s after Medicare and Medicaid became available was fueled largely by the for-profit sector, which moved quickly to exploit new profit opportunities. Nonprofits, partly because of more limited incentives, did not react as quickly. A sluggish response to new demands also produces inefficiency: when services that consumers value are slow to emerge, resources are not immediately put to their most valued uses.

Other efficiency arguments and considerations also enter the debate. Do nonprofits have the same incentives as for-profits to keep costs down? Why should their managers control costs if they cannot reap financial rewards from this control? Some have argued that leaders of nonprofit organizations are motivated by factors other than money (e.g., belief in the mission) and that these other motivations compensate for the lack of profit incentive. According to this argument, nonprofits are not as sluggish in responding to new demands or as slack in cost control as one might anticipate if financial reward were the only motive. The point of this discussion is not to resolve the question of whether nonprofits or for-profits are more desir-able in particular circumstances, but rather to illustrate how efficiency considerations are vital to analyzing such policy choices. (For more on this topic, see Steinberg and Gray, 1993.)

Heterogeneity, Excess Burden, and the Inefficiencies of Government The concept of information asymmetry is useful for comparing the relative efficiency of nonprofit and for-profit institutional providers. What happens when the choice is between governmental provision and private nonprofit provision? Since government must observe the nondistribution constraint, is not governmental provision as satisfactory as private nonprofit provision? This, too, is a complex issue that can be illuminated by focusing on economic efficiency. One question, of course, is whether government faces the same cost-control incentives as do private nonprofits. Presumably, if a government experiences rising costs, it can raise taxes to meet its expenses, or, in the federal case, it can simply increase its deficit. Access to the public treasury and the power to tax are factors that differentiate government provision from provision by nonprofits, which must pay their bills from existing revenues or go out of business. In this sense, government has weaker incentives to be efficient than nonprofit organizations.

A second source of governmental inefficiency stems from the side effects of governmental finance. Even though governments are restricted by a nondistribution constraint, donors may be reluctant to contribute voluntarily to an entity that has taxing power. Indeed, voluntary monetary contributions to government are negligible. Governments must rely on taxes, which, unlike voluntary contributions, distort the economy. A tax on personal income is a work disincentive; a tax on corporate income is an investment disincentive. To the direct payment of taxes, we must add these side effects as costs, and this constitutes what economists call the "excess burden" of taxation.

However, perhaps the most important reason that governmental provision is limited is politics, not inefficiency per se. Governmental decisions require a societal consensus (i.e., the support of more than half the electorate). But people disagree on the level of collective goods that should be provided by government. The frequency and intensity of this disagreement depends on the degree of diversity or heterogeneity within a given jurisdiction. Weisbrod (1975) argues that when a society is sufficiently heterogeneous, demanders of a high level of government services band together to support nonprofit organizations that can provide additional services on a voluntary basis. Conversely, in a homogeneous society, people agree on what should be provided by government, and there is no need for people to form their own organizations. In the latter instance, the nonprofit sector will be small.

Another way in which political systems accommodate heterogeneity of demand is through the formation of multiple governmental jurisdictions. If services are provided by many different local governments, variations in governmental provision across these communities can accommodate diverse demands. Citizens are free to move among local jurisdictions until they find a community that provides a package of services and taxation levels that they like (Tiebout, 1956). However, moving is costly and choices are often limited by employment opportunities and other factors. Moreover, public services are delivered in fixed packages (i.e., only one combination of police protection, fire fighting, day care, and public schooling is offered by a given jurisdiction), so that consumers cannot separate the services they like from those they don't. However, when nonprofits rather than government provide these services, people can choose among services without having to move to exercise their preferences (James, 1989).

Competition

Another important policy area of concern to leaders and managers of nonprofit organizations is that of competition in the provision of various kinds of goods and services. Generally, public policy favors competition, and economists argue that competitive markets are the most efficient means of allocating resources to their best uses. Major exceptions to this rule exist for some industries, such as utilities, where efficiency considerations require large-scale operation and hence regulated monopolies, and for goods and services whose characteristics preclude profit-making businesses from operating profitably or in a manner that is efficient for society. (See the discussion of market failure in Chapter 9.)

The nonprofit sector has important interests in a number of competition-related issues. These include competition between nonprofits and for-profit business as well as the question of competition and collaboration within the nonprofit sector.

Competition with For-Profits

Nonprofit and for-profit organizations compete in two types of markets: within mixed industries in service areas directly related to the nonprofit's mission, and in commercial areas not directly related to the nonprofit's mission but directly competitive with some for-profit firms. Each type of competition raises complex efficiency issues.

Competition between for-profits and nonprofits within mixed industries entails a number of important efficiency considerations. First, nonprofits and for-profits may occupy different niches within a given industry rather than compete head-to-head. Contract failure leads to one form of such market segmentation by sectors. If poorly informed consumers prefer to use nonprofit organizations and better-informed consumers feel they can obtain services closer to their preferences from for-profits, then these two forms complement each other and the arrangement is efficient: all consumers find their preferred service alternatives and can put their resources to their most highly valued uses.

However, if nonprofits and for-profits compete head-to-head, there may be other dangers, particularly in industries that produce different varieties of services for different groups of clients. For example, in the hospital industry, nonprofits have historically followed the practice of using profits from one area of service—say, elective surgeries—to fund public-benefit services such as care for the indigent, research, and medical education. In the absence of other servicing arrangements, this may have been a relatively efficient practice for allocating resources to charitable services that were not funded in any other way. However, as for-profit hospitals proliferated, they began to compete directly with nonprofits in those service areas that were producing profits. This practice has undercut the ability of nonprofits to subsidize such services. While the competition from for-profits may have induced nonprofits to become more efficient in those service areas in which they were challenged, overall the competition may have undercut economic efficiency by preventing hospitals from offering sufficient levels of public benefits (Eckel and Steinberg, 1993).

The second aspect of nonprofit/for-profit competition concerns the offering of commercial goods and services by nonprofits in competition with for-profit businesses. This competition may be healthy for three reasons. First, if nonprofits provide fair competition for businesses then they help spur all providers to become more efficient. Second, nonprofits may have real economic advantages in the provision of certain commercial services. For example, university bookstores and recreational facilities can easily employ inexpensive student labor. Similarly, nonprofits may be able to utilize existing plant resources and equipment to offer commercial services more cheaply. The photographic labs of medical schools, for example, can use their facilities to offer commercial photo processing. In these cases, nonprofits may actually enhance efficiency by offering selected commercial services at a lower real cost. Third, if nonprofits use their profits to subsidize their mission-related services, or if their commercial services directly enhance the mission-related services (e.g., Girl Scout cookie sales teach girls important lessons about responsibility), then, overall, resources may be allocated to their most valued uses.

However, a complicating factor is that nonprofits and for-profits are subject to different tax benefits and subsidies. If nonprofits receive greater subsidies than do businesses, then inefficient nonprofits may be able to compete despite having higher real costs. The potential for inefficiency exists when a nonprofit sells commercial services in competition with a business and those services are considered "related" to the mission of the nonprofit organization. In such a case, the nonprofit has a tax advantage because its commercial revenue is not subject to unrelated business income tax. If a commercial service is classified as "unrelated," however, the imposition of UBIT helps to avoid inefficiency by eliminating the nonprofit's tax advantage.

The threat of inefficiency remains in instances where nonprofits use the same facilities to offer both mission-related services and unrelated commercial services. The provision of commercial services by a medical school photo lab is an example of this. Allocating the joint costs of such facilities properly can be difficult from an accounting perspective, and businesses complain that nonprofits attribute too large a proportion of such costs to the commercial service so as to minimize profit estimates and avoid paying UBIT. In such cases, inefficiency can be introduced because businesses face higher net tax costs than do nonprofits, which gives nonprofits an artificial advantage.

Competition Among Nonprofits   Unlike for-profits, nonprofit organizations are often encouraged to cooperate among themselves instead of competing. Hence, they organize shared fund-raising mechanisms such as United Way; operate within federated networks of service provision; participate in planning councils; create joint projects and partnerships; form regional, statewide, and national associations to set standards and coordinate actions; and so on. However, contemporary public policy has yet to resolve what would be an appropriate competition policy for nonprofits. Recently, the Ivy League universities were prohibited from collaborating on offers of scholarships to particular students and exchanging other information in order to eliminate price competition and achieve diversity in their student bodies. However, Eckel and Steinberg's (1993) argument applies here. If nonprofit universities use their "monopoly profits" to subsidize balance in the student body, then efficiency may be enhanced rather than undermined by collaboration.

Another important area of competition policy is the domain of fund raising. Nonprofits in a given field of service or in a particular community frequently recognize that they are fishing from the same donor pool and that without a coordinated mechanism they will drive up the costs of fund development for everyone. In that case, they will reap much smaller net monetary gains that can be used for direct service provision. Thus, united funding arrangements can increase efficiency.

Typically, united funding organizations (UFOs) require that member organizations accept their UFO distributions in lieu of conducting an independent campaign; this practice reduces overfishing. UFOs also enhance efficiency in several other ways—by making giving convenient, by auditing member organizations to enhance donor confidence, and by saving donors the trouble of exploring the worthiness of competing causes. However, UFOs cannot fully realize these efficiencies because some organizations refuse to give up their independent fund raising (see Rose-Ackerman, 1980).

UFOs are controversial because they often have virtually monopolistic access to payroll deduction plans, forcing nonmember organizations to use costlier fund-raising methods. A monopolistic UFO may waste some of its cost advantage by becoming lax in its solicitation efforts, in its administrative operations, or in the care with which funds are distributed to recipient charities. Against these disadvantages, one must weigh the efficiency gains for member organizations and donors.

Taxation and Subsidy Policies

In order to encourage and facilitate the work of nonprofit organizations, various tax and subsidy incentives are provided through governmental policy. These include deductibility of donations from personal income taxes as well as postal and other direct subsidies.

Income Tax Deductions Prominent among tax and subsidy policies favoring nonprofits is the deductibility from personal income taxes of charitable donations to public benefit (i.e., 501(c)3) organizations. Economists have asked whether this provision, as currently constituted, is efficient (see Roberts, 1987).

Economists have an interesting way of analyzing the charitable deduction. They observe that the deduction provides incentives for donors to give more to charity by effectively lowering the "price" of giving. By this they mean that the cost to the donor of giving a dollar to charity is less than a dollar when the donor can recover part of that money through lower taxes. Thus, if a donor is in a 30-percent income-tax bracket, the cost of giving a dollar to charity is only 70 cents.

Tax incentives are a means that government commonly uses to encourage individuals or organizations to act in a particular way—in this case, to support charitable causes. However, economists have expressed concern about inefficiencies in the charitable deduction stemming from two sources: 1) the fact that the price of giving is different for different people, and 2) the fact that the price of giving money is different from the price of giving time (volunteering).

Income-tax rates are generally progressive—that is, they increase as taxable income increases. One implication of this is that the greater a person's income, the lower is his or her price of giving (i.e., the lower the net cost to give an additional dollar to charity). This means that the charitable deduction is biased toward allocation of resources to charities favored by wealthier members of society. Unless as a society we are prepared to make the judgment that such charities are more worthwhile, the charitable deduction is inefficient because it allocates more money to charities favored by the wealthy and less money to charities favored by the less wealthy than would be the case if the price of giving were the same for everyone. In addition to efficiency, fairness is an issue when it costs more for a poor person to donate a dollar to charity than it costs a rich person. Some have called the donation deduction an "upside-down subsidy." These are among the reasons why analysts such as Weisbrod (1988) have argued in favor of a system under which people would receive tax credits for their donations. A tax credit would give taxpayers a direct reduction of their taxes equal to some fixed percentage of their donations, regardless of tax bracket. Such a price-neutral system would not artificially distort the price of giving and would allow all individuals to allocate their charitable dollars under the same conditions, much as all consumers in a supermarket pay the same prices for available goods.

Giving Time Versus Giving Money Let us now consider the case of volunteering. Suppose that a taxpayer is in the 25-percent tax bracket and earns $10 an hour when he or she works. If the taxpayer itemizes deductions, then the tax system does not bias the choice between giving time and giving money:

- If the taxpayer volunteers for an hour and is equally productive as a volunteer and as a paid worker, he or she gives a gift worth $10 but forgoes only $7.50 in after-tax income.
- If the taxpayer works for an hour and gives $10 to charity, he or she deducts $10 and receives a $2.50 reduction in taxes. The net cost to the taxpayer is the same as if he or she had volunteered, namely $7.50.

However, consider the case of a non-itemizer with the same tax bracket and earning capacity:

- If the non-itemizing taxpayer works for an hour and gives $10 to charity, he or she receives no deduction. The net cost in this case is $10.
- If the taxpayer volunteers for an hour, he or she gives a gift worth $10 but forgoes only $7.50 in after-tax income. Thus the net cost is only $7.50.

Clearly, the tax code is biased in favor of gifts of time rather than money for those who do not itemize deductions. But why is this inefficient? People volunteer for many reasons, but the costs of volunteering influence how much they volunteer. The tax code can influence the taxpayer's choice between working and volunteering. Even if an extra hour of working produces the same value as an hour of volunteering, the taxpayer will be induced to volunteer more and work less (and give less cash) than would be efficient.

A second reason why the tax code produces inefficiency relates to the charity itself. The charity may be able to produce more value with more cash income and less volunteering, but the tax code inhibits such reallocation even though the real cost of the taxpayer's contribution is the same whether the contribution involves money or time. Again, resources are not put to their most highly valued uses. If the tax code were neutral with respect to giving cash and giving time, the allocation of these resources by the taxpayer and the charity would more closely reflect the actual value of the resources.

Subsidy Policies Direct subsidy policies can also cause inefficiency. An example is the postal subsidy available to nonprofit organizations. This subsidy is intended to help nonprofit organizations by lowering the cost of communicating with donors, clients, and other constituents. While its goal may be laudable, the postal subsidy artificially reduces the price to nonprofits of one particular means of communication. This may induce nonprofits to make inefficient choices in how they organize their communications budgets.

Consider the example of fund-raising solicitation. Suppose it costs 50 cents to raise a dollar by phone and 60 cents to raise a dollar by mail. If the government subsidizes the use of the postal service by, say, 25 percent, then the cost to the nonprofit of raising a dollar by mail will be only 45 cents (since the government pays the remaining 15 cents). Thus, the nonprofit will choose to use the mail rather than the phone, even though the real cost of using the mail is higher, and society will not be putting its resources to their best uses. (Note that we are ignoring here the additional costs associated with telephone fund raising, such as the annoyance people feel at being called during the dinner hour. If these costs are substantial, the postal subsidy may increase efficiency by shifting fund-raising activity from the telephone to the mails. On the other hand, there are also costs associated with producing, handling, and disposing of junk mail.)

Let's take this example further. How can public policy help the nonprofit be more efficient? The value of the subsidy to the nonprofit is 15 cents per dollar raised by mail. Suppose the nonprofit is raising $100 by spending $45. This costs the government $15. Suppose the government were to simply give the nonprofit $15. Then the nonprofit could spend $60 (the original $45 budget plus the unearmarked grant of $15) and could raise $120 by phone calls ($1 raised for each $.50 spent). The same resources would be used to produce greater results, and the inefficiency would be eliminated.

The exemption of nonprofit organizations from local property taxes probably creates inefficiencies as well. In suburbs and rural areas, where property tax rates are low, tax exemption does not provide many advantages to nonprofit organizations. However, in central cities, where tax rates are higher, exemption provides a substantial subsidy, and this difference in subsidy rates makes nonprofit organizations more likely to locate in central cities than they otherwise would be. Inefficiencies may develop as the central city is forced to raise tax rates to compensate for the loss of taxable property to exempt organizations. Higher taxes in turn may hasten the relocation of taxable businesses to the suburbs. On the other hand, nonprofit symphony orchestras and art museums may provide amenity values that increase the desirability of locating taxable businesses downtown, slowing or even reversing the decay of the urban tax base. Thus, the level of inefficiency created by nonprofits' exemption from property taxes depends on the difference between tax rates in neighboring communities and on the types of services provided by nonprofits.

MANAGEMENT ISSUES

Clearly, nonprofit leaders must be aware of the policy issues affecting nonprofit organizations, for these policies affect day-to-day operations as well as impel nonprofit leaders to seek policy reforms. Of more immediate concern to nonprofit leaders, however, are the managerial decisions and strategies they must oversee within their own organizations.

Volunteer Management

Typically, volunteer labor is regarded as "free" because volunteers do not earn salaries. This view leads to the assumption that nonprofit organizations should accept any and all volunteers who show up on their doorstep. Is this efficient? A careful economic analysis reveals that there are substantial costs associated with taking on volunteers, and that it is important to account not only for pecuniary, or "out-of-pocket," costs but for all economic costs associated with using valuable (scarce) resources. (We elaborate on these cost concepts in Chapter 6.)

Volunteers require supervision and guidance by paid staff. They may require space and supplies, reimbursement for travel, and other kinds of support costs. Volunteers may require training in the skills they need for tasks they are asked to undertake. If they are not compatible with the organization, they may be disruptive, causing losses in work effort and organizational effectiveness. Special recruitment efforts may be needed to find the right kinds of volunteers (Brudney, 1990).

On the other hand, volunteers, properly selected and strategically deployed, produce valuable benefits for nonprofit organizations. It is important to ask how many of what kinds of volunteers should be sought and accepted, and what it is worth spending to secure these volunteers? These are economic decisions that should be guided by a desire to put limited resources to their best uses. Accepting all comers will be inefficient if it produces more costs than benefits. Refusing volunteers and allocating no resources to their development is also likely to be inefficient because important opportunities and benefits may be lost. Finding the right level and mixture of volunteers and determining how much to invest in volunteers are issues that nonprofit managers and leaders must resolve if they are to use their resources in the most efficient way.

Fund Raising

The development of charitable donations is another important area of economic decision making for the nonprofit manager, and it is in many respects a controversial area. Managers must decide, for example, how much to spend on fund-raising efforts, which are often monitored by watchdog groups and donors concerned about administrative costs, and whether donations are really going to support programs. While donors' concerns about administrative costs are important, particularly if perceived high administrative costs discourage donations, there is an equally serious risk that nonprofits will underinvest in fund-raising efforts. Economic analysis can help illuminate this question by distinguishing between the set-up costs of a fund-raising effort and the incremental or marginal costs of soliciting additional funds. Such analysis shows that relatively high average fund-raising costs are not necessarily inefficient and that nonprofit organizations may be forgoing important funding opportunities by limiting themselves to circumstances where they can show that average costs are low (see Steinberg, 1988-89).

Other aspects of fund raising can also benefit from economic analysis. In the discussion of postal subsidies earlier in this chapter, we referred to one aspect of the question of alternative means of soliciting funds. Whether fund raising is subsidized or not, it is important to determine what combination of fund-raising methods will be the most efficient. Again, economic analysis can help by focusing on the incremental yields of different methods as more and more funds are raised.

Finally, one needs to consider the respective merits of joint, or federated, fund raising and fund raising by individual organizations. We mentioned this issue earlier in connection with competition policy. For the individual organization, too, this may be an important economic decision. What are the benefits and costs of joining a federated campaign? How can this decision be made sensibly? Again, economic analysis can help by evaluating the best use of an organization's limited resources and its competitive advantage vis-à-vis other organizations.

Many other nonprofit managerial decisions can benefit from economic analysis to determine efficient choices. These decisions may involve the level and pricing of services, the forms of revenues to be pursued, or the allocation of resources among programs, to name a few. Addressing these issues more precisely, as well as the policy issues considered above, requires sharper tools than we have been able to apply thus far in the discussion. The next several chapters will develop these tools.

SUMMARY

In this chapter we have seen how economic reasoning, particularly the concept of efficiency, can be applied to the analysis of public policy issues that affect nonprofit organizations as well as how it can be used by nonprofit managers to make more satisfactory operational decisions. In the policy arena, economics helps us understand the situations in which nonprofits have a competitive advantage relative to business or government entities; how competition among nonprofits and between nonprofits and business is affected by public policy; and how taxation and subsidy policies affect the behavior of nonprofit organizations as well as the resources available to them. In the nonprofit management area, economic analysis illuminates a number of important operational concerns, including the recruitment and deployment of volunteers and the level and form of fund-raising efforts.

REFERENCES

Brudney, Jeffrey L. *Fostering Volunteer Programs in the Public Sector*. San Francisco: Jossey-Bass, 1990.

Clotfelter, Charles T. *Federal Tax Policy and Charitable Giving*. Chicago: University of Chicago Press, 1985.

Clotfelter, Charles T. "Tax-Induced Distortions in the Voluntary Sector." *Case Western Reserve Law Review*, 39:3, 1988-89, pp. 663-704.

Eckel, Catherine C., and Richard Steinberg. "Competition, Performance, and Public Policy Towards Nonprofits." Chapter 2 in David C. Hammack and Dennis R. Young (eds.), *Nonprofit Organizations in a Market Economy*. San Francisco: Jossey-Bass, 1993.

Gidron, Benjamin, Ralph M. Kramer, and Lester M. Salamon (eds.). *Government and the Third Sector*. San Francisco: Jossey-Bass, 1992.

Hansmann, Henry. "Economic Theories of Nonprofit Organization." Chapter 2 in Walter W. Powell (ed.), *The Nonprofit Sector: A Research Handbook*. New Haven: Yale University Press, 1987.

James, Estelle (ed.). *The Nonprofit Sector in International Perspective*. New York: Oxford University Press, 1989.

Mauser, Elizabeth. "What Organizational Form Represents from the Perspective of Managers and Consumers." Paper presented to the annual meeting of the Association for Research on Nonprofit Organizations and Voluntary Action, New Haven, Conn., Oct. 1992.

Roberts, Russell. "Financing Public Goods." *Journal of Political Economy*, 95, April 1987, pp. 420-437.

Rose-Ackerman, Susan. "United Charities: An Economic Analysis." *Public Policy*, 28, Summer 1980, pp. 323-350.

Steinberg, Richard. "Economic Perspectives on Regulation of Charitable Solicitation." *Case Western Reserve Law Review*, 39:3, 1988-89.

Steinberg, Richard, and Bradford Gray. "'The Role of Nonprofit Enterprise' in 1993: Hansmann Revisited." *Nonprofit and Voluntary Sector Quarterly*, 22:4, Winter 1993, pp. 297-316.

Tiebout, Charles M. "A Pure Theory of Local Expenditures." *Journal of Political Economy*, 64, Oct. 1956, pp. 416-424.

Weisbrod, Burton A. "Toward a Theory of the Voluntary Non-Profit Sector in a Three Sector Economy." In Edmund S. Phelps (ed.), *Altruism, Morality and Economic Theory*. New York: Russell Sage Foundation, 1975, pp. 171-195.

Weisbrod, Burton A. *The Nonprofit Economy*. Cambridge, Mass.: Harvard University Press, 1988.

EXERCISES

1. If nonprofits develop in response to problems of asymmetric information, why are there no nonprofit automobile repair shops?

2. Elizabeth Mauser (1992) found that parents who placed their children in nonprofit day-care centers spent more time researching their choice than those who put their children in for-profit day care. What does this say about the contract-failure theory?

3. For each of the following situations, would you expect the nonprofit sector to be relatively large or relatively small compared to the government and/or for-profit sectors? Explain.

    a. Preferences for public services differ substantially among local communities but are homogeneous within each local jurisdiction.

    b. A new city has rapidly growing needs for social services, and the average resident lives in the community for only a couple of years before moving out.

    c. Property taxes are extremely high, but nonprofits are exempt from these taxes.

4. Suppose we were to eliminate the current tax deduction for personal donations and replace it with a matching-grant system. At the end of each year, each nonprofit would mail an (audited) statement to the government indicating the total amount of personal donations it had received that year. The government would then mail to the nonprofit a check representing a fixed fraction of donations. For example, if the matching rate were 30 percent and a charity received $100,000 in donations, the government would mail a check for $30,000.

a. This system is similar to a tax-credit system in terms of the resulting effective "prices" for giving. Explain.

b. There is at least one important difference between the effect of a tax credit and the effect of matching. Identify and explain the difference.

c. The matching grants would eliminate the pattern of "upside-down subsidy" in the current system of tax deductions. Explain why this is so and discuss whether this change is desirable.

CHAPTER 4

Analysis of Economic Functions: Total, Average, and Marginal

In economic analysis, important relationships among economic quantities such as costs, revenues, prices, input resources, and output goods and service levels are represented by a mathematical construct called a *function*. So, with apologies to Hagar in the accompanying cartoon, we need to delve a little into elementary mathematics.

A function is a representation, in mathematical, tabular, graphical, or other form, of how two or more quantities change in relation to one another. Before we learn about functions in economic analysis, we must first become familiar with the building blocks of functions, namely variables.

A *variable* is a quantity that takes on different numerical values in different circumstances. Thus, cost, revenue, price, and donations are all

Reprinted with special permission of King Feature Syndicate.

variables that can assume different positive or negative dollar values. Time, as measured in hours, minutes, or seconds, is also a variable.

In the construction of functions, we distinguish conceptually between two types of variables—independent variables and dependent variables. A *dependent variable* is a quantity whose value we want to explain or predict based on its relationship with other determining or influencing variables that we call *independent variables*.

For example, suppose we are interested in what influences students' attention spans in class. The attention span of students (measured by the percentage of time they are actually listening to the lecturer) becomes our dependent variable. We can suppose that the length of the class (measured in hours) is an influencing, or independent, variable. If we graph our dependent variable (usually on the vertical axis) against our independent variable (usually on the horizontal axis), the result will resemble Figure 4.1. This graph shows that, past some point, as classes get longer and longer, the attention span of students decreases. This example illustrates that a function can describe compactly—in this case, graphically—the relationship between a dependent and an independent variable in a way that facilitates an informed decision about how long the class period should be.

It is likely, however, that our dependent variable—student attention—is influenced by a number of variables, not just the length of the class. In general, it is important to distinguish among different types of independent variables—those under our control, which we call *choice variables*, and those beyond our control, which we call *environmental variables*. In the foregoing example, the length of the class is presumably a choice variable, since we can influence student attention levels by selecting its value. However, other variables not subject to our control, such as the weather, may also influence student attention. These are environmental variables.

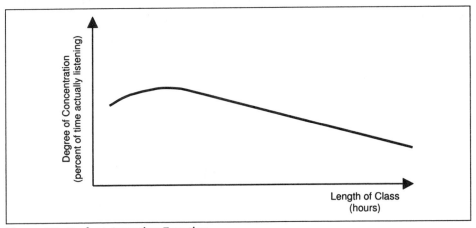

Figure 4.1 Student Attention Function

An example of a function from the economics of nonprofit organizations is the *donative revenue function*, which relates how much an organization receives in donations in a given time period (the dependent variable) to such influencing variables as how much is spent on fund raising (a choice variable) and the wealth of potential donors (an environmental variable).

To focus on the variables under our control, we usually depict the relationship between choice and dependent variables while holding environmental variables constant at some pre-specified level. Economists call this idea of holding other variables constant while studying the relationship between two particular variables *ceteris paribus* ("holding all other things equal"), and it enables us to simplify the discussion considerably by breaking our analysis into a sequence of steps. Figure 4.2 provides an illustration. The lower curve in this figure represents a donative revenue function for a charity during a recession, when the environmental variable Y, the level of income in the donor community, remains constant at a low level (Y_3). The upper curve illustrates the donative revenue function for that charity in good times, when donors enjoy income Y_1. The middle curve illustrates the function when donor income takes the intermediate value Y_2.

The figure shows that contributions increase with increases in fund-raising expenditure. However, the level of contributions (i.e., the height of the curves) is also influenced by the level of income in the donor community. At any given level of fund-raising expenditure, donations are higher when income is higher. Thus, if this organization spent $10,000 on fund raising

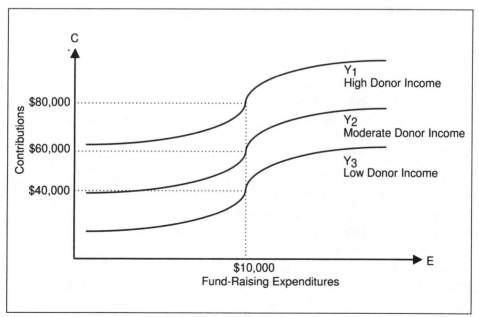

Figure 4.2 Donative Revenue Function at Different Income Levels

during a recession, it would receive $40,000 in donations. The same organization could obtain $80,000 in donations if it spent $10,000 on solicitation during an economic boom.

Now that we are familiar with dependent and independent variables, we can think of a function more precisely as a mathematical or graphical representation that shows how a dependent variable appears to change in response to changes in independent variables. We should be cautious about inferring causality, however. In reality, it is often unclear what causes what (e.g., does fund-raising expenditure increase donations, or do increased donations cause excited fund raisers to spend more?) and whether some third, unidentified variable (e.g., a hunger crisis spurring both donations and spending on fund raising) is influencing both the independent and the dependent variables. Correlation does not necessarily imply causation. These caveats notwithstanding, the reader may find it useful to think in terms of cause and effect when examining how a function summarizes the relationship between dependent and independent variables in an economic function.

In economics, there are many different types of important functions, including cost and revenue functions, production functions that relate inputs to outputs, demand and supply functions, and others. In addition, the relationships between particular dependent and independent variables, such as cost and quantity produced (which we will call output), may be represented in several different ways. In this chapter we will discuss three kinds of representation—total, average, and marginal—for two significant types of economic functions: cost functions and revenue functions.

OUTPUT

Economic functions depict the relationships among two or more economic variables such as costs, revenues, or amounts produced. One often-used variable is output. *Output* refers to the level of a good or service that is produced, as measured by some quantitative indicator.

In industries that produce manufactured goods, the concept of output is quite straightforward. Output can be measured by such indicators as the number of pairs of shoes, cans of fruit, tons of steel, or personal computers. Even when we are referring to goods, however, we must qualify output measurement by standardizing for *quality*. One personal computer is not the same as another, so we must indicate the quality or specifications that characterize any particular output unit we may be using. Similarly, in the provision of services, such as those offered by nonprofit organizations, we must attend to the quality issue. Here, the measure of output we select often requires more judgment than in the goods case and may depend on the purpose of our analysis. For example, in the performing arts we sometimes consider output as the number of performances given and at other times as the number of seats filled.

In general, we want to distinguish between outputs and outcomes. *Outputs* are variables that can be directly controlled by the producer because they depend primarily on the input resources (labor, capital equipment, etc.) and the technology that the producing organization employs. Thus, an *output function* depicts output as the dependent variable and inputs to production as the independent (choice) variables. *Outcomes*, by contrast, represent the social impact of outputs and depend not only on the outputs but on other (environmental) independent variables as well. Thus, an *outcome function* frames outcome as the dependent variable and output and environment variables as the independent variables.

Outcomes often reflect the overall mission of a nonprofit organization. Consider the following examples:

- The output of a meal program for children may be measured in terms of the number of meals served or the number of children served. The desired outcome is better child health, which is dependent not only on proper eating but on medical care, good housing, and other factors not within the program's purview.
- The output of a school may be measured by the number of courses offered or the number of students graduated. The desired outcome is a more skilled and educated population, which may depend not only on schooling but also on the upbringing of students and the economic opportunities to which they have access.
- The output of a theater may be measured in terms of the number of plays produced or the number of theatergoers served. The desired outcome may be greater arts appreciation in the community, which will depend on the socioeconomic character of the community as well as its access to theater.
- The output of a community foundation or a United Way may be the number of dollars raised or the amount of money given as grants. The desired outcome is a more prosperous and well-functioning community, which depends on many other socio-economic factors.

Several comments about outputs and outcomes are relevant here. First, notice that in some of the examples, a given organization or program may have multiple outputs (e.g., courses offered, students graduated) and particular outputs may be associated with multiple outcomes (e.g., skilled workers, informed citizens). While multiple outputs and outcomes techni-cally can be accommodated in our framework here, for explanatory purposes we focus primarily on single outputs and outcomes. (In Chapter 8, we will consider multiple outputs explicitly.)

Second, the examples suggest the importance of clearly identifying a measurable unit of output that is thought to contribute to better outcomes. Analyses of costs, revenues, and other important economic variables will all revolve around this measure. Output measures, which represent the direct products of organizations, are usually easier for an organization to define and measure than are ultimate outcome measures. While we would often like to focus directly on outcome, it is usually more practical to analyze managerial decisions as they affect output. Even where global measures of outcome such as poverty, unemployment, or child mortality rates are available (for example, from government bureaus), a manager will have trouble discerning any impact on such measures by his or her particular program or organization. Thus, practically speaking, the manager must make decisions in terms of output.

Nonetheless, in making such decisions, managers need to be sure that output positively influences outcome. If a clear case can be made that desired outcomes are positively associated with increased output, then economic analysis can help determine how much output is efficient. However, choos-ing a level of output or among alternative outputs may pose difficulties if there is no strong evidence that more output leads to better outcomes or that one output is more effective than another in achieving a desired outcome. For example, in order to increase the scientific literacy of students, should schools produce more hours of classroom instruction, or should they offer more field trips? Economic analysis can help structure how we think about this problem, but resolving the problem itself will require advances in the understanding of educational programs.

The various functions we will study next are generic and can be applied to different measures of output. The important thing to understand is that output is a measure of how much an organization produces of a particular good or service. Output is the key independent variable in several critical economic functions that we will study, including cost functions, revenue functions, demand functions, supply functions, and profit functions.

THE CONCEPT OF COST

The first type of function we will study is the *cost function*, which relates the value of resources used in the production of a good or service (cost) to the amount of the good or service that is produced (output). In Chapter 6 we will look more closely at the nature of cost, the concept of which is basic to economics. Here we provide a brief explanation.

Fundamentally, we define economic cost as the value of the opportunities that are lost when resources are put to one use instead of another. For instance, if a resource is committed to a given use—say, buying the toys used for children in a day-care program—the cost is the value of that same resource in its *next best use*. If the toys would otherwise have been bought by a family for use by its children, then the cost of their use in the day-care program is the value that the family assigns to the toys.

Note that *economic cost* is not the same as *accounting cost*. The amount paid for something may not equal the good's or service's worth in its next best use. However, in the case of the toys, the two are probably the same since, if the day-care center had not bought the toys, the family would have bought the same toys at the same price from other sources. On the other hand, suppose a worker in a hospital would be unemployed if he or she did not work at the hospital. In this case, the sum of the worker's wages and benefits (the accounting cost) is not an accurate estimate of the economic cost of using the worker's time because the worker cannot get another job at that wage. Rather, an appropriate estimate would be the wage in the next best available job or, if there is no such job, the value the worker assigns to additional hours of leisure. By contrast, the cost of a volunteer's time may be significant even though his or her wage is zero, since the volunteer is giving up scarce time that could be applied to other valued uses.

This discussion may seem esoteric for the hospital manager who has to pay the worker's wages and benefits, or for the administrator of volunteer services who does not pay dollar wages to his or her charges. However, it is important to take into account the volunteer's cost because, whether or not the cost shows up on the books, the volunteer knows intuitively that his or her work is not free. Rather, it consumes valuable leisure time. Administrators who ignore this cost risk losing volunteer effort.

This brings us to still another important point—that perspectives on costs may vary, depending on the nature of the decision or the decision maker involved. Economists make a distinction between *private costs* incurred by particular economic actors such as organizations, workers, or consumers and *social costs* incurred by society as a whole. The social cost of employing a worker who otherwise would be unemployed is very low, but the private cost to the employer may be much higher. On the other hand, while the private cost to the organization that employs a volunteer may be low, the social cost of using that volunteer's time may be much higher. (We will consider the distinction between social and private costs further in Chapter 9 when we discuss "externalities.")

COST FUNCTIONS

How do we represent the relationship between the output produced by an organization and the cost of producing that output?

Fixed and Variable Costs

To answer this question, we need to break the idea of costs down into two basic components, fixed costs and variable costs.

Fixed costs are those components of cost that do not vary or change with the level of output. *Variable costs* are those components of cost that do vary with the level of output. In other words, fixed costs are costs that need to be expended before even the first unit of output can be produced, whereas variable costs are the additional costs incurred as more and more output is produced. The following are some examples of fixed and variable costs.

- In order to produce a play, you need a theater, costumes, stage sets, a rehearsed cast, a crew, and management before even one performance can be offered. These are fixed costs. Then, for each performance, additional costs are incurred for the daily wages of ticket takers, ushers, clean-up crews, actors, and other staff; for the printing of programs; for utilities such as water and electricity; and for various other supplies and services. These are the variable costs that increase with the number of performances.

- In order to run a fund-raising campaign, you need an office, a desk, a telephone, a computer, some basic information resources, and perhaps a certain amount of an administrator's time. These are the fixed costs that need to be in place before a single dollar is raised. As more and more funds are solicited and secured, costs are incurred for the time spent by fund-raising volunteers or consultants, for phone calls and mailed letters, for supplies, for electricity and other utilities, for transportation to visit potential donors, and so on. These are the variable costs that increase with the level of funds raised.

Note that the classification of cost components into the categories of fixed and variable depends on the time frame in which costs are being considered. In particular, what may be a fixed cost in the short run may become a variable cost in the long run. In principle, if production decisions are made over a long enough period of time, there will be no fixed costs; all costs can be varied to accommodate production needs. The capacities of facilities can be modified, administrative staffs increased or decreased, and other resources adjusted to just the right level for the most efficient production. Indeed, technically we can define long-run costs as the costs incurred over a time period that allows all fixed costs to vary. For a given level of output, long-run costs per unit of output are lower than short-run average costs because they represent maximum flexibility in adjusting all inputs to their optimal levels. That is, over the long run, average costs will be lower because fixed costs can be adjusted to promote efficiency.

Consider the case of a school. In the short run, the facility costs may be fixed; there is no opportunity to expand or contract the size of the building to accommodate more or fewer students within a year's time. However, over a 10-year period, school capacity can be considered a variable cost that may be adjusted in anticipation of changes in the number of students served. On the other hand, even though the staff costs of a school are variable on a year-to-year basis, if we are analyzing costs within the time frame of say, one month, contract commitments or constraints on hiring for short periods of time may preclude changes, making this a fixed cost for that purpose. Thus, classification of cost components as fixed and variable depends on the time frame of the analysis.

Total, Average, and Marginal Cost Functions

Using the concepts of fixed and variable costs, we can represent the relationship between costs and output in three different ways.

Total cost is the sum of fixed and variable costs at a given level of output. The *total cost function* shows how total cost varies with the level of output.

Average cost is the cost per unit of output, calculated at a given level of output. Average cost is calculated by dividing total cost by the level of output. The *average cost function* shows how average cost varies with the level of output. (Note that average cost is more precisely called *average total cost,* since it is the sum of fixed and variable costs divided by output.) We can also compute *average variable cost* (equal to variable cost divided by output) and *average fixed cost* (equal to fixed cost divided by output). Average total cost is the sum of average fixed cost and average variable cost at any given level of output.

Marginal cost is the additional cost of increasing output by one unit at a given level of output production. The *marginal cost function* shows how marginal cost varies with the level of output.

Note that total cost is measured in units of dollars, while average cost and marginal cost are measured in dollars per unit of output. These units, and careful specification of the output measure, are important to remember in making proper comparisons.

Consider a dramatic example of these various cost measures. Suppose the fixed cost of producing a student play at a high school is $1,000 and the additional cost of producing each performance is $100. Suppose further that initially five performances are being considered. At this level of output:

fixed cost = $1,000;
variable cost = $500 at the five-performance level;
total cost = $1,000 + $500 = $1,500;
average cost = $1,500/5 = $300 per performance;
average variable cost = $500/5 = $100 per performance at the
    five-performance level; and
marginal cost = $100, the cost of a sixth performance.

How do we go from such calculations to representing total, average, and marginal costs as functions, and how are these functions related to one another? Let's consider a slightly more complicated example (represented in Table 4.1) depicting the costs and revenues of a Meals on Wheels program. The output measure for this program is the number of meals delivered per day to homebound people in need. The set-up or fixed cost is $15 for the availability of a van and driver (obviously a bargain!). The first column in the table shows the number of meals delivered. Note that the fixed cost (column 2) is by definition the same, regardless of the number of meals delivered. Column 3 shows the variable cost of meals and fuel for the van, which increases with the number of meals delivered. Column 4 shows the total cost (*TC*), which is calculated by adding the fixed cost in column 2 to the variable cost given in column 3. Column 5 shows the average cost (*AC*), which is found by dividing *TC* in column 4 by the output (number of meals) in column 1. Column 6 shows the average variable cost (*AVC*), which is computed by dividing variable cost (column 3) by output. Column 7 shows the marginal cost (*MC*), which is calculated by subtracting the total cost in column 4 in that row from the total cost in column 4 of the row below.

Let's take a closer look at the calculation of the marginal cost column. For the purposes of our analysis, we will represent the level of output (number of meals) by the variable Q. Now suppose that the number of meals delivered is six (i.e., Q=6). What is the marginal cost of producing that last (sixth) meal? It is the total cost (*TC*) of producing six meals minus the *TC* for producing five meals. Thus, we write:

$$MC(6) = TC(6) - TC(5) = \$31.50 - \$28 = \$3.50.$$

Thus, $3.50 appears in the table in column 6 at the level of output (Q) of six meals. To generalize the above equation for any level of output, we write:

$$MC(Q) = TC(Q) - TC(Q-1).$$

TABLE 4.1
Meals on Wheels: Cost and Revenue Functions

Meals /Day	Fix Cost	Var Cost	Tot Cost	Average Cost	AVC	Marg Cost	Tot Rev	Average Rev	Marg Rev	Profit
0	$15.00	$ 0.00	$ 15.00	—	—	—	—	—	—	($15.00)
1	15.00	3.00	18.00	$18.00	$3.00	$3.00	$ 6.00	$6.00	$6.00	(12.00)
2	15.00	5.50	20.50	10.25	2.75	2.50	12.00	6.00	6.00	(8.50)
3	15.00	7.50	22.50	7.50	2.50	2.00	18.00	6.00	6.00	(4.50)
4	15.00	10.00	25.00	6.25	2.50	2.50	24.00	6.00	6.00	(1.00)
5	15.00	13.00	28.00	5.60	2.60	3.00	30.00	6.00	6.00	2.00
6	15.00	16.50	31.50	5.25	2.75	3.50	36.00	6.00	6.00	4.50
7	15.00	20.50	35.50	5.07	2.93	4.00	42.00	6.00	6.00	6.50
8	15.00	25.00	40.00	5.00	3.13	4.50	48.00	6.00	6.00	8.00
9	15.00	30.00	45.00	5.00	3.33	5.00	54.00	6.00	6.00	9.00
10	15.00	35.50	50.50	5.05	3.55	5.50	60.00	6.00	6.00	9.50
11	15.00	41.50	56.50	5.14	3.77	6.00	66.00	6.00	6.00	9.50
12	15.00	48.00	63.00	5.25	4.00	6.50	72.00	6.00	6.00	9.00
13	15.00	55.00	70.00	5.38	4.23	7.00	78.00	6.00	6.00	8.00
14	15.00	62.50	77.50	5.54	4.46	7.50	84.00	6.00	6.00	6.50
15	15.00	70.50	85.50	5.70	4.70	8.00	90.00	6.00	6.00	4.50
16	15.00	79.00	94.00	5.88	4.94	8.50	96.00	6.00	6.00	2.00
17	15.00	88.00	103.00	6.06	5.18	9.00	102.00	6.00	6.00	(1.00)

Source: *Adapted from Apgar and Brown (1987).*

By making the above calculations for each level of output, we compute the numbers in columns 4, 5, and 6 of Table 4.1 for all levels of output (rows of the table). Such a table is one way to represent cost functions. In particular, columns 4 and 1 together represent the total cost function $TC(Q)$, columns 5 and 1 represent the average cost function $AC(Q)$, and columns 7 and 1 represent the marginal cost function $MC(Q)$.

Another way to represent such functions is through graphs. For the Meals on Wheels program described in Table 4.1, the graphs in Figure 4.3A show the total as well as the fixed and variable costs as functions of output, while Figure 4.3B shows the average, average variable, and marginal cost functions. (The figures also contain revenue functions, which we'll discuss later in the chapter.) These graphs are obtained by plotting output Q (column 1 in Table 4.1), measured in meals per day, along the horizontal axis and the particular cost value, measured in dollars per day and in dollars per meal per day, respectively, along the vertical axis.

Why is it permissible in these graphs to connect the dots between the integral numbers representing different levels of output (whole meals)? That is, why do the graphs suggest that one can produce 2.5 meals as well as 2 meals or 3 meals? The answer is that we are measuring output on a per-day basis so that, for example, 2.5 meals per day can be produced by producing 5 meals over a two-day period. Thus, every fractional output is producible

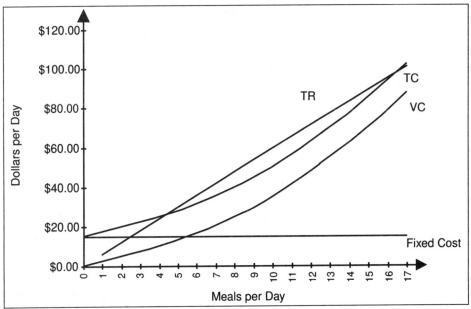

Figure 4.3A Meals on Wheels Example

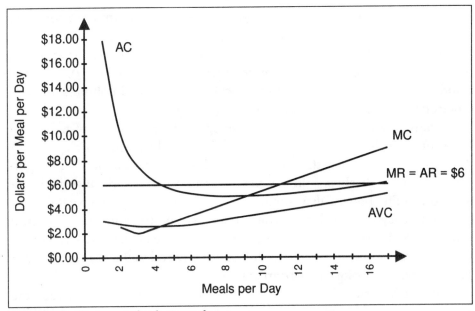

Figure 4.3B Meals on Wheels Example

because we are considering rates of production (output) rather than absolute levels. (Even 3.14159 meals/day is permissible, though obviously pi is just for dessert.)

Key Relationships

Graphical representations of cost functions help us to see certain relationships among total, average, and marginal costs that are difficult to appreciate by looking only at tables or even equations. Here we want to note several of these relationships because they help us to understand these functions better and will give us new, intuitive insights into the nature of cost functions and how they can help us think about resource allocation decisions.

1. The height of the marginal cost curve (*MC*) follows the slope of the total cost curve (*TC*) and the slope of the variable cost curve (*VC*).

Recall our definition of marginal cost as the difference in total cost as one goes from one level of output to another. Now note that if the *TC* curve is steep, costs are much higher for producing another unit; if it is relatively flat, the marginal cost is small. If the total cost curve becomes steeper, this means that marginal costs are increasing. If it becomes less steep, then marginal costs are falling. In Figure 4.3 (and Table 4.1) we can see that from a level of output $Q=0$ to $Q=3$, total cost *TC* becomes less steep and *MC* declines. From $Q=3$ on to higher levels of output, *TC* becomes steeper and steeper and *MC* rises over this range. Thus, marginal cost is reflected in the *slope* of the total cost curve.

Now observe that the slope of the variable cost curve (*VC*) is the same as that of the *TC* curve (see Figure 4.3A). The only difference between these curves is in their height, and this difference equals fixed cost. Thus, where the *TC* curve becomes steeper or less steep, the *VC* curve follows it exactly. So, if the slope of the *TC* curve reflects the marginal cost, the same is true of the slope of the *VC* curve. Thus, we can compute marginal cost $MC(Q)$ by calculating $VC(Q)-VC(Q-1)$ at each level of output Q.

One may wonder, however, why *VC* and *TC* do not increase uniformly with output in this Meals on Wheels example. This is the same as asking why marginal costs are not constant over the whole range of output. The short answer is that it is uneconomical to prepare only one or two meals in a kitchen designed to produce more than that. Preparing two meals requires only a little more effort on the part of a cook, and involves only slightly higher energy and cleaning costs, than preparing one meal. This would explain why marginal cost declines from $Q=0$ to $Q=3$. However, as more meals are produced, they may have to be delivered to increasingly remote locations, and this costs more. After a while, this factor takes over and the marginal cost of meals at higher levels of output ($Q=3$ and beyond) increases.

2. Where the *MC* curve is above the *AC* curve, average costs are rising; where the *MC* curve is below the *AC* curve, average costs are falling.

Note in Figure 4.3B (and Table 4.1) that until an output of $Q=8$ meals is reached, average cost (*AC*) is higher than marginal cost (*MC*), while at outputs above nine meals, *MC* is higher than *AC*. Note also that below eight meals, *AC* is falling while above nine meals *AC* is rising. This relationship between *AC* and *MC* *always holds*. (Indeed, such a relationship always holds between any pair of marginal and average functions, whether they involve cost, revenue, or other quantities.) Why? Because if the cost of an additional unit of output (meal) is greater than the average cost at the current output, then the next unit of output will raise the average cost. Conversely, if the cost of an additional unit is lower than the average cost, the next unit of output will lower the average cost. In the case of our example, at an output level of 5 meals per day, the average cost is $5.60 while the marginal cost is $3.00. Thus, increasing output to 6 meals lowers the average cost to $5.25. In contrast, at an output level of 13 meals, the average cost is $5.38 while the marginal cost is $7.00. Thus, increasing output to 14 meals increases the average cost to $5.54.

Where average costs are falling (because marginal costs are lower than average costs), there are economies to be exploited by expanding production. Over such a range, producing more output lowers the average cost of each unit. On the other hand, where average costs are rising (because marginal costs are higher than average costs), there are diseconomies of further production, and each additional unit produced increases the average cost per unit. When we are analyzing long-run cost curves where plant, equipment, and all other inputs are variable so that we can estimate the advantages of operating at different physical scales of production, we use the terms *economies of scale* or *diseconomies of scale* to describe the reduction or increase in average (per-unit) cost resulting from expanding or contracting production.

In a less exact sense, the terms *economies of scale* and *diseconomies of scale* are sometimes used to describe production decisions in the short run as well as when not all inputs can be varied. A closer examination of the *AC* curve in Figure 4.3B sheds some light on this situation. The fall and rise of the *AC* curve, as output increases, reflects two basic factors: First, as we discussed earlier, the variation in marginal cost as production increases pulls average cost up or down. In addition, the average cost falls, very steeply at first, as production rises, partly because the fixed costs of production (*FC*) are being spread over more and more units of output. This is what people often mean when they refer to lowering costs by "spreading the overhead." While this phenomenon is technically not the same as an economy of scale, because the scale of production itself is not being adjusted, it is sometimes loosely referred to as such.

3. The *AC* and *MC* curves cross each other where *AC* reaches its minimum.

Note in Figure 4.3B that the average and marginal cost curves intersect each other where output Q equals 9, and that here *AC* reaches its lowest value. This follows from relationship 2, as discussed above: *AC* keeps getting smaller with additional output as long as *MC* is less than *AC*. When *MC* rises to the point where it is equal to *AC*, then producing the next unit of output will no longer lower the average cost; *AC* will have reached its minimum. At that point there is a crossover: *MC* will become greater than *AC*, and *AC* will begin rising rather than falling with additional output.

The point of minimum average cost is an important one. It represents the level of output (meals in this case) that can be produced at the least possible cost per unit, within the time frame considered. If the objective of a government agency is to produce a given level of output—say, a certain number of meals—at the lowest possible total cost, then there is an optimal number of organizations that the government should employ to deliver the desired number of meals. If, as in the current example, *AC* is minimized when Q = 9, the government should contract with 10 providers if it wants to provide 900 meals. Note that 900 meals could be supplied by 8 providers or by 12 providers, but in either case it would be impossible for all suppliers to produce at the point where average costs are lowest.

Note the implication here for government policy: it is not always best for government to require consolidation of service providers. Perhaps fixed costs could be reduced if each city had only one ambulance service or police station, but the added variable costs from longer travel distances would likely outweigh this effect, not to mention the reductions in service quality that would occur. Similarly, one large soup kitchen might have lower average production costs for meals than a dispersed set of neighborhood centers, but if one counted the added variable costs of distribution incurred by recipients having to travel to the kitchen, the actual average cost of the kitchen might well be higher.

Finally, the question of what scale of production is most efficient is much more complicated than identifying the situation in which average cost is minimized. For the individual organization, for example, the revenue as well as the cost side must be considered. To get some insight into how this works, we extend our Meals on Wheels example to include revenues as well as costs.

REVENUE FUNCTIONS

In a manner similar to our treatment of cost functions, we can represent how the revenues acquired by an organization change as the level of its output varies. The nature of revenue functions depends on the source of revenues and on how the organization is paid. As with costs, we can make the distinction between *fixed revenues,* which do not vary with the level of output, and *variable revenues,* which do change with the level of output.

Examples of fixed revenues include grants or budget allocations given to an organization as a lump sum that are not explicitly tied to how much the organization produces; returns on investments or endowments that come in regardless of what a nonprofit organization produces; and a certain level of donations that a charitable organization may attract on the basis of its past reputation, even if it produces no services.

Examples of variable revenues include those received per unit of sale of goods or services; reimbursements received from government or other third-party payers based on services provided; and incremental donations received as a consequence of providing additional levels of service.

Note that there are certain areas of ambiguity in classifying fixed versus variable revenues for nonprofit organizations. Some types of revenues, such as sales income and reimbursements for services, are clearly variable. Others, such as income from existing endowment, are clearly fixed. And there are revenues (e.g., charitable contributions) that, while not explicitly connected to the level of output, are likely to vary with output. Thus, within a given time period, a portion of charitable contribution revenue is probably fixed, while another component probably depends on how much service is produced or how much donors perceive the organization as offering. Here again, the time period within which "fixed" and "variable" are defined becomes important. Within a period of a few months or a year, charitable contributions probably are not greatly affected by the output level of services. Over a period of several years, however, they probably are.

In any case, as with costs, we can compute the three basic revenue functions.

Total revenue (TR) is the sum of fixed and variable revenues at a given level of output.

Average revenue (AR) is the revenue per unit of output, calculated at some given level of output. Average revenue is computed by dividing total revenue by the level of output. If there is a component of fixed revenue, then it may also be worthwhile to compute *average variable revenue (AVR)*, equal to variable revenue divided by output.

Marginal revenue (MR) is the added revenue obtained as a result of increasing output by one unit at some given level of output production.

Let's return to our Meals on Wheels example, as illustrated in Table 4.1 (on page 59) and Figure 4.3 (on page 60). Suppose that the meals produced are sold at a uniform price of $6 each and that the organization is able to sell as many meals as it produces at this price. Under these conditions, columns 8, 9, and 10 in Table 4.1 display the *TR, AR,* and *MR* functions, respectively. In this case, there is no fixed revenue, just variable revenue resulting from the sale of meals; thus, *AR* and *AVR* are the same. We can see as well that since the meal price stays the same (i.e., the price of each additional meal is the same regardless of how many meals are sold), *MR* remains constant at $6. Since there is no fixed revenue and *MR* is constant, *AR* (or *AVR*) is also constant at $6. That is, the average revenue brought in per meal is $6, no matter what the level of output. These relationships are shown graphically by the lines *TR, MR,* and *AR* in Figures 4.3A and B. The *TR* function is a straight line, and the *MR* and *AC* functions are the same horizontal line at the $6 level.

This is the simplest imaginable revenue structure. (More general revenue functions are analyzed later in this chapter.) Yet it is a meaningful example because it represents the revenue opportunities of a small organization in a large market that must behave as a "price taker." That is, no matter how much it produces, within a wide range of output, the organization will have no influence on the market price. If it raises its price, it will not be able to sell because other firms will sell at the lower ($6) market price. If it lowers its price, it will hardly be noticed and will spite itself by decreasing its revenues.

THE PROFIT FUNCTION

For any given level of output we can calculate the profit by subtracting total cost from total revenue. Thus, in equation form, the *profit function* is

$$Profit\ (Q) = TR(Q) - TC(Q)$$

This function is calculated in the last column of Table 4.1 and is graphed in Figure 4.4. Notice that the organization can make a profit by producing between 5 and approximately 16 units of output (meals). Producing outside

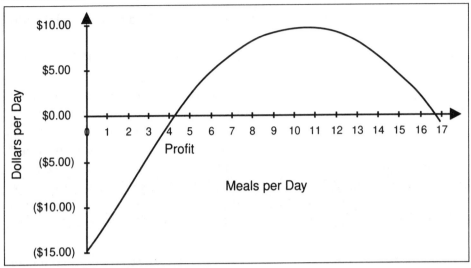

Figure 4.4 Profit Function

this range produces net losses. At $Q = 5$ and $Q = 16$, the organization barely breaks even. The maximum profit is produced when the organization produces an output between 10 and 11 meals. There is an interesting and important relationship between the cost and revenue functions at the output where profit is maximized. Namely: **Profit is maximal where marginal cost (*MC*) is equal to marginal revenue (*MR*).**

First, it is important to understand why this is so: If *MR* were greater than *MC*, then expanding output would bring in more revenue than cost, and profit would be increased. For instance, in our example, if output is increased from 5 to 6 meals, then profit is increased by $2.50, the difference between the marginal revenue ($6) and the marginal cost of the sixth meal ($3.50). Therefore, profit cannot be maximum where *MR* is greater than *MC*.

Similarly, if *MC* were greater than *MR*, then profit could be increased by contracting output. For instance, when output is decreased from 13 to 12 in our Meals on Wheels example, then profit is increased by $1, the difference between the marginal revenue forgone ($6) and the saving of the marginal cost of the 13th meal ($7). That is, producing one less unit would increase profits. Hence, profits cannot be maximum where *MC* is greater than *MR*. The only possibility, then, is that profit is maximal where *MR* equals *MC* (around 11 meals in our example).

If one wants to make as much money as possible, one keeps producing more output until one reaches the point where the revenue taken in just offsets the cost of producing one more unit. To go further means producing additional units whose costs exceed the revenue they bring in; not to go that far means forgoing additional profits from units that can be sold for more than they cost to produce. The preceding rule for deciding how much to produce in order to maximize profits is just one example of what economists call "analysis at the margin." (In Chapter 5 we will explore how analysis, or "thinking," at the margin can guide a variety of important resource allocation decisions.)

Let's return to the Meals on Wheels example and ask a different question. What if the organization is a nonprofit that decides its mission is to produce and deliver as many meals as it possibly can? How much output will it be able to produce? Referring to Figure 4.4, we can see that the organization can produce up to $Q=16$ and still break even. An agency with the objective of maximizing output subject to breaking even financially will decide to produce 16 meals, compared to 11 meals for the profit-maximizing agency. This is one instance where the different motivations between the nonprofit and for-profit sectors may lead to different levels of service. However, there are a number of interesting qualifying points here.

First, the goal of pure output maximization is by no means universal among nonprofits. Nonprofit organizations may require profits in order to build their endowments and reserve funds, to finance capital expansion, or to subsidize other outputs. (An example of the latter is using profits from the sale of art reproductions to finance new acquisitions.) Thus, a nonprofit may choose to make some profit rather than produce the highest possible level of service.

Second, it is not clear that maximizing service is the best thing to do from the viewpoint of society. Note that every unit produced and sold after $Q=11$ loses money because the marginal cost of producing that unit exceeds what people pay for it. If the price people pay is taken as an indication of what people think the unit is worth, then an organization producing more than 11 units may be allocating resources inefficiently, and the additional units are best not produced. However, if there are reasons to believe that such units have value above the price that consumers pay, then, from society's point of view, additional output beyond that which maximizes profit may be efficient. (In Chapters 5, 8, and 9, we will introduce the concepts of "beneficial demand" and "externalities" to deal with social benefits not incorporated in the price system.)

The Meals on Wheels example shows that, under some conditions, there is no level of output that would allow the organization to make a profit or break even. If the prevailing price were reduced from $6 to less than $5 per meal in Table 4.1, there is no level of output for which average revenue (revised column 9) will exceed average cost, or for which total revenue (revised column 8) exceeds total cost. At the $5 price, the organization can sell nine units (the profit-maximizing level where price equals marginal cost) and just break even (since both revenues and costs equal $45). However, even if the prevailing price is less than $5, the organization may wish to continue operations in the hope of breaking even when conditions improve. This would be the case if fixed costs needed to be paid whether or not any output were produced, and if average revenue at least exceeded average variable cost (*AVC*) so that variable costs could be covered and some contribution made toward paying fixed costs.

In particular, if the available price in our example is more than $2.50, an output level can be set for which average revenue will exceed average variable cost. For example, suppose the prevailing price were $3 per meal. Then the organization would sell five units (where *MC* equals $3), and revenues would exceed variable costs by $2 ($15 minus $13). The $2 margin could go toward paying part of the fixed cost. However, if the available price were less than $2.50, there would be no level of output at which revenues could exceed variable costs. Thus, the organization would be best off shutting down because production would involve additional losses over and above fixed costs. In short, the *shutdown rule* for organizations needing to break even through the sale of their output at a prevailing market price is:

> **Cease production if, at the profit-maximizing production level where the prevailing price equals marginal cost ($P = MC$), that price (average revenue) does not exceed average variable cost ($P < AVC$).**

The shutdown rule represents an important idea for nonprofit managers. Later in this chapter and in Chapter 8, we will encounter other versions of the shutdown rule, including one that applies to fund-raising efforts.

THE DEMAND FUNCTION

The Meals on Wheels example is particularly straightforward because it assumes a simplified revenue structure under which the organization can sell as much as it can produce at a given constant price. This is often not the case, especially when organizations produce a large share of the total output in the markets in which they sell. Thus, if the organization in the Meals on Wheels example were the only producer in its area, it might very well affect the price it could charge: as it produced more and more output, it would have to lower its price in order to sell that output.

Economists describe this phenomenon by saying that organizations may face *downward-sloping demand curves*. What they mean is that the price people are willing to pay for a good or service declines as more of that good becomes available. In other words, people will buy more if the price falls and less if the price rises. Thus, we can characterize the *demand function* as the quantity Q that people want to purchase at each possible price P.

The demand function, shown in Figure 4.5, is usually represented by a curve or line sloping downward from left to right, with price P on the vertical axis and output Q on the horizontal axis. At any point (P,Q) on this curve, Q represents the amount that would be purchased if the price were set at P.

It is worth noting that the inverse relationship—how much people are willing to pay (P) for each additional unit of output (Q)—is also of interest to us. In fact, the normal convention is to represent demand mathematically as $P(Q)$, "price as a function of quantity," rather than the other way around. This way of characterizing the demand function is the foundation for valuing the outputs of nonprofit organizations. In particular, *marginal willingness to pay* reflects the economic value consumers attribute to outputs that interest them, given a certain level of purchasing power or income. Hence, *demand* is not simply a function of what people need but also of what they can afford and what they prefer to have within the constraints of their resources. This is one reason why market prices may not accurately reflect social valuations; social judgments sometimes incorporate distributional concerns and individual needs not reflected in what people are willing to pay in the marketplace. We will develop these ideas more fully in later chapters.

Consider now the relationship between demand and the revenue received by organizations selling the given output Q. When the price is set at P, all Q units are sold at this price, so that P (the demand) is the average revenue $AR(Q)$ brought in for these Q units. Thus, we can see the following

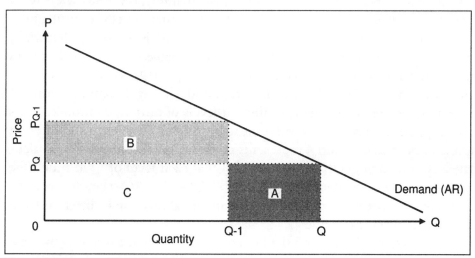

Figure 4.5 Demand Function

relationship among demand P, total revenue $TR(Q)$, and average revenue $AR(Q)$:

$$TR(Q) = P(Q) \times Q, \text{ and}$$
$$AR(Q) = TR(Q)/Q = P(Q).$$

In short, the demand function represents the average revenue function, and total revenue is just average revenue (demand) multiplied by output. Note that this assumes that all output is sold at one uniform price P. In economists' terms, this means that there is no *price discrimination*—that is, sellers cannot charge different prices to different purchasers. If they can, the revenue functions are more complicated but can still be analyzed in a similar way. (We will discuss various opportunities for price discrimination by nonprofits in Chapter 8.)

In fact, for nonprofits, determination of pricing policies can be a complex issue. For instance, normally a producing organization will choose to sell its output at some point on the demand curve. However, selling at points (combinations of P and Q) below the demand curve is also feasible; it simply means that the seller is receiving less for the output than consumers are willing to pay for the quantity sold. Profit maximizers would never do this, but a nonprofit concerned about distributional issues (e.g., a university seeking a balanced student body) may choose to do it. As we will discuss later, selling at a price below what the market demands requires other ways of rationing services than just prices. Suffice it to say that in such cases the revenue functions will take a different form than those presently being discussed.

To return to the straightforward situation of selling output along a declining demand curve: how do we calculate marginal revenue (MR)? What additional revenue is brought in by selling another unit of output under conditions where the price changes with output? This is a somewhat tricky question, which we will answer by referring to Table 4.2. This table shows the relationship between demand (AR or P), output (Q), total revenue (TR), and marginal revenue (MR) in a situation of declining demand. Column 1 represents the price obtained at different levels of output, column 2 shows the output level Q, and column 3 is the total revenue TR obtained at different levels of output. Column 4 represents the marginal revenue $MR(Q)$ calculated by subtracting $TR(Q\text{-}1)$ from $TR(Q)$ at each level of Q in much the same way as we calculated $MC(Q)$ from $TC(Q)$ and $TC(Q\text{-}1)$ in the previous discussion of marginal cost. Notice that marginal revenue is different from demand or average revenue.

Why is this so? Why isn't the incremental revenue from selling the next unit the same as the price that is paid for it? The answer is that for every

TABLE 4.2
Computing Marginal Revenue

Average Revenue (P)	Quantity (Q)	Total Revenue (TR)	Marginal Revenue (MR)
$10	1	$10	$10
9	2	18	8
8	3	24	6
7	4	28	4
6	5	30	2
5	6	30	0
4	7	28	(2)
3	8	24	(4)
2	9	18	(6)
1	10	10	(8)

additional unit sold, the price goes down, as does the revenue obtained for previous units (again, assuming no price discrimination). So if you sell three units, you only receive $8 for each and a total of $24, rather than $9 for each and a total of $18 for selling two units. Thus, the (marginal) revenue added by the sale of the third unit is $6 ($24 minus $18). In general, the marginal revenue is equal to the price obtained from the next unit sold (P) minus the loss due to the price decrease for previous units (the change in price multiplied by the original quantity). This effect is illustrated in Figure 4.5.

Total revenue (TR) at a given level of output (Q) is represented graphically by the area of the rectangle between the origin and the demand curve at that quantity. Two such TR rectangles are illustrated in Figure 4.5. The rectangle consisting of boxes B and C represents total revenue when Q-1 is sold, because the area of this rectangle is length (here equal to,P_{q-1}) multiplied by width (here equal to Q-1). Similarly, the rectangle consisting of boxes A and C represents the total revenue when amount Q is sold. The difference between these two TR rectangles, or $(A + C) - (B + C) = A - B$, measures the marginal revenue brought in by the sale of the Qth unit. Box A represents the sale of the Qth unit. (Note that its length is, by construction, one unit, so that the area equals 1 times P_q, or simply P_q.) Box B represents the loss of potential revenue from earlier units of production. (Its width is the change in price necessary to sell the next unit [$P_{q-1} - P_q$], and its length is the number of units previously sold [Q-1]).

In sum, in Figure 4.5 we see that going from Q-1 to Q units sold gains the revenue represented by box A but loses the revenue represented by box

B. Figure 4.6 shows that the marginal revenue function $MR(Q)$ is always below the average revenue or demand function $AR(Q)$ because of the losses represented by box B in Figure 4.5. In fact, it is possible that, for some range of output, MR will be negative (when box B exceeds box A in area). Under these conditions, the revenue gained by selling an additional unit will be more than offset by losses on the sale of previous units. (We will investigate the conditions under which this will occur in Chapter 8.)

The fact that MR is, in general, different from demand has important implications for pricing and output decisions. Figure 4.7 depicts the cost and revenue functions for an organization that faces a declining demand function. Here again, the choice of level of output depends on the objective of the organization, but the rules of analysis are the same:

- To maximize profit, increase output Q until MR is no longer greater than MC, but merely equal to MC; this occurs at output level $Q = A$ in the diagram.
- To maximize output, increase output until TC equals TR or AC equals AR (break-even point). This occurs at level $Q = C$ in the diagram.

Again, the profit-maximizing level of output is considerably less than the maximal output that can be produced while breaking even. However, the more interesting result here is that the level of output (A) at which profit is maximized is different from the level (S) at which demand $P(Q)$ is equal to MC (as it was in the previous example). This is an interesting observation because up to level S of output additional units can be sold at prices higher

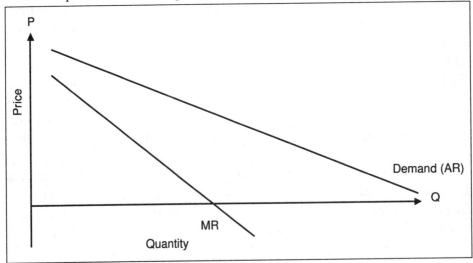

Figure 4.6 Average and Marginal Revenue Functions

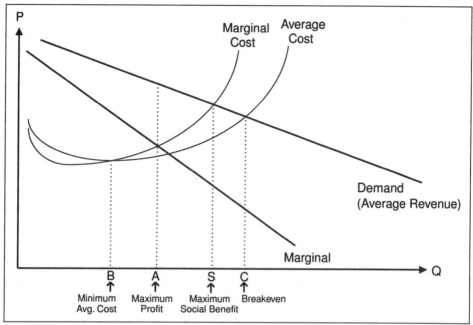

Figure 4.7 Output Under Different Organizational Objectives

than the cost of producing them. Thus, it can be argued that society places a net positive value on producing the added units of output from *A* to *S*, and that such expansion would be efficient. Nonetheless, a profit-maximizing firm would not produce those units. A nonprofit firm attempting to maximize social benefits might do so, however. If there were further reasons (external benefits, discussed in Chapter 9) to produce even more, the nonprofit might expand output to *C* units.

In the Meals on Wheels example, there were no fixed revenues and the price was independent of the quantity sold. Thus, price, average revenue, average variable revenue, and marginal revenue were all the same thing. We have just seen that when the price or demand depends on quantity, marginal revenue is distinct from the price, but price is still the same thing as average revenue. Now, we also consider the possibility of fixed revenue and revisit the shutdown rule.

Average revenue (*AR*) consists of two components—average fixed revenue (*AFR*) and average variable revenue (*AVR*). When fixed revenues are present, the price on the demand curve is the same as average variable revenue, but both are less than average revenue. Therefore, we must be much more specific in our shutdown rule:

Shut down production if, at the profit-maximizing level of positive output, *AVR* is less than *AVC*.

In reality, this shutdown rule is the same as the earlier one, since average variable revenue is identical with the price. However, this form of the rule provides an additional insight. As we mentioned before, an organization may want to remain in business even though it is losing money. This is the case when the net revenues from operating offset a share of fixed costs so that losses are reduced by operating.

The interesting and new implication here is that, assuming its sales are intended solely as a means of raising funds, an organization might want to shut down its sales operation even if it could stay open and operate at a profit! Specifically, if at the profit-maximizing level of (positive) output (where *MR* equals *MC*) variable revenues are lower than variable costs, an organization could nonetheless enjoy positive overall profits if the excess of fixed revenues over fixed costs outweighed the difference between variable costs and revenues. Despite its ability to stay open and avoid bankruptcy, this organization would do better to shut down and devote its entire (nonoperating) profit, unencumbered, to direct pursuit of its organizational mission. Regardless of whether the organization is making or losing money, operating losses will hurt it and can be avoided by shutting down.

An example illustrates this possibility. Suppose that an organization can sell its services at a fixed price of $10 and that the best level of production at this price (if the organization stays open) is 5 units of output. Suppose, further, that fixed costs are $5, the total cost of producing 10 units is $60, and fixed revenues are $100. Under these conditions, the organization would have profits of $95 (calculated by subtracting fixed costs from fixed revenues) if it shut down. If it stayed open, its total revenues would be $150 ([5 x $10] plus $100) and its total costs would be $60, so its maximal profits would be $90 ($150 minus $60). By eliminating its money-losing sales activity, the organization can spend more on its organizational mission. Our shutdown rule provides correct guidance in this case, because average variable revenue (price) is $10, which is less than the average variable cost of $11 (calculated by subtracting fixed costs from total costs and dividing the result by the quantity).

The alert reader will have noticed two related problems with this analysis. First, the organization's mission may be to sell the service in question, rather than to use it to finance some other charitable activity. Second, short-run fixed revenues may evaporate if the organization stops producing that mission-related service. What would be the point of making grants or donations to support an activity the organization had discontinued? We deal with both these possibilities in the section on advanced pricing issues in Chapter 8.

SUMMARY

We have covered a lot of territory in this chapter. We have defined output and cost, and we have shown how economic variables such as cost, revenue, and demand can be related to the level of output through the construction of cost, revenue, and demand functions. We have described the different forms of these functions—total, average, and marginal—and we have demonstrated a number of ways in which these functions can be analyzed to arrive at decisions about the quantity of output to produce. One analytical principle we applied to output decisions was *analysis at the margin*. We will apply this powerful principle to other situations in Chapter 5.

REFERENCES

Apgar, William C., and H. James Brown. *Microeconomics and Public Policy.* Glenview, Ill.: Scott, Foresman, 1987.

Gill, Richard T. *Economics.* Mountain View, Calif.: Mayfield Publishing Co., 1993.

EXERCISES

1. Given the following cost data for a local symphony orchestra, complete items a-e.

Output (concerts per season)	Total Fixed Cost	Total Variable Cost	Total Cost	Average Variable Cost	Average Cost	Marginal Cost
0	$150	0	_____	N/A	N/A	N/A
1	150	60	_____	_____	_____	_____
2	150	90	_____	_____	_____	_____
3	150	107	_____	_____	_____	_____
4	150	122	_____	_____	_____	_____
5	150	140	_____	_____	_____	_____
6	150	165	_____	_____	_____	_____
7	150	192	_____	_____	_____	_____
8	150	268	_____	_____	_____	_____
9	150	382	_____	_____	_____	_____

a. Fill in the blanks in the table. Note: Place the marginal cost *between* any consecutive quantities next to the higher quantity. For example, if you decided that the marginal cost between the quantities of 12 and 13 was $45, and if the table were a bit longer, you would put a $45 next to a quantity of 13.

b. On a sheet of graph paper, plot and label the average variable cost, average cost, and marginal cost curves. Fractional outputs are allowed, so you can connect the dots when drawing these curves.

c. If your diagram is correct, *AVC* declines first and then rises. Why is this pattern typical?

d. Does the marginal cost curve intersect the average cost curve where *AC* is rising, where it is falling, or at *AC*'s minimum point? Explain.

e. If fixed costs were $300 instead of $150, how would your *MC* curve be affected?

f. Given the following data on demand, fill in the blanks in the table, placing marginal revenue between any two quantities next to the higher quantity and assuming that there are no fixed revenues.

Quantity Demanded	Price	Total Revenue	Marginal Revenue
0	$40	_____	_____
1	39	_____	_____
2	38	_____	_____
3	37	_____	_____
4	36	_____	_____
5	35	_____	_____
6	34	_____	_____
7	33	_____	_____
8	32	_____	_____
9	31	_____	_____
10	30	_____	_____

g. Given the cost and revenue data in the second table, how many concerts per season should this orchestra give if its goal were to maximize profits? (Be sure to check the shutdown rule.) How big would profits be at this point?

h. In the long run, the $150 becomes a variable cost rather than a fixed cost. There are no other long-run changes in the cost or demand functions. Given this added information, what do you think the orchestra would do when it reached the long run?

2. Suppose you are organizing a fund-raising campaign for your favorite charitable organization. Consider the costs of organizing and running such a campaign and answer the following questions.

a. Describe a single method you will use to raise funds (e.g., a mailing, a dinner, a telephone campaign) and specify the time period over which this activity will take place.

b. List all the different types of costs you will incur in carrying out the fund-raising campaign.

c. Assume that your output measure is "number of dollars raised." Identify the components of cost that are fixed (i.e., do not vary with the level of output) and those that are variable (i.e, do vary with the level of output).

d. Explain which of the fixed costs would become variable if you considered operations over a longer period of time.

e. Using your best judgment, or data to which you may have access, make quantitative estimates of the fixed and variable costs at different levels of output and display these costs in a table.

f. From the numbers in your table, calculate total, average, and marginal costs at each level of output and display these costs as three additional columns in your table or in a separate table.

g. Draw in a single graph the average and marginal cost curves, showing how these quantities vary as output changes.

h. Using your graphs or table, determine the optimal level of the campaign: How much should you spend, and how much money will you make?

3. Suppose you are organizing a conference for a professional society to which you belong. The society finances the conference with participant registration fees plus a foundation grant explicitly designated for the conference. The costs of the conference involve renting a facility, organizing the program and securing speakers, and providing materials and meals for each participant.

a. Using graphs, describe the total, average, and marginal revenue functions.

b. Classify costs as fixed and variable components and graph the total, average, and marginal cost functions.

c. Using (a) and (b) as a guide, draw a graph showing a circumstance where the conference loses money but the society is better off financially holding the conference than canceling it.

d. Graph an alternate situation in which the society should cancel the conference if it insists on avoiding losses.

e. Show a circumstance where the conference makes a positive profit. What can you say about the relationship between the conference fee and marginal cost and the relationship between average variable cost and the conference fee in this case?

CHAPTER 5

Thinking at the Margin

In Chapter 4, we introduced the economic concept of the *margin*. In particular, we learned how to calculate marginal costs and marginal revenues and demonstrated how the analysis of these marginal functions could help a manager decide how much of a good or service to produce. This mode of analysis, which we call "analysis (or thinking) at the margin," is one of the most powerful ideas underlying microeconomics. In this chapter, we look further into the application of this concept to resource allocation decisions faced by nonprofit managers.

OUTPUT AND PRICING DECISIONS

First, let us review and extend what we learned earlier about analyzing marginal costs and marginal revenues in order to determine how much to produce and what price to charge. Recall that such decisions hinge on the organization's objective in providing a particular good or service. In Chapter 4 we considered several possibilities, including maximum profit, maximum output, minimum cost, and maximum social benefit.

Let's dispense with two of these objectives—maximum output and minimum cost—because, as we explain below, these generally are not very satisfying criteria. We need to ask, Why produce at maximum output? What is the underlying reason for producing as much as possible? There may well be a virtually unlimited need for some service such as day care or artistic performances, but in allocating scarce resources to such services we want to be sure that the services are valued enough to justify whatever level of production is chosen. The objective of maximizing output, which only seeks the highest level of production that is financially possible and says nothing about the value of that production or the efficiency of such a decision (i.e., whether resources would be put to their most highly valued use if we maximized output), doesn't make that clear.

To understand the problem better, we can apply our idea of thinking at the margin. If a nonprofit organization produces as much output as possible and then allocates that output according to established priorities based on some indicator of client needs, it presumably will allocate the last unit it produces to the least needy of its clients. If, instead, the organization cuts back production of that last unit, resources are freed for other uses that may be more important. For example, suppose a nonprofit employment agency offers training courses to unemployed individuals, giving priority to the financially neediest. If the agency simply maximizes the number of courses it offers, it will be accommodating clients whose financial needs are less and less pressing as it nears its maximum capacity. Thus, it should begin to ask itself whether it should invest its funds elsewhere, such as in a job placement service that would benefit its needier clients more, instead of in yet another course offering.

A similar argument applies to the minimum average cost rule. As we observed earlier, the average cost may reach a minimum point at a fairly modest level of service. Should we resist expanding beyond that point even if people highly value the provision of additional units? Should we even produce that much if people do not value the service very much? Again, the minimum cost rule says nothing about the most efficient level of provision (i.e., the level that would put resources to their most highly valued uses).

The two remaining rules are more meaningful because they do juxtapose the value of services produced with the cost of producing those services. The maximum profit rule asks that services be expanded until the producing organization achieves its maximum financial surplus, while the maximum social benefit rule asks that overall net value of services be maximized. Application of each of these rules involves thinking at the margin. Either or both rules may be applicable to nonprofit organization services, depending on the circumstances.

Maximizing Profit

It is appropriate for a nonprofit organization to seek to maximize profit from certain services or activities that are specifically intended to produce net revenues that the organization can use to support its mission-focused activities. Thus, museum gift shops, university bookstores, and church bake sales may use the rule of maximum profit to guide their output and pricing decisions. Any fund-raising activity per se may be appropriately framed as an exercise in maximizing profit. As we mentioned earlier, the rule for maximizing profit is as follows:

To maximize profit, expand output to the point where marginal revenue just equals marginal cost.

This point is illustrated by output level Q_1 in Figure 5.1A. This output level would be sustained by charging a price P_1 corresponding to Q_1 on the demand or average revenue function. (Recall that a profit maximizer will always choose a price on the demand curve, not below it, in order to get the highest possible price for the output sold.) Note that at Q_1, MR equals MC and production beyond this point would result in units of output (at the margin) that cost more than they command in revenue. Failure to reach this level of production would forgo marginal units of output that would bring in more revenue than they cost. Thus, either deviation from the point where marginal revenue just offsets marginal cost will reduce profit.

As suggested by the shutdown rules discussed in Chapter 4, there is one important caveat to this rule: in some circumstances it may not be possible to make a profit at all. That is, setting MR equal to MC results in a negative profit because the demand function (AR) lies below the average (total) cost curve (AC) for all levels of output. While setting MR equal to MC results in the smallest possible loss, given that production takes place, it may be better in this instance for the organization to shut down production entirely. Figure 5.1B illustrates the case where the organization runs a loss but the profit-maximizing (loss-minimizing) price P_0 is greater than the average variable cost (AVC) at corresponding output Q_0. Here, continuing to produce can help pay for part of the fixed costs, and the organization will do better to continue production. If this were not the case, the organization should shut down.

Maximizing Social Benefit

The computation of social costs and benefits is a major subject that we will discuss in detail in our treatment of cost-benefit analysis in Chapter 10. For now, we already have some analytical tools that allow us to examine how a nonprofit organization wishing to maximize benefits for society might approach decisions about output and pricing. Depending on the circumstances, we can assume one of two things about the demand function (AR) in Figure 5.1A. One possibility is that the function accurately represents how

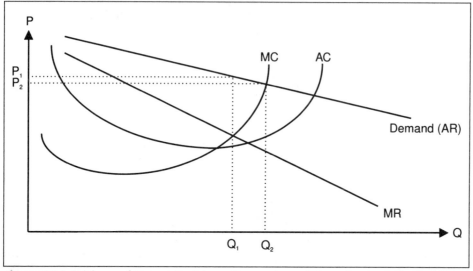

Figure 5.1A Pricing and Output Decisions: Circumstance Where Service Is Profitable

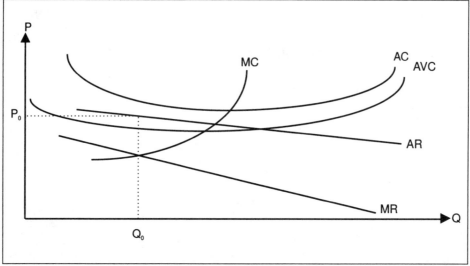

Figure 5.1B Pricing and Output Decisions: Circumstance Where Service Is Unprofitable at All Levels

society values the good or service at issue. A second possibility is that the function does not represent the full value of the good or service.

Consider the first possibility. As we discussed in Chapter 4, the demand function can be interpreted as the amount consumers are willing to pay for additional units of the good or service. For example, the value placed on art reproductions sold in a museum gift shop may be closely approximated by the demand for those items (willingness to pay) on the part of museum visitors. Under this assumption, the museum shop could use the following *output and pricing rule*:

To maximize social benefit where the demand function adequately represents the value that society places on the good or service, choose a level of output at which demand equals marginal cost.

The rationale here is that producing any less would mean that some consumers—those who are willing to pay more for additional (marginal) units of the good or service than it costs to produce them—would not be accommodated. So, too, producing any more than the level at which demand equals marginal cost would mean production of marginal units that cost more than anyone is willing to pay for them. Either deviation from the level at which demand equals marginal cost would therefore be inefficient.

In Figure 5.1A, this solution is represented by output Q_2 and price P_2. It is interesting to observe that applying this rule results in higher output and a lower price than if one were to apply the maximum profit objective (where MR equals MC). One can thus argue that when an organization faces a downward sloping demand curve (and therefore can influence the price it charges by varying its output), the profit-making objective will result in a less efficient allocation of resources than the "demand equals marginal cost" rule. In particular, the profit maker will not produce the additional output from Q_1 to Q_2 even though those units provide more benefit than they cost to produce.

This raises a perplexing question for nonprofit managers. Should they sacrifice additional profits in a service such as a museum gift shop in order to increase societal benefit, or should they try to make as much profit as possible? The answer of course must depend on how the additional profits would be used to produce other benefits, whether alternative funding can be procured to produce those benefits, and how those other benefits compare to those forgone by restricting the output level of the gift shop (Eckel and Steinberg, 1993).

One additional nuance of the output and pricing rule is important for nonprofit organizations. In some cases, while the demand curve may be a good representation of social benefits, the organization may choose not to charge prices along this curve. For example, for reasons of equity it might decide to charge a lower price or to give the good away free, rationing it in some other way than by charging fees. The rule still applies in principle, however: The same level of output should be selected as that which would be chosen if demand were set equal to marginal cost. What counts here is what people are willing to pay, not what they actually pay.

What about cases where demand is not an adequate measure of social benefit? This is probably more the rule than the exception for nonprofits, since many nonprofits serve needy clients or produce public goods whose value is greater than the amount their consumers demonstrate they are willing to pay. For example, while there is a clear market demand for preschool education, part of the benefit from that service flows to society at large in the form of healthier, better-educated, less disruptive children who ultimately become more productive citizens. But market demand reflects only what parents themselves are willing to pay, not what other citizens may also be willing to contribute. Thus, making price and output decisions based solely on market demand is likely to underallocate resources to this important service.

We can extend our thinking at the margin to address this case. One way is to supplement the market demand curve with estimates of the additional public benefits associated with each unit of service. For example, for each additional child served in day care, how much does society benefit? This might be estimated by the level of subsidies government provides, or it might be an internal estimate of what the nonprofit organization calculates this value to be and what it may be willing to provide in subsidy from its own sources. (See the discussions of these approaches in Chapters 8 and 9.) Figure 5.2 graphs such a situation by drawing above the demand curve a line labeled *MSB* (*marginal social benefit*). Marginal social benefit is determined by adding the estimated marginal external benefit to the private demand (average revenue) curve. If we can estimate such a function, we can subscribe to the following rule:

To maximize social benefit where external as well as private benefits are involved, choose the level of output where marginal social benefit is just equal to marginal cost.

Indeed, we can adopt this as the universal rule (superseding the output and pricing rule given above), with the caveat that sometimes *MSB* is the same as the demand curve and sometimes it is not. Figure 5.2' shows that using this rule leads to producing even more output (Q_3) than if we simply set price (private benefit) equal to marginal cost (Q_2). And, of course, the resulting price P_3 is lower than P_2. However, as the graph suggests, we have to be careful in using this rule so that the organization is not jeopardized financially. In the figure, for example, AC exceeds AR at output level Q_3 where social benefit is maximized. Unless the organization can subsidize the difference from other sources, it may have to decide to set output at level Q_4, the most it can produce while still breaking even.

The possibility that, when social benefits are taken into account, a nonprofit agency may want to produce beyond its financial means prompts us to revisit briefly the rule about maximizing output that we earlier dis-

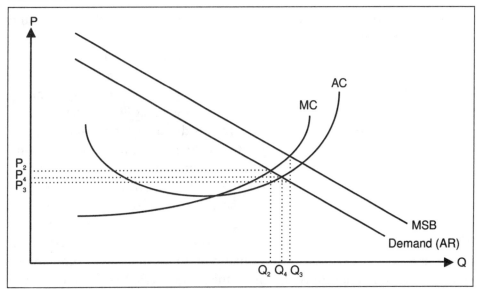

Figure 5.2 Circumstance Where Maximum Social Benefit Requires Maximum Output

missed. In particular, a nonprofit in such a circumstance may wish to maximize its output as a way of trying to achieve the objective of maximizing social benefit. How should an agency decide whether to maximize its output? Again, we can apply thinking at the margin:

> **If, at maximum feasible output (i.e., at the financial break-even point where AR equals AC), producing another unit of service would yield a marginal social benefit greater than or equal to the marginal cost, then maximizing output is justifiable.**

This condition holds in Figure 5.2. Producing another unit of output beyond Q_4 does yield a marginal social benefit greater than its marginal cost. This situation may well apply to services for which there is a strong need and of which there is a limited supply, such as emergency relief for hurricane victims, supplies of rare blood, or health-care or preschool services in poor rural areas. The key, however, is to ask the question about the last unit of production to ensure that maximum output is justified. Essentially, we are still using analysis at the margin to make the decision, even though the maximum output rule may be a handy shortcut in some instances. However, caution should be used in maintaining a maximum output objective over a long period of time, even if the objective is initially justified by the rule just discussed. Such an objective may become part of the organization's culture and may persist even after circumstances have changed and the rule no longer warrants pursuit of that objective.

In Chapters 9 and 10, we will study the concepts of public goods and external benefits and costs and will develop the methodology of cost-benefit analysis. This will introduce more sophistication into decision making about output levels where market demand is an insufficient (and often absent) indicator of value. In this wider framework, we will again employ thinking at the margin to equate marginal social costs with marginal social benefits. For the present, however, we summarize this discussion by reiterating that one of several rules may be appropriate for the nonprofit manager wishing to set price and service levels efficiently. For activities explicitly intended for fund-raising or commercial purposes, the maximum profit rule would apply. For an activity intended as a public service, the rule of setting demand equal to marginal cost will apply where demand accurately reflects social benefit. Where it does not, a more general rule of setting marginal social benefit equal to marginal cost, using additional estimates of public benefits to supplement private demand, is appropriate. All of these cases employ thinking at the margin to ensure that the last unit of output produced has a value greater than its incremental cost.

FUND RAISING

Fund-raising activity is the classic example of a situation in which the profit-maximizing rule can be applied to the operations of a nonprofit organization. If we characterize the output of fund-raising activity as *the number of dollars raised*, then a key question is, How much should an organization spend on fund raising? This question is easily analyzed by thinking at the margin, using the profit-maximizing rule developed above. In particular, consider the diagram in Figure 5.3, which shows the average and marginal cost functions and the average and marginal revenue functions for a fund-raising program.

Since the output is dollars raised, the average revenue received per unit of output (i.e., per dollar) is, by definition, $1. Thus, the *AR* function is a constant horizontal line at the level of $1. Similarly, the marginal revenue associated with each additional unit of output (i.e., $1 raised) is the same constant horizontal line at the level of $1. The cost curves are more conventional. As drawn, they illustrate that the initial dollars to be raised may cost more than $1, but that eventually the marginal cost of raising a dollar, and subsequently the average cost of raising a dollar, dips below $1. It is in this region, where average cost is below average revenue (i.e., less than $1), that fund-raising activity is worthwhile (unless one enjoys fund raising just for the sport!). Eventually, at higher levels of (output) Q, dollars become more difficult to raise and the marginal and then average costs of fund raising again

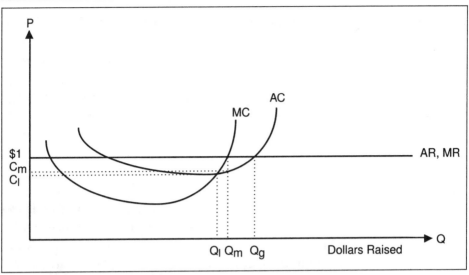

Figure 5.3 Optimal Fund Raising

rise above the average and marginal revenue line. At this level of activity, fund raising is no longer worthwhile.

Following our principle of thinking at the margin, we can see that net funds raised (profits) will be maximized at the point where marginal cost equals marginal revenue (i.e., where the marginal cost rises to \$1 at level Q_m). Up to this point, every dollar spent brings in more than \$1 in revenue. Beyond that point, every dollar spent brings in less than \$1. Clearly, then, the logic of thinking at the margin determines the fund-raising level Q_m that will bring in the most net funds. At this level, raising a dollar costs C_m dollars. Thus, one should spend C_m times Q_m dollars in order to bring in Q_m dollars.

Again, we have the caveat of the shutdown rule to ensure that the solution produced by comparisons at the margin is better than not producing at all. In this case, the rule can be stated as follows:

> **If, at the level of fund raising where marginal contributions received equal marginal fund-raising costs and average variable contributed revenue is less than the average variable fund-raising cost, the fund-raising campaign should be suspended.**

The foregoing analysis is interesting in light of ongoing debates about the administrative costs of fund raising. In particular, charities are chastised for administrative costs that represent too high a percentage of funds raised, while charities with very low average fund-raising costs are applauded. However, Figure 5.3 shows that in order to raise the most net funds, a nonprofit should *not* seek to minimize its fund-raising costs. If it did so, it would raise only Q_1 dollars at the point where AC is lowest. (Note that because AR is a constant, equal to \$1, Q_1 is also the point where the ratio of costs to revenues $C_1 = AC/AR$ is lowest.) At this point, the nonprofit would raise fewer net funds than if it expanded to raise Q_m at an average cost of C_m. That is, by operating at the lowest average cost (and the lowest ratio of funds spent to funds raised), the charity is missing the opportunity to raise more net funds. Thus, charities with the lowest average fund-raising costs are not necessarily the most efficient or making the best use of their fund-raising resources.

One can argue, of course, that if the average cost of fund raising is too high, donors may become wary and give less money. However, this would ultimately be reflected in the shape of the cost functions experienced by the organization. (The curves in the graph would become higher relative to the revenue line.) But the logic of analysis at the margin would continue to apply to determine the most efficient output and cost levels.

Of course, there is also a danger that an organization will err in the other direction. Charities often set fund-raising goals or targets and then focus simply on funds raised, not on how much it costs to raise those funds. Thus, an organization that sets its goals so high that it essentially seeks to maximize the gross level of funds it could possibly raise may actually bring in as much as Q_g in Figure 5.3, where AC equals AR. However, in the process of raising funds, such an organization would spend all those funds! Unfortunately, this has been known to happen.

Finally, it is important to realize that one cannot simply compare one charity with another in terms of the costs and levels of fund raising, since each charity faces different fund-raising conditions and hence different cost functions. To suggest that a given charity should minimize its fund-raising costs or is inefficient simply because its average ratio of costs to revenues raised is high is not correct. The appropriate approach is to determine whether the last dollar allocated to fund raising brings in \$1, no more and no less. This rule can be extended to cover many real-world complications: the time lag between solicitation and receipt of funds (especially in connection with bequests and other forms of planned giving), the effects of fund raising on volunteers, and the opportunity to advocate and educate while raising funds (see Steinberg, 1988-89). Although it is not possible to discuss all the nuances of the issue in this book, the principal lesson is clear: Thinking at the margin can help nonprofit managers avoid the traps of "average thinking" in fund-raising management, assessment, and regulation.

It is also possible for charities to be inefficient in their fund raising by using the wrong combination of fund-raising techniques or by not making the most efficient use of their input resources. Next, we will discuss how analysis at the margin helps us to avoid such situations.

ALLOCATING RESOURCES TO ALTERNATIVE INPUTS AND PROGRAMS

Another important application of thinking at the margin relates to the decisions nonprofit managers must make about allocating resources to alternative uses within the organization. These types of decisions fall into several categories. For example, managers must choose the right combination of input resources needed to produce a given service. Telephones, supplies, people, and physical space are needed to run an advocacy campaign. What combination of these will be most efficient in producing as much output (measured, say, by the number of citizens contacted) as possible for a given budget expenditure?

Another type of decision is the choice among different programs designed to achieve the same goal. For example, a Meals on Wheels program and a cafeteria program in which disabled people are brought to a common location for meals are two different ways of delivering food to those who cannot shop or prepare meals for themselves. What combination of such programs is most efficient in delivering as many meals as possible for a given expenditure of funds?

The problem can be stated as follows: Suppose we have a certain budget and wish to allocate this budget between two uses (inputs or programs), which we will label t and v. Suppose, further, that the price of a unit of t is P_t and the price of a unit of v is P_v. What combination of inputs t and v will allow us to achieve the highest possible level of output Q? In order to solve this problem by thinking at the margin, we need new terminology. In particular, we define the *marginal product* associated with each input as follows:

> MP_t, the marginal product of t, is the additional output (Q) produced by employing an additional unit of input t (with all other inputs held constant).

Similarly,

> MP_v, the marginal product of v, is the additional output (Q) produced by employing an additional unit of input v (with all other inputs held constant).

For example, if t were telephones and v were volunteers in an advocacy campaign, and Q were the number of contacts made per day, then MP_t would be the number of additional contacts that could be made if we added one telephone. Similarly, MP_v would be the number of additional contacts that could be made if we added one volunteer.

Note that the marginal product of a given input is a function not only of the level of that input but of all other inputs as well. For example, suppose a public radio station has 10 phones for its fund-raising drive. Holding the number of phones constant at this amount yields one level of marginal product (additional output) for the eleventh volunteer (say, $100) and a different level for the twelfth volunteer (say, $90). However, if the number of phones is increased to 12, the marginal products of the eleventh and twelfth volunteers will be different again (perhaps $120 and $105, respectively, because they no longer have to share a phone).

Now that we understand the concept of marginal product, let's see how it can help in the decision to allocate alternative inputs efficiently. We can allocate inputs efficiently if we are guided by the following rule:

> **For a given level of budget expenditure, select levels of t and v such that MP_t/P_t equals MP_v/P_v.**

Note that the ratios of marginal product to price (MP/P) of each input represent the amount of additional product achieved per additional dollar spent on that input. For example, if it costs 50 cents (P_v) to attract an additional full-time-equivalent (FTE) volunteer, and if that volunteer increases output by five units (MP_v), then $1 spent on volunteers will bring in two FTE volunteers, yielding an increase in output of approximately 10 units (twice the marginal product for volunteers). Alternately, if it costs $5 to attract an FTE volunteer, then an additional $1 spent on volunteers will bring in only 0.2 FTE volunteers and will increase output by only one unit (a fifth of the marginal product for volunteers). So, another way of stating the above rule is:

> **Choose levels of inputs t and v such that the additional output (Q) obtained by spending another dollar on t is the same as the additional output that results from spending another dollar on v.**

The logic here is just another application of thinking at the margin. If we selected amounts of t and v such that the above relationship did not hold, then it would be possible to obtain more output for the same budget by shifting resources toward t and away from v, or vice versa. For example, suppose we could obtain two meals per dollar by spending one more dollar on a cafeteria program, whereas we would obtain only one meal by spending that dollar on Meals on Wheels. Then, in order to obtain the greatest possible output for our budget, we should shift a dollar from Meals on Wheels to the cafeteria program. After doing this, we should ask the same question again: Should we shift another dollar from the cafeteria to Meals on Wheels? As long as it was possible to obtain more meals by shifting dollars from Meals on Wheels to the cafeteria program, we should continue to do so.

Eventually, we would expect to reach a point where another dollar for the cafeteria program would produce the same number of additional meals as another dollar for the Meals on Wheels program. This is the *point of efficient allocation*. If we went further, we would find that we could obtain more meals from an additional dollar allocated to Meals on Wheels than from a dollar allocated to the cafeteria plan. This would be inefficient and we would have to cut back allocation for the cafeteria program until our two allocations were once again equally productive.

But why should we expect that the yield of the cafeteria program will diminish as we increase its budget? The answer is that, like any input or program, the cafeteria program is probably subject to *diminishing returns*. That is, beyond a certain level of expenditure, additional dollars spent on a given input are likely to have less and less impact. For example, at a budget level of $1,000, an additional dollar spent on the cafeteria program may yield two meals delivered, but as additional dollars are spent on the program the yield may drop to 1.5 meals, and so on. This happens because, as the program expands, it may become subject to congestion, administrative complexities, or other factors that inhibit its productivity. Similarly, the Meals on Wheels program is likely to experience diminishing returns because, as it expands, it must reach out to less accessible populations over a wider geographic area, making delivery of additional meals more expensive. Even if one of these programs (say, the cafeteria program) is the more effective alternative at some budgetary level, as this alternative is expanded its yield is likely to drop to a point where the other program (in this case, the Meals on Wheels program) becomes equally effective.

The same phenomenon occurs when one is choosing between direct inputs such as volunteers and phones in a fund-raising campaign. If volunteers are added and the number of phones is kept constant, the volunteers' productivity will drop as they share phones or begin to get in one another's way. And if phones are added while the number of volunteers remains constant, the productivity of the phones will eventually drop because there are not enough people to answer them all.

If diminishing returns do not prevail, or if one alternative dominates another over a wide range, an exception to the above rule for allocating the budget can occur: we may shift every dollar from Meals on Wheels to the cafeteria program and still not reach equality. That is, the marginal product of the cafeteria program may continue to exceed that of the Meals on Wheels program. In this instance, the most efficient decision would be to allocate the entire budget to the cafeteria plan and eliminate the Meals on Wheels program.

The marginal product allocation rule is really common sense, but it requires thinking about the marginal units of inputs and outputs rather than the average or total quantities involved at any given level of output.

FUND-RAISING APPLICATION

Consider a fund-raising program that uses two means of soliciting funds: direct mail and advertisements in the media. The output of this program, Q, is measured in dollars raised. Table 5.1 displays the marginal products MP_m and MP_a for each mode of fund raising at different levels of expenditure. For example, at a level of expenditure of $2 on direct mail, an additional dollar would bring in $9 in funds. Similarly, at an expenditure level of $5 on media ads, an additional dollar would bring in $5 in funds. Note also that the numbers in the table illustrate the effect of diminishing returns: the marginal product of each input declines as more is spent on it.

How can we apply the marginal product rule to determine how much we should invest in direct mail as compared to media advertising? The answer depends, of course, on how much money we have to spend. Suppose we have a budget of $10. We can determine how to allocate this $10 by considering one dollar at a time. Where should the first dollar go? Since a first dollar devoted to advertising brings in $20 (as compared to only $10 for direct mail), we should put that first budget dollar into advertising. Similarly, we should allocate the second and third dollars to media ads. Once we reach the level of the fourth dollar, the situation becomes a toss-up. The next dollar spent on either ads or direct mail brings in $10. Since we are already using ads, we may as well allocate the fourth dollar to ads, but the fifth dollar should be allocated to direct mail, which will bring in $10 (compared to only $5 for the next dollar for advertising). Similarly, the sixth through ninth dollars should be allocated to direct mail. The tenth dollar is a toss-up again, since at this level another dollar to either method will bring in $5. We may as well allocate this last dollar to direct mail rather than switching back to ads. This uses up our $10 budget. In all, we have allocated $6 to direct mail and $4 to media advertising, and we have brought in a total of $108, found by adding up all the marginal products MP_m from 1 to 6 and MP_a from 1 to 4 in the table. The most money we can raise with a $10 budget using the best combination of the two alternative programs is $108.

We can follow this logic for any given level of fund-raising budget. Table 5.2 shows the results of doing this. Note that the total yield (total revenue) is $108 for a budget of $10, as we have just calculated. Note also that the

TABLE 5.1
Allocating Fund-Raising Expenditures Among Alternative Methods
(in thousands of dollars)

Direct Mail		Media Ads	
Expend$_1$	MP$_m$	Expend$_2$	MP$_a$
Start		1	20
		2	18
		3	15
		4*	10
1	10 ←		←
2	9		
3	8		
4	7		
5	6		
6*	5 →	5	5
		6	4
7	4 ←		
8	3		
9	2 →	7	2
		8	2
		9	2 Stop
10	1	10	1
11	0.5	0.25	11

*Optimal expenditures for a $10 total budget level

optimal combination of direct mail and fund raising changes as the budget changes. Finally, note that Table 5.2 lists the marginal revenue (MR) and total revenue (TR) associated with each level of budget up to $18. At any given level of budget, *MR* is the same as the *MP* for the alternative method selected for additional allocation at that level. Thus, at budget level $5, the last dollar is spent on direct mail, bringing in $10, and so on.

The marginal revenue column is revealing because it brings us back to our previous analysis of how much we should spend and what level of output (funds raised) we should seek to attain. In particular, note that up through a budget of $18, an additional dollar spent on one method or another brings in more than a dollar of funds raised. If we were to increase the budget to

TABLE 5.2
Optimal Combinations of Fund-Raising Methods for Different Budget Levels
(in thousands of dollars)

| | $'s spent on: | | $'s raised: | |
Budget	Direct Mail	Media	MR	Total Yield (TR)
1	0	1	20	20
2	0	2	18	38
3	0	2	15	53
4	0	4	10	63
5	1	4	10	73
6	2	4	9	82
7	3	4	8	90
8	4	4	7	97
9	5	4	6	103
10	6	4	5	108
11	6	5	5	113
12	6	6	4	117
13	7	6	4	121
14	8	6	3	124
15	9	6	2	126
16	9	7	2	128
17	9	8	2	130
18	9	9	2	132

Stop Here (MP = 1) — Optimal Budget Level

$19 by allocating an additional dollar to fund raising, we would bring in only one more dollar in return. Thus, the optimal fund-raising budget in this case is $18, yielding the highest net return: $132 −$18 = $114.

SUMMARY

In this chapter we have used the logic of "thinking at the margin" to analyze two important kinds of decisions facing managers of nonprofit organizations. The first type of decision involves choosing the most efficient levels of service and the prices that correspond to those levels. The second type of decision involves allocating a limited budget among alternative inputs or programs so as to achieve the highest possible level of output. We also observed, as in the case of fund raising, that the two kinds of decisions are related: for any particular level of budget, resources should be allocated among inputs (or alternative programs) in the most efficient way possible to achieve maximum output. Once this allocation is ensured, we can determine what level of service is most efficient in achieving the organization's goal, be it the goal of maximum profit in the case of fund-raising initiatives or the goal of maximizing social benefit in the case of mission-related services.

REFERENCES

Apgar, William C., and H. James Brown. *Microeconomics and Public Policy*. Glenview, Ill.: Scott, Foresman, 1987.

Eckel, Catherine C., and Richard Steinberg. "Competition, Performance and Public Policy Towards Nonprofits." Chapter 2 in David C. Hammack and Dennis R. Young (eds.), *Nonprofit Organizations in a Market Economy*. San Francisco: Jossey-Bass, 1993.

Gill, Richard T. *Economics*. Mountain View, Calif.: Mayfield Publishing Co., 1993.

Steinberg, Richard. "Economic Perspectives on the Regulation of Charitable Solicitation." *Case Western Reserve University Law Review*, 39:3, 1988-89, pp. 775-797.

EXERCISES

1. Explain how you would apply the principle of "thinking at the margin" to the following nonprofit management situations:

   a. Determining how many volunteers to recruit for a fund-raising event.

   b. Deciding on the size of a committee being formed to develop a strategic plan.

   c. Deciding on the size of a newspaper ad to recruit for an open position in your organization.

   d. Deciding how to allocate an increase in the annual grant from United Way to a variety of organizational uses.

   e. Deciding how to distribute an annual budget cut across different departments of your organization.

   f. Determining whether to undertake a fund-raising campaign or a commercial venture in order to increase organizational resources.

2. For the fund-raising example discussed in the text and illustrated by Tables 5.1 and 5.2, explain why the alternatives of direct mail and media advertising may be subject to diminishing returns.

CHAPTER 6

The Concept of Cost

In Chapter 4, we introduced the definition of economic cost as the value of opportunities that are lost when resources are put to a given use and hence become unavailable in their "next best use." This idea of *opportunity cost* is fundamental to economics; all costs are opportunity costs. In most circumstances, however, we need not give explicit attention to calculating lost opportunities because the value of these opportunities is well represented by the market price of the resources being used. Thus, if we use pencils and paper in our offices, the cost of these resources can be accurately assessed by referring to their price in the store. The value of the opportunities lost corresponds to the price that some other customer would have paid to use the pencils and paper.

In some cases, however, market prices do not accurately portray the cost of using a particular resource. In such cases, we need to think explicitly about the opportunity costs associated with use of the resource. Otherwise, we may undervalue or overvalue the resource and hence use more or less of it than would be efficient (i.e., than would lead to allocating resources to their most highly valued uses).

In this chapter, we review the circumstances under which prices fail to reflect opportunity cost, and we use the concept of opportunity cost to consider how to account for costs that are incurred at different times. That is, how do we value costs incurred now in comparison to costs incurred later?

This is a key question affecting resource-related decisions (e.g., regarding investments in new programs where high short-term costs may need to be incurred in order to reap long-term benefits).

WHEN PRICES FAIL TO REFLECT COSTS

There are a variety of circumstances in which nonprofit managers must make decisions about the use of resources, the prices of which do not accurately reflect their opportunity value. Some of these circumstances are obvious, and others less so, but they tend to fall into one of two categories. First, nonprofit managers utilize some resources that are scarce within the organization but are not internally priced in a manner that accurately reflects that scarcity. In such cases, the organization is unlikely to use its resources efficiently in pursuit of its own goals. Second, nonprofit managers use some resources whose value to society is not well represented by their price because of the poor functioning (or absence) of external markets for these goods and services. In such cases, managers may make resource decisions that will not be efficient from society's point of view.

Unpriced Resources

The most obvious examples of resources whose value is not well represented by their prices are resources that, by definition or circumstance, have no price at all. In the nonprofit world, such resources are common, especially volunteer time and donated goods. The case of volunteer labor is especially interesting and important and is dealt with later in this chapter.

Donated goods are an example of resources that are internally scarce but may not be properly valued within the organization. Their value can be estimated in a fairly straightforward manner, however. If the goods are similar to goods sold in the marketplace, then the prices of those goods in the marketplace may provide a fairly accurate estimate of opportunity value. That is, if the goods had not been donated they might have been sold to consumers who value them at their market price. If the donated goods were substandard, used, or different in some other way from those normally sold, then some adjustment might have to be made in this estimate. Nonetheless, the market price of similar goods would likely serve as a useful proxy for estimating the cost of the donated goods. We sometimes call such a proxy a *shadow price*.

Other unpriced resources include common resources such as clean air, water, and sewerage and public services such as police protection, social and educational services, and the legal system. These are examples of resources about which nonprofit managers are likely to make inefficient social decisions. There are at least two reasons for this. First, such services are often provided by government and supported not by user fees but by taxes that depend on an organization's sales, profits, land use, or some other factor essentially unrelated to the organization's utilization of services. Second, nonprofit organizations are often exempt from these taxes. Thus, there are no clear market prices that the nonprofit can use to estimate these costs. Nonetheless, additional use of the services involves opportunity costs, and efficient decision making, from society's point of view, requires that these costs be taken into account. This poses problems, however, because the nonprofit manager may have little incentive to account for such costs, and because the opportunity costs may be difficult to estimate even if the manager is conscious of them.

Finally, even a conscientious nonprofit manager must apply the subtleties of "thinking at the margin" to estimate accurately the costs of using publicly provided services. In cases such as water and sewerage, the nonprofit's usage clearly creates an added cost for the government for each additional user. In other cases—for example, use of a public park that is already available for use by others—the nonprofit's additional usage may involve very small opportunity costs. For example, the cost of using the park for an outing for handicapped children may be limited to the additional cleanup needed, and the nonprofit manager may be justified in limiting cost estimates related to this item.

Resources Budgeted Elsewhere

The problem of accounting for use of public resources such as police and fire protection is similar to the internal accounting problem involved when the use of certain resources by one department is reflected in the budget of another department. For example, expansion of a day-care program by the child-care division of a multipurpose human service agency may involve increased costs for administrative departments such as payroll, benefits, and maintenance, or even other service departments such as family counseling. The child-care division manager may not see the additional resource costs imposed by the expansion program, or these costs may not be accurately reflected in the department's formula for overhead charges. Nonetheless, costs borne by others in the organization represent real opportunity costs. Ignoring these costs in departmental decision making will lead the organization to allocate its internal resources inefficiently.

Another example of costs budgeted elsewhere is costs borne by users. For example, converting from a Meals on Wheels program to a central cafeteria service moves transportation costs from the organization's budget to the budgets of consumers. Replacing an institutional program for handicapped children with a program that provides in-home family-based care imposes additional costs on family members in the form of lost work time and the cost of additional supplies or equipment. These, too, are real opportunity costs. Ignoring these user costs will lead the nonprofit organization to allocate resources inefficiently from society's point of view.

Absence of Internal Markets

Costs imposed on other divisions of an organization are an example of how estimating the costs of resource use becomes a problem when an organization has no internal market system. (Indeed, one of the reasons for having an organization in the first place is to avoid the *transaction costs* associated with carrying out all exchanges and resource decisions in a market environment [see Williamson, 1975]. We will deal more extensively with the concept of transaction costs in later chapters. These costs are very important in determining what kinds of organizational arrangements are most efficient in particular circumstances.) The lack of an internal market leads to problems even with resources that have well-defined market prices because, in the absence of internal prices, there may be a temptation to use these resources inefficiently within the organization.

One area of concern is the use of talented personnel for alternative purposes. For instance, nonprofit organizations often draft "star performers" for fund-raising appearances. Nobel Prize-winning professors, famous conductors of symphony orchestras, and renowned physicians associated with large medical centers may thus be employed. The wage rates of these individuals represent the value of their work in their profession or craft. If such talented individuals are used extensively for public appearances in fund-raising campaigns, the opportunity cost can be estimated as the value of the work they could have done in their fields had their time not been usurped for resource development purposes. This is not to say that such practices are necessarily inefficient, only that the opportunity value of the time of these individuals should be taken into account in decisions to use them.

Note, however, that opportunity value may be different from the wage rate for a couple of reasons. First, the fund-raising appearances may be after hours, during time that would not have been used for work. In this case, one needs to estimate how highly the individual values additional hours of leisure and how much he or she values the satisfaction derived from volunteering for fund raising. The latter value can be deducted from the former in estimating a net opportunity cost for volunteering leisure time. (See the section "Application to Volunteer Time" below.) Second, wage rates may not always be reliable measures of opportunity cost even in estimating the value of lost work time in one's profession. For example, some individuals' current salaries reflect past accomplishments more than present productivity. However, these nuances do not obviate the basic point—that reasonable estimates of opportunity value are needed if an organization is to make efficient decisions about the use of its star staff's time. Because there may be no internal price mechanism for disciplining these decisions, such individuals may be recruited for fund-raising duty without consideration of opportunity value.

Another instance where the lack of an internal market requires explicit attention to the value of lost opportunities is the use of floor space within an organization. For example, suppose a musical arts organization proposes to allocate space in its building to a day-care facility for its employees. One problem may be that there is no internal pricing system, and therefore no price index, available to estimate the internal cost of space allocated to day care instead of other uses. Second, even if there is an internal price system, it may be based on the organization's mortgage payments rather than on an accurate estimate of the external market value of the floor space. Thus, the internal price may not reflect the real value of the space in other possible uses, including use by outside renters. Such limitations to any internal market for space force us to ask the more basic question, What benefits would be lost if the space were taken from its next best (possibly current) use and applied to day care? This is the question that always needs to be asked in order to obtain a valid estimate of the value of resources used.

While the lack of an internal market in cases such as the use of space or star performers primarily affects how efficiently the organization is able to allocate its internal resources, it also affects the efficiency with which social resources are deployed. While using its space inefficiently, for example, a nonprofit may be precluding the use of some of that space by other organizations that would put it to a more highly valued use.

Missed Opportunities

Suppose an organization has a fixed program budget or limited space in which to expand and must choose among mutually exclusive program initiatives—that is, alternatives such that choosing one requires passing up the others. For instance, suppose a community hospital must choose between implementing a new kidney dialysis unit and building a prenatal clinic. The direct costs of undertaking either alternative may be straightforward, involving construction, equipment, staff, supplies, utilities, and the like. However, there is another category of cost that is more difficult to estimate: the benefits lost by not implementing the unchosen alternative. As we will discuss in Chapter 10, estimating these benefits may not be easy, but it is essential to making efficient decisions about the effective use both of scarce internal resources and of society's resources. The organization must account for the net benefits it fails to produce by forgoing the unchosen alternative. These benefits are a part of the opportunity cost but are not reflected in the price of the resources used, since there is probably no competing organization bidding for those resources in order to pursue the other alternative.

Inaccurate Prices

Sometimes the prices attached to resources appear to be fairly clear and straightforward and yet do not accurately reflect opportunity value. For example, the opportunity cost of employing a worker who would otherwise be unemployed is not accurately reflected by the prevailing wage paid. The opportunity value may be the value that the worker assigns to leisure, his or her next best use of the time. Prices that do not reflect opportunity cost are often caused by rigidities in the marketplace, such as set wage schedules for particular kinds of jobs (irrespective of the productivity of the people who occupy them) or explicit government policies (such as taxes and minimum-wage laws) mandating payments that do not reflect actual resource use. In such situations, it is useful to apply new terminology. In particular, we define a *transfer payment* as follows:

> **A transfer payment is a shift of resources from one person or group to another that does not entail the net consumption or creation of resources.**

Examples of transfer payments are taxes, gifts and donations, welfare payments, excess profits, and other payments in excess of opportunity value. Transfer payments are entered as costs in a bookkeeping sense but are not costs in an economic sense because they do not signal the use of valuable resources. They merely move resources from one organization or individual to another.

How does the concept of transfer payments apply to the nonprofit manager wishing to obtain accurate opportunity-cost estimates of particular resources? Consider the following examples:

- Employing a worker may require paying that worker the going wage even if the worker has no other job prospects. The real cost of the resource, however, is the value the worker assigns to his or her leisure time, the best available alternative use. The organization still incurs the financial cost of employing the worker, but the net cost to society is only the opportunity cost. The rest of the wage represents a transfer payment from the organization to the worker. Similarly, if the worker has alternative employment prospects, but at a lower wage, the difference between the present and alternative wages represents a transfer payment.

- If an organization pays taxes on supplies or property, these taxes represent transfers from the organization to the public sector.
- If an organization buys supplies from a monopoly supplier that makes profits over and above the level of profits needed for that supplier to stay in the industry, the proportion of the price paid that goes to excessive profits represents a transfer from the organization to the monopoly supplier.
- If an organization charges rent for the use of some of its space, and if that space would otherwise go unused, the rent (less the costs of cleaning, maintenance, and administration) is a transfer payment from the renter to the organization.
- If an organization pays subsidized postal rates, the difference between the real cost of postal service and the price paid represents a transfer payment to the organization from the government (i.e., the public at large).
- If an organization receives a gift of money or goods, the gift represents a transfer payment from the donor to the organization. (A cost is incurred only when the gift is utilized to secure resources used to carry out the organization's work.)

The problem with transfer payments is that to the nonprofit organization itself they often look like real costs. The otherwise unemployed worker still "costs" the agency the amount equal to his or her wages and benefits. The purchase price of a good supplied by a monopoly and the taxes paid to government still come out of the organization's budget. This is why the costs and benefits of a given activity or decision may look different to an organization than they do to an analyst making the calculations from society's point of view.

Consequently, nonprofit managers and leaders face an interesting problem in deciding how much of a resource to use or what quantity of a service to produce. Should the organization take society's view, as consistent with the public-benefit mission of nonprofit organizations, or should it take the more narrow view of a private entity? In an environment of constrained budgets, it may be hard to decide to use the postal service less because no one has taken into account its real cost, or to employ more otherwise unemployed workers because their real cost is lower than their wage. Such decisions may be efficient in a social sense, but they would make it more difficult for the organization to promote its own mission.

Joint Costs

Some resources used by a nonprofit contribute to the provision of more than one service, activity, or output. For example, the office of financial administration at a university serves many departments, centers, and programs. The costs incurred in using such a shared resource are called *joint costs*. The question is, How do we account for joint costs in making decisions about one service or another? What is the opportunity value of using a shared resource?

The usual accounting answer is to assign some "fair" or proportional share of overhead costs to each activity. Thus, each department might be charged on the basis of its floor space, number of students, and so on. However, such a "price" may inaccurately portray the opportunity value associated with using the resource—say, when a new program is added or an existing one is expanded. It is likely that such an incremental expansion will not require a proportional increase in the size of the financial administration department. To use the terminology explained in Chapters 4 and 5, the marginal cost of this service is likely to be less than the average cost. Thus, the accounting price (average cost) will not reflect the opportunity value (marginal cost) of the expanded use.

Moreover, the estimation of the cost of the financial department may be influenced by the tax system. If the university is deciding whether to expand its profit-making bookstore, it may find it expedient to charge the store with more than its share of joint administrative costs so as to minimize unrelated business income tax liability. This, too, would be a distortion of the concept of opportunity cost.

In order to make efficient incremental decisions in the presence of joint costs, it is necessary to consider directly the principle of opportunities forgone. The decision to expand a university program may appear to be very costly because the new program is required to pay a substantial proportion of central administrative costs. However, this accounting cost may mask the fact that the decision benefits the university, since the marginal costs of central administration are low. In this case, part of the payment to central administration will be a transfer from the program to administration over and above opportunity cost.

In any case, it is clear that proper accounting for joint costs is needed for the nonprofit organization to allocate its internal resources efficiently and that such accounting may also affect how the organization influences the allocation of social resources through the calculation of its tax liabilities.

Sunk Costs

Another misleading indicator of cost is historical expenditure on a given program or activity. Despite their sometimes contrary reputations, economists try to be forward-looking. They focus on future opportunities and on the consequences of losing those opportunities as decisions are made. Thus, they are careful to ignore costs that have already been incurred and about which nothing can be done. For example, suppose an organization wants to build a new facility and pays a consultant a nonrefundable fee to develop a plan before the project is begun. Once the plan is completed, the cost of that plan should not enter the decision of whether to go ahead with the building. The consultant's fee is a *sunk cost* and has nothing to do with future resource expenditures.

Training of employees is another example of a situation involving sunk costs. The decision to move an employee from one type of work to another should not take into account the amount of training the employee may have received in order to do his or her present assignment. More relevant are the cost of training that the employee may need for the new assignment and the cost of training that may have to be provided to the employee's replacement in the old job. These costs may differ from the cost of the employee's original training.

In decisions involving real estate or other durable assets, historical costs are irrelevant. One mistake that many nonprofits make is to neglect depreciation and other factors that cause opportunity costs to diverge from historical costs for certain categories of physical assets. For example, university art and library collections are variously valued using historical cost, replacement cost, resale value on liquidation, or productivity in current use (Hansmann, 1990). Attempts by the accounting profession to impose uniformity here have caused much controversy (Suhrke, 1991).

APPLICATION TO VOLUNTEER TIME

How do the foregoing ideas about the accurate valuation of resources apply to volunteer time, one of the unique and most important resources available to nonprofit organizations? Clearly, this subject is important to nonprofit managers, who must try to make efficient decisions about developing and deploying this key resource. We can make several observations about this issue.

Potential problems are associated with valuing volunteer time at the rate of wages for paid workers. Recall from Chapter 2 that gross estimates of the value of volunteer resources in the U.S. economy were obtained by multiplying estimates of hours worked by the average (after-tax) wage rate for nonagricultural workers (Hodgkinson et al., 1992). This is probably the best we can do at the aggregate level, given the present state of the data. However, we may be able to improve upon these estimates at the level of individual organizations. What nuances can be introduced into the calculation in order to improve such estimates?

First, it is clear that we can be more sophisticated at the organizational level by inquiring specifically about who the volunteers are as well as about their employment prospects. Thus, even if we use wage rates as estimates of the value of volunteer time, we can be more specific about the alternative opportunities available to various groups of volunteers.

Second, it is not clear that volunteers would necessarily be working if they were not volunteering. Inquiring about this helps us to develop a more accurate estimate of the opportunity value of volunteer time. If the volunteer would otherwise remain at home or engage in leisure activity, the opportunity value may be substantially lower than the alternative wage.

Third, it is possible that if volunteers were not working for the present organization they would be volunteering for another organization. In this case, we need to ask about the individual's next best volunteer opportunity and then estimate the benefits the volunteer would have produced in those activities. This is only a reasonable approximation of the opportunity value of that volunteer time, however. Given that there is no well-functioning market for volunteer time, additional effects may need to be accounted for. For example, the organization for which the volunteer might have worked may now have to attract a less productive volunteer or expend more effort on volunteer recruiting. In a refined estimate, the decrease in benefits associated with use of the less productive volunteer, the additional recruiting costs, and any lost opportunities for that volunteer would have to be added to the original estimate.

Fourth, part of the cost of volunteering may be offset by the benefits that volunteers receive. For example, volunteer ushers get to attend the concert or the opera. Volunteer teaching assistants gain experience or training that enhances their employability. Thus, we may think of the net cost of using these volunteer resources as being the opportunity cost of their use in the next best alternative, less the benefits received by the volunteers in their present employment (assuming that those benefits would not be available in the other opportunity). (For an overview of the complexities of valuing volunteer time, see Steinberg [1990].)

Fifth, volunteer labor is not free, even in out-of-pocket cash terms. Volunteers require recruitment, nurturing, supervision, and some rewards (see Brudney, 1990). If improperly selected or utilized, they may impose costs on the organization in the form of disruptions. These costs must be accounted for in decisions to use volunteer resources.

Noting these factors will help the nonprofit manager reach a more realistic estimate of the cost of volunteer time and hence to allocate that resource more efficiently. In addition, certain factors in the environment can, over time, change the costs of using volunteers. For example, suppose that income-tax rates increase, making it less attractive to work. This makes volunteering more attractive. The higher tax rate makes it easier to recruit volunteers because the cost to volunteers of giving their time becomes lower. Using after-tax wage rates to estimate the cost of volunteer time would account for this effect.

One area of managerial decision making in which it is especially important to have a good estimate of the cost of volunteer time is the allocation of volunteers and paid workers among different tasks in the organization. For example, some nonprofit organizations, in an effort to minimize their apparent fund-raising costs, allocate their volunteers primarily to fund-raising solicitation and their paid staff primarily to service delivery, even if volunteers are scarce and paid staff are skilled in fund raising. This practice is obviously inefficient in light of our discussion of how marginal analysis is used to allocate alternative inputs to production (see Chapter 5). The right combinations should be determined by applying the rule equating the ratios of marginal product to the price of each input (volunteers vs. paid staff) in the production of fund raising or service delivery. However, in the case of volunteers, we have no explicit price. Hence, we need to estimate a "shadow price" for volunteers by computing the opportunity value of their time using the principles we have just cited.

TWO EXAMPLES OF THE CONCEPT OF OPPORTUNITY COST

To illustrate the role of opportunity cost in nonprofit management, let us consider the various kinds of opportunity costs associated with programs and initiatives that may be undertaken by nonprofit organizations. In our study of cost-benefit analysis in Chapter 10, we will be more detailed in our approach to such matters. For the present, we simply want to get the flavor of these considerations.

Example 1: A Residential Treatment Program. Suppose a nonprofit family service agency administers a program for teenage delinquents that provides residential and treatment services. The costs associated with providing this program are likely to include:

- direct budgeted costs such as salaries and benefits of paid workers, supplies, food, maintenance, and other expenses;
- the cost of administration incurred by the host organization;
- the time costs incurred by individuals who volunteer in the program;
- indirect costs incurred by other agencies, such as security provided by police in the neighborhood, court costs associated with

the referral process, the costs of services provided by the school system, and so on;
- costs to offenders, including lost employment while in the program and the value they assign to lost liberty; and
- costs incurred by families in connection with visiting and other obligations that may be imposed on them.

Note that the organization may choose not to take account of all these costs if it makes decisions from a narrow organizational perspective. In particular, indirect costs, costs to offenders, and costs to families might be ignored in this instance. However, if the organization takes a wider view of its social responsibility, it should include these costs in its decision making.

Example 2: A Deaccessioning Program in a Library or Museum. Suppose a library or museum is considering selling part of its collection. The costs associated with such a decision are likely to include:

- the benefits that may be lost to researchers, connoisseurs, or others denied access to the sold inventory (the benefits would be the smaller of (1) the value researchers place on access and (2) the added transportation and other costs associated with visiting the collection in its new private locations, if such visiting is possible);
- the labor and other costs associated with administering the deaccession process; and
- the value of the time of volunteers who provide assistance.

On the other hand, the costs of not undertaking the deaccession program might include:

- lost benefits associated with alternative use of the space housing the current inventory (e.g., if the current inventory is not sold, there may be no space for new acquisitions); and
- loss of benefits that could be obtained from the funds received by selling part of the current inventory (e.g., the proceeds from deaccessioning might be used to purchase new items for the collection or to fix a leaky roof).

THE OPPORTUNITY VALUE OF TIME

A very important application of the concept of opportunity cost involves situations in which costs are incurred at different times. In these situations, we must ask, Does a dollar spent now have the same value as a dollar spent a year from now? This is an important issue for nonprofit managers because different projects or programs may have very different expense profiles over time, and a given program's profile of expenses or costs may differ significantly from its profile of services or benefits. Thus, we need a method that lets us weigh costs incurred at different times against each other.

A host of nonprofit managerial decisions involve choosing whether to expend resources now or later:

- How much should be spent now on soliciting planned gifts in order to reap returns later?
- In a crisis, should part of an endowment be spent or should it be preserved to retain future investment returns?
- How should resources be allocated between finding new donor prospects and concentrating on current donors?
- Should a building for the headquarters of a regional association be bought or leased?
- To what extent should workers be given time off and tuition benefits for continuing education in order to increase future productivity?
- In a budget crunch, is it wise to defer routine maintenance of plant and equipment?
- Should time be taken out for a staff retreat when staff is needed to service clients?

All these and other cases require choices regarding the timing of scarce organizational resource allocation. There are two basic reasons why resources spent at one point in time have a different value than do resources spent at another point in time: *lost opportunities* and *inflation*.

Lost Opportunities
Even if there were no inflation, consumption of scarce resources today would be costlier than consumption in the future. If we consume resources now, they cannot be devoted to expanding productive capabilities for the future. Thus, banks pay interest on savings to compensate savers for deferring their consumption so that funds are available for investment in future production. Consider the following example:

If we spend $100 now, it costs us $100. If we wait and spend the $100 a year from now, we can invest the $100 now and allow it to grow to $110 by next year. We can then spend the $100 and have $10 left over. In effect, *the original $100 will be worth $110 next year. Similarly, $100 received next year is worth only $100/1.10, or $90.91, this year. The greater value of an expense incurred this year instead of next year results from the loss of the opportunity to invest it. This phenomenon is completely unrelated to inflation. We are assuming, however, that everyone involved has the opportunity to borrow or invest at the going rate, so that at the margin the interest rate represents the trade-off people are willing to make between having a dollar now and having a dollar next year.*

The calculation we just made is called *discounting* from one year to the next so that all costs (or revenues or other dollar-denominated quantities) are converted to their opportunity value in a single reference year (i.e., the present one). Discounting reduces all costs into the common measure of reference year dollars and allows us to add all costs over time in a consistent way. Here's how the calculation is made in general for costs incurred over a period of several years:

Say we have the following stream of costs: A_0 in year 0 (present time, the reference year); A_1 in year 1; A_2 in year 2; A_3 in year 3. Suppose further that we want to add up A_0, A_1, A_2, and A_3 in terms of the common measure of dollars in year 0. This will give us the present value *of this stream of costs. Assume that we can invest dollars from one year to the next at the interest (or discount) rate r. (Here we express r as a decimal rather than a percentage; that is, a 10 percent rate would be written as 0.1.) Following the preceding logic, we make the following calculations: A_0 is worth A_0 in terms of year 0 dollars; A_1 is worth $A_1/(1+r)$ in terms of year 0 dollars; A_2 is worth $A_2/(1+r)$ in terms of year 1 dollars or $A_2/(1+r)^2$ in terms of year 0 dollars; and A_3 is worth $A_3/(1+r)^3$ in terms of year 0 dollars. In general, the present value of a cost A_n in year n is equal to $A_n/(1+r)^n$ (in year 0 dollars). Moreover, the present value of the stream of costs A_0, A_1, A_2, A_3 is:*

$$PV = A_0 + A_1/(1+r) + A_2/(1+r)^2 + A_3/(1+r)^3.$$

The present value of a stream of costs over any period of years can be calculated using this method.

There is a shortcut to this calculation in the special case where there is a very long stream of identical costs year by year. For example, suppose we want to determine the present value of a stream of payments of *B* dollars every year from now into the indefinite future. The formula for this is:

$$PV = B/r \quad \textit{(where r is the discount rate).}$$

To see why this is so, imagine that a donor's estate promises to deliver $100 a year to a charity in perpetuity and that the interest rate is 10 percent. The present value of this stream must be $1,000, for if we had $1,000 today we could place it in the bank, collect $100 each year in interest, and never exhaust the principal. Conversely, if we borrowed $1,000 today, our credit rating would remain sound if we paid $100 in interest each year forever.

Perpetuities are rare in the real world, but this formula is nonetheless useful for approximations. As a rule of thumb, any project that has the same annual costs for 20 or more years has a present value fairly close to (slightly less than) that given by the perpetuity formula.

Inflation

If we use dollars to measure cost, then we need to be sure that the value of this measuring rod remains constant. Unfortunately, the purchasing power of the dollar (or any currency) changes over time because of inflation (or deflation)—that is, changes in general price levels in the economy as a whole. Inflation is affected by the money supply and by the growth and productivity of the economy. The effect of inflation is to make the purchasing power of a dollar in a given year lower than its purchasing power in the previous year.

We can compare dollar expenses in one year with those in another in one of two ways. First, we can change all dollars into constant dollars (e.g., 1990 dollars) by multiplying by the appropriate price index correction factor. Thus, if inflation from 1990 to 1991 was 5 percent, then we can convert dollars spent in 1991 to 1990-equivalent dollars by dividing the 1991 values by 1.05. (A dollar in 1990 had the same purchasing power as $1.05 did in 1991.) Another alternative is to keep all dollar amounts in "current" numbers and to utilize current or "nominal" interest rates in making comparisons between dollar expenses in different years.

The interest rate charged by banks (i.e., the nominal rate) reflects both of the factors involved in comparing resource use at different times—forgone opportunities and inflation. If annual inflation is expected to be 10 percent, banks will charge at least that much for a one-year loan because they do not wish to lose purchasing power over the period of the loan. Typically, the nominal interest rate is higher than the expected inflation rate because, in lending funds, the bank is forgoing other investment opportunities that would allow the purchasing power of the money to grow despite inflation. This forgone real investment return represents the "real" rate of interest. Thus, we have the following relationship:

nominal interest rate = real interest rate + expected inflation rate

We can apply the present-value calculation in two ways. One way is to use the actual (current) dollar figures for A_0, A_1, A_2, and so forth (amounts spent now and in years 1, 2, etc.) and the nominal interest rate observed in the market. Alternatively, we can employ inflation-corrected values of A_0, A_1, A_2, and use the real rate of return by removing the inflation factor built into the market rate. Thus, if inflation is 4 percent and the nominal r observed is 10 percent, then the real rate of return is 6 percent. It is important not to mix current dollar figures with the real rate of return as the discount factor, or to mix constant dollar figures with the observed, inflation-inclusive nominal interest rate. We always need to be dealing consistently either in constant dollars or in current dollars as we make the present-value calculation.

For example, suppose a development officer of a foundation is given the following choice by a donor: the foundation can receive an endowment of $100,000, given in a lump sum immediately, or an annual gift of $30,000 a year (in current dollars) for the next four years. Which alternative should the development officer choose? The answer depends on the interest rate at which the foundation can invest the funds.

If the nominal rate r is 5 percent, then the present value of the annual gift is as follows:

$$PV = \$30,000/1.05 + \$30,000/(1.05)^2 + \$30,000/(1.05)^3 + \$30,000/(1.05)^4 = \$106,379.$$

Since this is greater than $100,000, the present value of the endowment, the foundation officer should choose the annual-gift plan.

However, if the nominal rate r is 10 percent, then the PV of the annual gift is $95,096. In this case, the foundation officer should choose the endowment of $100,000. Conversely, if this example is considered from the viewpoint of the donor wishing to preserve as much value as possible for him- or herself, the donor should give the endowment if the rate is 5 percent and the annual payments if the rate is 10 percent.

This example illustrates an important principle: as the discount (interest) rate rises, future costs (or benefits) become less important than short-term costs. As we will see in more detail in Chapter 10, the choice of an appropriate discount rate can have profound effects on economic decisions. If we use a low rate, we count future costs and benefits prominently. If we assume a high rate, we discount the future heavily and count short-term costs more prominently. Because program initiatives differ in their time profiles of benefits and costs, the choice of discount rate ultimately will influence our assessment of a program's efficiency.

SUMMARY

All costs are opportunity costs. However, some costs are not well gauged by prices observed in the marketplace. In particular, there are a variety of circumstances in which prices are either absent or misleading. In these circumstances, one must explicitly determine the opportunity value of the use of resources by explicitly calculating their value in their next best use.

Aggregating costs incurred over different periods of time also involves consideration of lost opportunities. Such costs can be measured on the common scale of present-year dollars by calculating the present value of the stream of costs to be incurred at different times in the future. The present-value calculation compares the lost opportunities associated with dollars spent or received in the future and in the present.

REFERENCES

Apgar, William C., and H. James Brown. *Microeconomics and Public Policy.* Glenview, Ill.: Scott, Foresman, 1987.

Brudney, Jeffrey L. *Fostering Volunteering Programs in the Public Sector.* San Francisco: Jossey-Bass, 1990.

Brudney, Jeffrey L., and William D. Duncombe. "An Economic Evaluation of Paid, Volunteer, and Mixed Staffing Options for Public Services." *Public Administration Review*, 52:5, Sept./Oct. 1992, pp. 474-481.

Gramlich, Edward M. *Benefit-Cost Analysis of Government Programs.* Englewood Cliffs, N.J.: Prentice Hall, 1981.

Hansmann, Henry B. "Why Do Universities Have Endowments?" *Journal of Legal Studies*, 19, 1990, pp. 3-42.

Hodgkinson, Virginia A., Murray S. Weitzman, Christopher M. Toppe, and Stephen M. Noga. *Nonprofit Almanac 1992-1993: Dimensions of the Independent Sector.* San Francisco: Jossey-Bass, 1992.

Steinberg, Richard. "Labor Economics and the Nonprofit Sector: A Literature Review." *Nonprofit and Voluntary Sector Quarterly*, 19:2, Summer 1990, pp. 151-169.

Suhrke, Henry. "Nonprofits Advising the FASB." *Philanthropy Monthly*, Jan./Feb. 1991, pp. 33-34.

Williamson, Oliver. *Markets and Hierarchies.* New York: Free Press, 1975.

EXERCISES

1. Choose a service program or initiative provided by a nonprofit organization with which you are familiar.

a. After reading reports or talking to someone in charge of the program, list all the different kinds of costs associated with providing the program.

b. Which of these costs are well measured by market prices?

c. Which of these costs require indirect estimates because they are not adequately represented by market prices? How would you make those estimates using the concept of opportunity cost?

d. What expenses, if any, are incurred that are really transfer payments rather than actual costs?

2. A nonprofit cemetery offers families of the deceased two options for the maintenance of gravesites: (1) an annual fee of $25 per year, or (2) a one-time immediate charge of $500 for perpetual care.

a. If families are able to earn an interest rate of 10 percent on their savings, which plan is more economical for them?

b. Which plan would be more economical if the interest rate were 4 percent?

3. Ralph's Pretty Good Charity decides to hold a raffle to raise funds. The winner of the raffle will receive a total of $1 million, payable in 20 annual installments of $50,000 each. Unfortunately, Ralph is able to sell only 900,000 raffle tickets at $1 each. When Ralph learns from his banker that the nominal interest rate will remain at 10 percent over the next two decades, his face breaks out into an enormous smile. Has he gone crazy, or has Ralph's raffle produced a financial bonus? Explain.

4. A nonprofit social-service agency is trying to decide whether to put its resources into a residential-treatment program or into a day program for the elderly. The agency has a limited budget and can pursue only one of the options. In calculating the cost of the residential program, should the agency count the benefits lost by not opening the day program? Explain.

CHAPTER **7**

Analysis of Markets

One cannot fully understand the nature of individual nonprofit organizations, for-profit firms, workers, volunteers, consumers, or donors without understanding the economic environments in which they interact. That is the task for this chapter. First, we define markets and describe various market structures. Then we examine the forces that determine prices and quantities exchanged within these various types of market structures. In our discussion, we introduce the idea of a supply function and elaborate further on the demand function, because the interaction of supply and demand often determines market outcomes. We consider this interaction in both the short-run and the long-run equilibrium in each type of market structure, and we characterize how markets adjust from short-run to long-run conditions under various assumptions about the entry and exit of new suppliers. This, in turn, allows us to understand how nonprofit organizations should make price and quantity decisions under various market conditions, and it sets the stage for an analysis of the effects of taxes, subsidies, and regulations as discussed in Chapter 8.

TYPES OF MARKETS

A market is not necessarily a physical entity; fundamentally, a market is a "conceptual space" where items of value are exchanged. Usually we think of markets as places where goods or services are traded for money. In the nonprofit world, this sort of market is commonplace, but other forms of exchange can also be viewed as markets:

- Donors exchange their money for premiums, prestige, tax breaks, and the satisfaction of having done a good thing. Nonprofit organizations compete in the market for donations.
- Volunteers trade their time for experience, training, camaraderie, knowledge about the internal workings of the organization, and the satisfaction of working for the common good. Nonprofit organizations compete in the market for volunteers.
- Skilled managers, service providers, and fundraisers are scarce. Nonprofit organizations compete in various labor markets for the available talent.
- Nonprofit hospitals, day-care providers, nursing homes, universities, and counseling centers compete with for-profit and/or government providers as well as with one another in the markets for their respective mission-related services.
- Universities compete in the markets for housing services, food services, and bookstores. Many other nonprofits sell commercial goods and services peripherally related to carrying out their missions.
- Nonprofit lobbyists and advocacy organizations compete in the public-policy arena, which may be thought of as a market for ideas and influence over legislation.
- Government contracts are awarded to nonprofit and for-profit providers in a bidding market. Government and foundation grants are also scarce and are competed for in a marketplace.

Effective nonprofit management requires an understanding of the competitive structures in the various markets in which nonprofit organizations participate. There is a well-established terminology to describe the various possible structures for monetized markets (where goods, services, or inputs are traded for money), which we discuss in the following pages. Analyses of market structures for donations, volunteers, and ideas are less well developed and represent frontier areas for research. Nonetheless, the basic concepts presented here apply and will be illustrated in the following discussion of these topics.

Monopoly, where there is only one seller of a good or service, is the easiest market structure to describe and analyze. Even this simple concept is complicated, however, for the definition of the good or service being exchanged and the geographic scope of the market are often fuzzy. For example, in the town of Josephson Junction there is exactly one Catholic elementary school but several Protestant, Jewish, and secular private elementary schools. There are several other Catholic schools in the town of Parocchio, which is 15 miles away. Clearly, there is a monopoly if we look at the local market for Catholic education, but there is no monopoly if we look at the markets for private education and for elementary education in general, or if we broaden our concept of the geographic scope of the market. Whether we should treat the market as monopolized depends upon the extent to which these alternatives compete with one another. There is probably little competition between Catholic and Jewish schools for Catholic students, but the schools compete actively for the broader class of students disenchanted with public schools. Whether Catholic students regard themselves as buying from a monopolist depends upon their willingness to commute 15 miles.

Sometimes there is no lack of willingness to commute, but nonprofit organizations either agree among themselves or are told by governments or other funders to divide up the market into geographical "catchment areas." In contrast, a mutual agreement by for-profit firms to divide up a market is illegal under U.S. antitrust laws, highlighting the role of governmental policy in determining market structure.

At the opposite extreme from monopoly is *perfect competition*, where no sellers believe that they can safely depart from the price established in the broader market. In this market structure, organizations would not raise their price above the market level, for then their customers would flock to a cheaper provider. There is no financial incentive for any organization to consider lowering the price it charges, because in this market structure each organization can sell all it wants to at the prevailing price. Under perfect competition, the market shares of individual sellers are so small that an increase in any one firm's output would not saturate the market and force down the price. Moreover, as we shall see, offering a lower price in this situation will lead to financial ruin in the long run, since prevailing competitive prices will reflect the minimum revenue needed to break even.

Clearly, the monopolistic and perfectly competitive market structures are both rather extreme; it is hard to think of many real-world goods that are traded in totally monopolized or perfectly competitive markets. However, many markets are close in structure to one or the other of these extremes, so that by describing these two endpoints we can say something meaningful about the real-world "in-between" cases.

The characteristic that defines the difference between these polar cases is the organization's belief about its freedom to set prices. A monopoly can choose the price/quantity combination at which it will sell, constrained only by consumers' willingness to pay. In contrast, a perfectly competitive organization believes the market price is a fact of life (*price-taking* behavior) and can only choose what quantity to sell at the prevailing price.

Why would an organization believe it had no control over price? The usual assertion in elementary economics textbooks is that price taking results when the number of firms is large and the product being sold is homogeneous—that is, when there are no differences in real or perceived quality or in the convenience of purchasing that would lead consumers to think twice before turning to a lower-priced competitor. Recently, economists have realized that this is not an iron-clad test for price taking. If there is only one seller at present but that seller has no particular advantages—such as brand-name loyalty, proprietary production techniques, control of some essential input, legal protection against competition, or the like—then that seller would have to take the price as given. Should this "monopolist" attempt to raise prices, other providers would enter the market and force the price back down. Thus, the number of *potential* competitors may say more about market structure than the number of actual competitors. Markets in which there are many potential but few actual competitors are said to be *contestable*, and managers in contestable markets must behave as if they were in a perfectly competitive market.

In between monopoly and perfect competition are a variety of imperfectly competitive markets. When there are exactly two providers, we have a *duopoly*. Three providers make a *triopoly*, and any small number (greater than one) of providers constitutes an *oligopoly*. There is relatively little understanding of how oligopolies behave, for oligopolists can adopt differing strategies and counterstrategies. A duopolist could raise prices above their competitive level if its competitor matched the price increase, but it would lose all its customers if its competitor did not. Thus, oligopolists may behave like perfect competitors, like monopolists, or in a more complicated and fluid fashion than either. The mathematics of strategies and counterstrategies for duopolists is described by the field of *game theory*, originally developed to better understand oligopolies but now used to study a variety of multiparty cooperative and competitive situations in economics and politics ranging from nuclear brinkmanship to labor-union strikes (see Shubik, 1982).

Another intermediate case is provided by a structure known as *monopolistic competition*. In this market structure, each producer has a monopoly on its particular version of a common product (e.g., a brand of toothpaste), but producers with new versions of the product can enter freely. New versions of the product or service differ from the older versions in real or perceived quality, in style, in convenience of selling location and hours, and possibly in philanthropic character (social benefits conferred as a result of production). For example, in the financial industry one credit card seems just like another, but corporations differentiate their cards in terms of service quality (e.g., how widely the card is accepted, how easily complaints are serviced) as well as in how usage benefits charitable causes (through cause-related marketing). In higher education, there are many colleges and universities offering similar services, but each provides a different combination, style, and quality of coursework, and colleges differ in the degree to which they help low-income students or emphasize community service.

Monopolistic competitors can raise their prices a bit without losing all their customers because they each produce a unique version of the product. Nonetheless, they cannot raise their prices indiscriminately to secure extra profits, because at some point people will switch to substitute versions of the product. The monopolistically competitive market is thus, in a real sense, contestable.

Market structures are also defined for cases where the number of buyers is limited. A single buyer constitutes a *monopsony*, and a few buyers make an *oligopsony*. When a single buyer confronts a single seller, we have *bilateral monopoly*. When the government "purchases" social services by putting them out to competitive bid, there is one buyer (the government) and many sellers (the bidding nonprofit or for-profit firms), so the market is monopsonistic. When there is only one potential bidder for a government contract, we have a bilateral monopoly. Monopsony can also arise in input markets such as labor services; for example, one cannot be employed as a Catholic priest unless one works for a branch of the Vatican. Here, the church is effectively a monopsonist unless parishes are free to compete for priestly services. Just as monopoly gives the seller control over price, monopsony gives control over price (and other contract conditions) to the buyer. There are no clear-cut predictions for the outcome of negotiations under bilateral monopoly, for, as with duopoly, a variety of patterns of strategic interaction are possible.

Markets differ as well in their organizational mix. A *mixed-sector duopoly* consists of one for-profit and one nonprofit firm selling the same product. Also possible are nonprofit duopolies (two nonprofit firms), for-profit duopolies (two for-profit firms), mixed-sector monopolistic competition (a variety of for-profit and nonprofit firms each occupying a different niche), and any other sectoral combinations one could imagine.

Finally, we have various structures of collaboration that alter the competitive nature of a market—for example, *united fund-raising arrangements* (e.g., through United Way), where members refrain from competitive solicitation efforts but otherwise compete in service markets; *public-private partnerships,* where separately incorporated for-profits, nonprofits, and government agencies share decision making and risks for specified projects or programs; and *mixed-sector joint ventures*, such as a university collaboration with for-profit medical-technology and pharmaceutical companies. While economic theory is not well developed for all these possibilities, the following basic principles will nonetheless help nonprofit managers gain important insights for setting their strategies under different circumstances.

CONCEPTS OF EQUILIBRIUM

Equilibrium values are the prices and quantities we expect to see in a particular market once it reaches a stable level of operation. Generally, we use the term *equilibrium* to describe what we expect over a set period of time when both demand and the technology of production are relatively firmly established and any shifts are predictable. This construct is usefully applied in most for-profit market situations and works for most nonprofit markets as well. For example, the methods for providing emergency shelter care are well established and even the need for such shelter varies predictably with the weather, government policies, and the state of the local economy.

In perfectly competitive markets, each seller (or buyer) takes the price of the product or service as given and decides only on quantities to offer for sale or to purchase. Equilibrium is achieved if a price can be found that harmonizes these respective offers—that is, if a single equilibrium price can be found such that the quantity offered for sale and the quantity desired for purchase are the same. At this price, we say that the "market clears." In a monopoly, the seller chooses from among the set of possible market-clearing prices and quantities described by the demand curve. To predict the equilibrium requires knowing the objective function for the monopolist firm. Then the equilibrium prices and quantities can be computed by the rules developed in Chapter 6: profit maximizers choose a quantity that equates marginal revenue with marginal cost ($MR = MC$) and a price on the demand curve above this point, whereas social welfare maximizers choose a quantity that equates marginal benefit with marginal cost ($MB = MC$) and a price to clear the market at this point. Equilibrium in an oligopolistic market is somewhat more complicated (see Shubik, 1982). Fortunately, the perfect competition and monopoly models will serve us well for analyzing most market situations.

From these various manifestations of equilibrium, we arrive at a general definition of equilibrium in markets with nonprofit organizations:

For a given market structure defined by product demand, technology of production, and specified objective functions for participating

nonprofit organizations, equilibrium is the expected set of outputs and prices that result from the interaction of purchasers and supplying organizations in the marketplace.

Note that simple price-quantity combinations may not characterize non-profit markets in equilibrium. For example, nonprofits may choose to offer complex price schedules such as sliding-scale fees in order to accommodate their various clients, or they may choose to ration services by allowing queuing rather than by raising prices. In general, the concept of market clearing has somewhat less general application to nonprofit equilibrium than to equilibrium in markets comprised of for-profit firms only, since nonprofits may offer their services at a reduced price despite their inability to serve all customers at that price. For example, free medical care provided by a nonprofit clinic would not be provided to relatively affluent patients despite their eagerness to purchase at that price. (Some of these nuances will be discussed further in Chapter 8.)

An important distinction can be made between short-run and long-run equilibrium. As we suggested in Chapter 4, the *long run* is defined not by any specific length of time but by the rapidity with which fixed costs can be converted into variable costs in a particular industry. During the period of a lease, rental costs are fixed. When the lease comes up for renewal, an organization can avoid these costs by not renewing, or it can choose to employ the property as a factor of production by renewing the lease and paying rent. If rent were the only fixed cost, the long run would be reached the day after the lease expired. There are as many short runs as there are sources of fixed costs, but generally we simplify by having only one source of fixed costs (and hence one short run) to speak of. For example, we may speak of an organization that can vary the number of employees in the short run but is restricted to operating with its existing building. In the long run, this organization can vary the size of its facility as well.

In contrast to for-profit firms that derive their revenues strictly from sales, many nonprofit organizations derive a significant part of their funding from fixed revenues, such as grants or gifts not tied to output. Thus, it makes sense to extend the definitions of "long run" and "short run" to the fixity of costs and revenues in the nonprofit context. Here, the short run includes a period of time during which donations would continue, based on past reputation, even if the nonprofit stopped providing services. In the long run, however, donations are contingent on continuing evidence of service provision and so would become variable revenues.

Long-run equilibrium is determined by using long-run cost and demand functions, and short-run equilibrium is determined by short-run functions. However, the difference in equilibria does not depend solely on differences in the cost functions of individual firms or on long-term shifts in demand, but also on differences in the number of organizations in the market. The number of organizations can be thought of as a fixed quantity in the short run, but we need to make additional assumptions to determine how this factor is limited in the long run. For-profit-sector economists distinguish the condition of *free entry and exit*, in which the number of firms is perfectly variable, new firms can produce as cheaply as old firms, and no special penalty is paid by exiting firms, from the condition of *barriers to entry and exit*, in which legal or cost barriers preclude new firms from entering or leaving the market. These economists also consider various intermediate forms of restricted entry. However, to date we know relatively little about the nature and determinants of nonprofit entry and exit, although speculations and hints abound in the ongoing work of researchers. For this book, we will analyze the two extremes without a clear notion of where, between these two poles, most nonprofit industries fall.

SHORT-RUN EQUILIBRIUM UNDER PERFECT COMPETITION

Earlier (in Chapters 4 and 5) we studied the market demand curve, which describes how consumers adjust their desired purchase quantities depending on price. Below, we develop the corresponding *supply curve*, which describes how producers and sellers adjust their desired production and sales levels depending on price. Then we show how supply and demand interact to determine market equilibrium in both the short and long runs.

Under perfect competition, buyers and sellers are price takers. Calculating marginal revenue for a price-taking firm is particularly simple. The extra money that a perfect competitor derives from the sale of an additional unit is simply the price at which that unit is sold. (Recall the Meals on Wheels example in Chapter 4.) Perfect competitors do not have to worry that by selling an extra unit they will have to drop the sales price for all the earlier units they sell, for individual firms control a negligible part of competitive markets. In effect, individual firms see such a small slice of the market demand curve that it looks horizontal (at the given price) over the range of potential firm production levels, so that price, average revenue, and marginal revenue are all identical and do not depend on the firm's decisions. As was explained in Chapter 4, this simple marginal revenue function leads to an equally simple rule for competitive profit-maximizing firms: Choose a quantity of production that equates price with marginal cost ($P = MC$). Produce this quantity if, at that level, price exceeds average variable costs ($P > AVC$); otherwise, shut down and produce nothing.

We derive an organization's supply curve by repeated application of this rule at the different prices the organization might be faced with. The left half of Figure 7.1 illustrates the cost functions for a single competitive firm. If the organization faces a price of P_1, the candidate quantity that makes P equal MC is Q_1. However, P_1 is lower than the average variable cost at Q_1, so the best this organization can do when faced with such a low price is to shut down. At prices P_2, P_3, and P_4, the candidate quantities are Q_2, Q_3, and Q_4, respectively, and all these quantities are worth producing because the price exceeds average variable cost. When one continues the process with additional prices, it rapidly becomes clear that

> **The competitive organization's short-run supply curve is the same as the *MC* curve for all prices greater than or equal to *AVC*. Competitive suppliers will offer a quantity of zero for all prices lower than the minimum of *AVC*.**

Now suppose this organization is one of 100 identical suppliers, each possessing the same cost curves, that constitute the industry in question. This allows us to derive the short-run supply curve for the industry, for in perfect competition all organizations face the same price. If all organizations faced a price of P_2, they would each produce Q_2, so the total supplied would

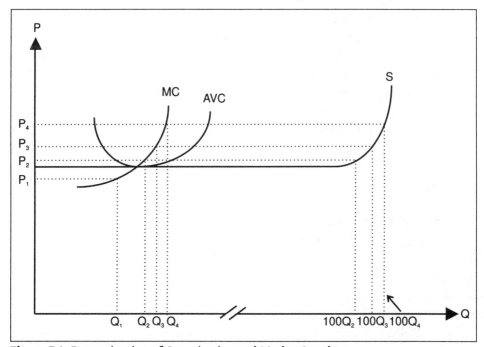

Figure 7.1 Determination of Organization and Market Supply

be $100 \times Q_2$. Repeating this process for other prices yields the market supply curve illustrated in the right half of Figure 7.1. What we did was add the quantities produced by each organization at a given price, a process known as *horizontal addition*. If all the organizations are identical, this addition is the same as multiplying the quantities produced by any one supplier by the number of suppliers at each price. Even if costs are not identical across organizations, we have shown the following result:

The short-run market supply curve is the horizontal sum of short-run firm-level supply curves.

Now that we have detailed how sellers respond to various prices, we are ready to show how prices harmonize the interests of buyers and sellers to determine an equilibrium. Figure 7.2 illustrates the typical short-run supply and demand curves in a competitive market. P^* is the equilibrium price, because at that price the quantity that sellers would like to offer for sale (Q^*) is exactly equal to the quantity that buyers would like to buy. P_1 is not an equilibrium price, because at that price the quantity supplied (Q^S_1) greatly exceeds the quantity demanded (Q^D_1) and goods will pile up on the shelves or potential services will be unused. If all organizations are faced with a rapidly accumulating inventory or excess capacity at some price, we will not expect that price to persist, even in the short run. Some seller will drop its price, competitors will be forced to follow suit, and the price will drop to P^*. As the price falls, sellers reduce the quantity they offer and buyers are willing to buy a larger quantity. This process continues until the two offers match. Likewise, P_2 is not an equilibrium price, because at that price the quantity demanded (Q^D_2) greatly exceeds the quantity supplied (Q^S_2). If consumers are lining up to buy a product or service, competitive for-profit sellers will raise prices a bit and still sell out because consumers cannot find the product available from a lower-priced competitor. As prices rise, sellers increase the quantity they offer for sale and buyers reduce their desired quantities, until once again we reach the short-run equilibrium price and quantity. Thus:

Equilibrium prices and quantities in perfectly competitive markets are determined by the intersection of supply and demand curves.

While supply and demand are defined in terms of desired quantities sold or bought at given prices, either can be interpreted in inverse fashion. We have already noted that the height of the demand curve can be interpreted as the maximum marginal willingness to pay—that is, as the most a consumer would willingly pay for one additional unit of output. Similarly, the height

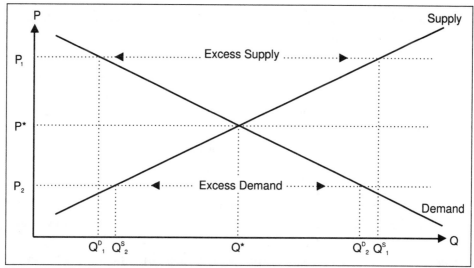

Figure 7.2 Equilibrium of Supply and Demand

of the supply curve can be interpreted as the minimum marginal willingness to sell, or the minimum payment that would make the supplier offer an additional unit for sale.

COMPARATIVE STATICS

Equilibrium is by definition stable but not eternal. We have assumed that many factors remain constant while price adjusts to equilibrate the market. If the positions of the supply and demand functions change, then the market moves to a different equilibrium based on the new conditions. The comparative static approach simply compares these two equilibria without trying to understand the dynamic adjustment process that moves a market from one equilibrium to another. While this approach has the disadvantage of ignoring possible speculative price spirals, selling panics, and other chaotic and sometimes catastrophic adjustment paths, it has the virtue of simplicity and is descriptively accurate for most markets where speculation is not the driving force. In addition, while little is known about price dynamics in for-profit markets, even less is known about dynamics in nonprofit markets. We do not yet know whether, as some allege, nonprofit organizations are too slow to recognize and react to changing market conditions, or whether they just take a longer-term perspective than for-profit managers when choosing their patterns of adjustment. (There is some evidence that nonprofits do react more slowly; for example, for-profit nursing homes expanded much faster than nonprofit homes at the advent of Medicare and Medicaid [see Vladeck, 1980].)

At least five different kinds of factors or conditions affect the positioning of the demand and supply functions:

Changes in the prices of inputs change each supplier's cost functions and hence move the supply curve. For example, if labor contracts mandate an increase in the wage rate, this raises each organization's marginal and average cost functions. Hence, the schedule of minimum marginal willingness to sell (supply curve) shifts upward. This shift of the supply curve from S_1 to S_2, illustrated in Figure 7.3A, leads to a new equilibrium with a higher price and a lower quantity exchanged. In contrast, if formerly paid workers agree to perform their regular duties as volunteers, supply will shift in the opposite direction, the equilibrium price will fall, and a larger quantity will be sold.

Changes in technology that reduce the cost of production shift the supply function downward. An increase in worker productivity due to technological enhancements shifts each organization's marginal and average cost functions downward, causing the market supply curve to shift downward as well. This shift is also illustrated (in reverse) in Figure 7.3A if we think of S_2 as the initial supply curve and S_1 as the new supply curve. As the diagram reveals, this kind of technological advance lowers the equilibrium price and increases the equilibrium quantity.

Changes in consumer tastes can shift the demand function in either direction. If, for example, the music of Chopin suddenly enjoyed a surge of popularity, the number of classical-music concert tickets that would be bought at any given price would increase, and the demand curve would move to the right. This case is illustrated in Figure 7.3B, which shows that an increase in demand leads to an increase in both equilibrium price and quantity. Alternatively, if newly environmentally conscious consumers switched to products without extensive packaging, the demand curve for waste management services would shift to the left. In Figure 7.3B this would be illustrated by a shift from D_2 to D_1, with changes in equilibrium from (P_2, Q_2) to (P_1, Q_1). Thus, a decrease in demand reduces both the equilibrium price and quantity.

Changes in wealth or income can shift the demand function. When people become wealthier, they wish to purchase more of most goods and services at any given price, increasing the market demand in these markets. Theater tickets, vichyssoise, luxury cars, and cosmetic surgery fall into this category, where an increase in wealth will shift demand to the right and thereby increase the equilibrium price and quantity. However, the demand for some goods falls when income or wealth increases: bleacher-seat tickets, cold

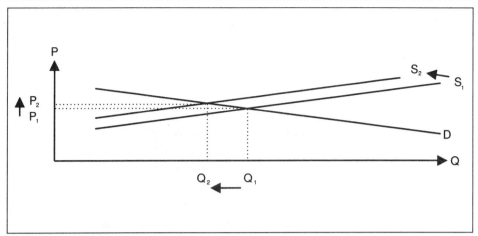

Figure 7.3A Changes in Market Equilibrium: Supply Function Shifts

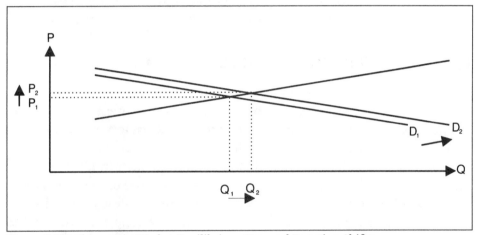

Figure 7.3B Changes in Market Equilibrium: Demand Function Shifts

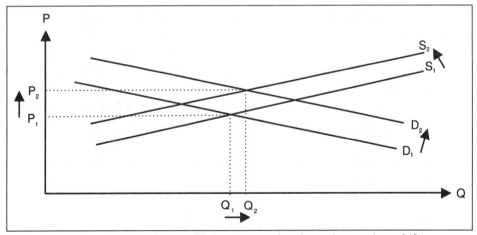

Figure 7.3C Changes in Market Equilibrium: Demand and Supply Functions Shift

watery gruel, bus tickets, and medical treatment for malnutrition. An increase in income will decrease demand, equilibrium price, and equilibrium quantities for these goods and services.

Changes in tax, subsidy, or regulatory policy can shift either or both curves in either direction. For example, a housing code regulation requiring foster-care agencies in a given locality to meet minimum space and fire prevention standards will increase cost and hence decrease the quantity of services supplied at each possible price. This same regulation will increase the quality of the product and may attract added customers from neighboring jurisdictions at any given price. With supply decreasing and demand increasing, we cannot be certain whether the equilibrium quantity will rise or fall (this depends upon which curve-shifting has greater impact), but we can be certain that the equilibrium price will rise, as Figure 7.3C makes clear. (We will analyze the impact of other tax, subsidy, and regulatory policies in more detail in Chapter 8.)

PERFECT COMPETITION IN THE LONG RUN

As a market enters the long run, four changes occur: (1) fixed costs become variable costs, (2) fixed revenues become variable revenues, (3) the size of physical facilities (and the amount of other fixed factors of production) changes, and (4) the number of supplier organizations changes.

The first two changes have already been dealt with in Chapter 4. An organization should shut down in the long run if its long-run average variable costs exceed its long-run average variable revenues. With no fixed costs, long-run average variable costs are synonymous with long-run average total costs. With no fixed revenues, long-run average revenues include revenues from both sales and donations. In the long run, the shutdown rule makes eminent sense—shut down if you cannot at least break even so that overall revenues exceed costs.

We postpone for a moment discussion of the third source of change, facility size. First we need to say more about the impact of entry and exit on long-run equilibrium. If there are sufficient barriers to entry and exit, the number of firms is fixed in the long run. But if there is free entry, we have the following paradoxical result:

Economic profits are zero in long-run competitive equilibrium with free entry and exit.

Why would any firm, especially a for-profit firm, remain in business if it expected to receive zero profits? The key here is that we are talking about

economic profits, which count the value of all forgone activities and investments as costs. To say that profits are zero is to say that there is no other
economic opportunity offering a greater return. Anytime profits in an
industry are positive it means that a new entrant could do better in the
industry than it could anywhere else. Anytime profits are negative, entrepre-
neurs could profit by switching to another line of business. Thus, the
conclusion that long-run profits are zero with free entry and exit follows
directly from our definition of profits.

We are now ready to illustrate how a market adjusts from one long-run
equilibrium to another. Suppose that, as in Figure 7.4, the day-care market is
perfectly competitive and in long-run equilibrium, where the typical organization produces q_0 at price P_0 (left-hand side of the diagram). In turn, the price
P_0 is determined by the intersection of the market supply (S) and demand (D)
curves (right-hand side of the diagram), and the market equilibrium quantity
Q_0 results. Because we have supposed that this is a long-run equilibrium, we
know that profits are zero, so P_0 must equal the AC at q_0. Prices and quantities
will remain at these equilibrium values until one of the curves moves.

Now suppose that a sudden in-migration of families with young children increases the demand for day-care services to D_1. In the short run, this
will increase the equilibrium price to P_1. Why? Because at the initial price
with the new demand curve, we have a shortage that bids the price up. The
price rise will increase the firm and market quantities to q_1 and Q_1, respectively. The typical supplier earns positive economic profits because the new
price is greater than average total cost at the new quantity.

As we move toward the long run, these positive profits will attract new
entrants to the day-care industry. At the same time, some incumbent suppli-

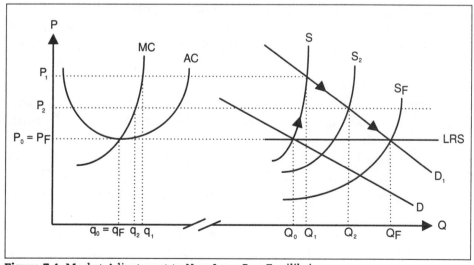

Figure 7.4 Market Adjustment to New Long-Run Equilibrium

ers may wish to adjust their facility sizes. In order to keep things simple, assume that there is only one facility size available, so that the long-run and short-run cost curves are identical. Then the increase in the number of firms moves the market supply curve to the right to position S_2. Why? Because, at any given price, 101 identical suppliers will produce a greater total quantity than would 100 firms. The horizontal summation moves to the right as we increase the number of organizations over which we sum. With the new supply curve, the equilibrium price falls to P_2 and each supplier reduces its production to q_2, but the increase in number of organizations dominates the reduction in production at each organization so that the market equilibrium quantity increases to Q_2. As we can see, profits, although smaller, are still positive, so that entry of new suppliers would continue and the supply curve would continue to creep to the right.

When will this process end? It will end when profits are once again zero. But what price and quantity does this lead to? The answer depends on whether the entry of new suppliers causes a change in the cost functions of existing suppliers. The simplest and most common assumption is that the cost functions are unaffected by entry. We have been implicitly assuming this by not changing the location of the curves on the left side of Figure 7.4 as the market supply curve moved to the right. Under this assumption, the long-run equilibrium price (P_F) with the new demand curve is the same as that with the old demand curve (P_0), and each supplier produces the same quantity ($q_F = q_0$) as well. However, market quantity goes up to Q_F. Connecting the intersections, we derive the long-run supply curve, which illustrates the quantities willingly supplied in the long run when the number of suppliers can adjust. Here, the long-run supply curve is horizontal.

Another possibility is that the increase in the number of suppliers raises the price of production for all suppliers. This could occur if one essential input (for instance, well-adjusted adults who are good at nurturing other people's children) were scarce, so that the expansion of the industry would drive up the wages of day-care workers. This would result in an upward-sloping long-run supply curve, although the curve would still be flatter than the short-run supply curve, and an increase in demand would cause a small increase in price in the long run.

Another possibility is that an increase in the number of suppliers would lower the costs of production. This could occur if there were sufficient economies of scale in supplying an input crucial for our output of interest. For example, it is quite expensive to produce solar power cells on a small scale, so that if the solar electric-generating industry contained only a few firms, each would have to pay a high price for raw materials. If the number of firms increased, it would be possible to use more efficient assembly-line techniques in the production of power cells, which would lower their price and make solar generation of power possible at lower cost. In the nonprofit world, a similar situation can occur with ticket-sales services for arts organizations. Automated ticket-purchasing systems are expensive but become more efficient as volume increases. If more arts organizations enter the market, demand for this service increases and costs decline. In such a case, the long-run supply curve is downward-sloping even though the short-run supply curve is upward-sloping. This situation is the only case where an increase in demand would cause a decrease in price in the long run.

The foregoing discussion of long-run competition points to the importance of profits in the performance of competitive industries, even those involving nonprofit organizations. In particular, we can conclude that

> **When there is free entry, profits are a temporary phenomenon. Profits signal that demand has increased in a particular market and will attract the added resources necessary to meet the increase in demand.**

Thus, even for nonprofits, profit can serve the function of helping markets adjust to new levels of demand. Conversely, we can also see the importance of economic losses in helping markets adjust to reduced demand in the long run. For an industry that starts in long-run equilibrium but then experiences a permanent decrease in demand, losses signal that resources should move away from that industry toward more highly valued uses. In the example illustrated in Figure 7.4, the exit of suppliers will then raise the price back to its initial level. (As an exercise, the reader should trace the path of adjustment in Figure 7.4, from Q_F to Q_0, assuming demand drops from D_1 to D.)

EQUILIBRIUM IN MONOPOLY

What does the monopoly supply curve look like? This is a trick question because there is no such thing. We saw in Chapter 5 (although we hadn't yet introduced this terminology) that if there are barriers to entry, the profit-maximizing monopoly firm picks its price on the market demand curve after choosing to produce the quantity that makes MR equal MC. We don't have to answer the question suggested by a supply curve (i.e., How much would suppliers like to sell at each possible price?), because monopolies are price setters, not price takers. The same rule applies in the long run, when long-run MC is substituted for short-run MC, because we have assumed that entry is impossible.

But suppose the market is contestable. One possibility is that the market is perfectly competitive but has only one competitor. In this case, any attempt to exercise market power would attract enough competitors to render that effort futile. Thus, the foregoing analysis of perfect competition suffices to characterize long-run equilibrium in this case as well. Another possibility is that the market is monopolistically competitive, but with only one competitor. Here, the long run would feature several monopolists, each setting prices and quantities according to the long-run marginal costs and revenues, and setting MC equal to MR for each of their differentiated products.

EQUILIBRIUM AND OBJECTIVE FUNCTIONS

In Chapter 5, we considered three possible objective functions for what we now see was a monopoly supplier: profit maximization, welfare maximization, and quantity maximization. We saw that if demand accurately reflects marginal social benefits, the profit-maximizing monopoly produces too little and the quantity-maximizing monopoly generally produces too much. Now we can consider these same three possibilities for firms in competitive markets. Then we will discuss how to revise our conclusions when price does not reflect marginal social benefits.

We have seen that profit-maximizing monopolies underproduce in order to maintain their profits. Although they have the power to sell more, their fear of driving their own price down restrains them from doing so. In contrast, perfect competitors produce the socially optimal quantity, for no single supplier worries about driving its competitors' prices down, and each supplier owns too small a part of the market to worry about driving its own price down. In both short-run and long-run equilibrium, the quantity picked by a profit maximizer equates marginal cost with price (and hence with marginal benefit). This is just the rule we established in Chapter 5 for ascertaining whether production levels are socially optimal. We reinterpret that rule here as follows:

> **In perfectly competitive markets, nonprofit managers with social objectives should operate just like for-profit firms if they believe the demand curve accurately reflects marginal social benefits.**

What about nonprofit organizations that wish to maximize the quantity they produce as long as they can at least break even? In the short run, they would select a quantity that makes P equal AC, so their short-run firm supply curve would trace out the AC curve above its minimum and would lie to the right of a profit maximizer's supply curve. In the long run, entry of profit-maximizing for-profits (or nonprofits seeking to maximize their financial surpluses) would drive this price down, and nonprofit output maximizers would expand until they reached their AC curve minimum. But this is precisely where, by a different route, the for-profit firms will end up, because, as shown in Chapter 4, MC equals AC where AC is at its minimum. Choosing a quantity that makes P equal MC is the same as picking a quantity that makes P equal AC if MC equals AC. This leads to a surprising conclusion:

> **If there is free entry (by profit-making firms or by nonprofits seeking to maximize financial surpluses), nonprofit firms have two choices in the long run: to maximize profits (and just break even) or to go out of business. Regardless of the organization's objective function, profit maximization is essential for survival in a perfectly competitive environment.**

This is no problem here when the nonprofit manager believes that the demand curve accurately reflects marginal social benefits, as may be the case for certain arts or recreational services, for example. However, nonprofit organizations with social objectives that are not reflected in demand curves, such as providers of social services or those with output-maximizing objectives, may need the state's protection from competition in order to pursue those objectives and survive. There are some exceptions: there may be natural barriers to entry; entry may occur very slowly so that departures from long-run equilibrium can persist for a long time; and donations, tax benefits, or exclusive government contracts may or may not provide a cushion that protects nonprofits from the homogenizing force of competition. (See Steinberg [1993] for greater detail.)

One further observation is in order. Suppose the competitive market is restricted to nonprofit organizations alone. For example, suppose the day-care market features free entry—but only for nonprofit suppliers. Will the result be any different in the long run? The answer would seem to depend on the objectives pursued by the competing nonprofit organizations. However, a reasonable assumption is that at least some of the competitors will behave as profit maximizers, attempting to maximize their financial surpluses for whatever purposes. If this is the case, those competitors will drive the market, pushing prices down to minimum average cost in the long run (in the same way that for-profit firms would), and the result will be the same.

SUMMARY

In isolation, it is not hard to figure out how an individual for-profit firm or nonprofit organization should decide on a price and quantity to produce for any set of goals it might want to pursue. However, organizations operate in markets in which competition restricts their options to a smaller set of "survivable behaviors" that may or may not support their objectives. In some cases, competition forces even malevolent organizations to contribute to the good of society or go out of business. For example, competition helps preclude suppliers from charging exorbitant prices for shabby services. In other cases, competition destroys the ability of nonprofit organizations to provide unique social benefits. For example, a day-care center wishing to extend its services to all unserved preschoolers in its vicinity will find itself losing money. Nonprofit organizations must be cognizant of current and latent competition in all the markets they participate in—for sales, inputs, donations, volunteers, and grants—in order to accomplish their missions.

REFERENCES

Shubik, Martin. *Game Theory in the Social Sciences.* Cambridge, Mass.: MIT Press, 1982.
Steinberg, Richard. "Public Policy and the Performance of Nonprofit Organizations: A General Framework." *Nonprofit and Voluntary Sector Quarterly,* 22:1, 1993, pp. 13-32.
Vladeck, Bruce C. *Unloving Care.* New York: Basic, 1980.

EXERCISES

1. Think of the process of charitable giving as a market in which nonprofit organizations compete for the funds offered by donors. In particular, nonprofits supply satisfactions to donors in exchange for financial contributions. If Q is the supply of donor satisfactions (tangible expressions of recognition, services provided for which the donor can claim credit, etc.), draw the supply curve for these satisfactions, using Figure 7.1 (on page 123) as a model and assuming that many nonprofits compete for donor contributions. What can you assume about the objective function for nonprofit organizations in this situation?

2. Continuing the example above, use Figure 7.2 (on page 125) to characterize the market for donations. Assume that the demand curve represents how much donors will give, at the margin, for each level of satisfactions that nonprofits can offer them. Discuss how this market moves toward equilibrium. That is, what happens if nonprofits ask for a high level of contributions for the satisfactions they are prepared to supply, but donor demand is low and contributions fall short? Alternatively, what happens when nonprofits ask for very modest donations and cannot meet the demand for donor satisfactions at this "price"?

3. Pursuing the example further, and assuming that entry into this market is not restricted, describe how the long-run supply curve will differ from the short-run supply curve as more nonprofits enter the competition for donations. What does the long-run supply curve look like? Is it more likely to be vertical or horizontal? Why?

4. If the market for donations is perfectly competitive, how will this affect the ability of individual nonprofits to raise funds in the long run? How does your reasoning in this case help us to understand the justification for united fund-raising arrangements? If all nonprofits raised funds through United Way, would you characterize the market as competitive or monopolistic? How would long-run net proceeds (profits) in this case differ from those in markets without united fund-raising arrangements?

5. Local PTAs depend on volunteers to raise funds and administer their activities.

    a. Characterize the market for these volunteers in terms of supply and demand curves such as those pictured in Figure 7.2. If Q is the number of volunteer hours, what is the interpretation of P on the vertical axis?

    b. If the wage rate that these volunteers can earn in the paid labor market rises, how is the supply curve for volunteers likely to shift? Illustrate the shift in a diagram modeled after Figure 7.3A (on page 127). What will be the effect on the number of volunteer hours and the "price" nonprofits will have to pay to attract or retain volunteers?

    c. Suppose the demand for PTA programs increases significantly, leading to an increased demand for PTA volunteers. Illustrate how this shift will affect the number of volunteers and the price nonprofits must pay for them.

6. There are several dozen nonprofit and for-profit theaters in the entertainment district of the city of Thespian that offer serious dramatic performances. However, ever since Computers, Inc., closed its nearby facility and many laid-off employees moved away, these theaters have all run annual deficits. In this market, how are the strategies and objectives of nonprofits likely to differ from those of the for-profit theaters? In the long run, what are the likely ways for this market to adjust, in terms of the number of theaters, how much they produce, what they charge, and how well they do in terms of profit or loss? Use a diagram such as that in Figure 7.4 (on page 129) to illustrate your reasoning.

CHAPTER **8**

Applications of Market Analysis

In this chapter we consider some advanced applications of market analysis. First, we examine how selected governmental policies (taxes and subsidies) affect competitive equilibrium. Then we examine the markets for inputs, illustrate the added complications in the nonprofit sector resulting from interactions between paid- and volunteer-labor inputs, and consider the impact of the minimum wage on this labor market. Last, we survey some of the complexities of nonprofit pricing, including use of sliding-scale fees and other forms of "price discrimination," the effects of sales revenues on donations, the effects of subsidized prices on recipient behavior, and the pricing of one service to cross-subsidize another.

TAXES AND SUBSIDIES

The primary purpose of taxes may be to raise revenues for the government, but taxes in particular markets have sometimes intended, sometimes unintended effects on market equilibrium. In this section, we examine the impact of sales taxes and excise taxes (sales taxes that are specific to a particular industry) on competitive equilibrium and consider the circumstances where we expect the tax will be passed on to consumers and those where the seller will absorb the tax. This division of the tax burden among the parties ultimately affected is known as *economic tax incidence*. Nonprofit managers who care about the well-being of their customers or have vested interests in various tax policies (such as taxes on sales of tickets for performances in the arts) need to understand tax incidence. Next, using the same framework, we analyze government subsidies that are proportional to sales, for these subsidies are, in effect, negative excise taxes. Finally, we briefly discuss the differential tax rates applied to (generally) tax-exempt nonprofits and taxable for-profit businesses in the same industry, and offer some insights into the controversy surrounding alleged unfair competition between nonprofits and businesses.

Sales and excise taxes are of two types: ad valorem and per-unit. An *ad valorem tax* is a percentage markup on the price—for example, a 6 percent sales tax. A *per-unit tax* is a fixed-value markup on the price—for example, a tax of 6 cents per gallon on gasoline. Under either approach, the tax on an item priced at $1 per unit would be the same (in this case, 6 cents), but if the price rose to $2 per unit, the sales-tax liability would increase to 12 cents while the per-unit tax liability would remain at 6 cents.

Sales and excise taxes may apply to products sold by nonprofit organizations (e.g., computers sold by a university bookstore or fee parking in a nonprofit hospital's lot) or to products bought by nonprofits (e.g., utility taxes paid on telephone or electricity usage by a social service agency). If the nonprofit organization has some market power, it has some control over tax incidence. To protect consumers, the organization can reduce its pre-tax price for the product it sells; to protect its bottom line, the organization can pass on the tax costs of products it buys. However, as we demonstrated in Chapter 7, nonprofits in competitive markets with free entry have less choice. We will now show that the shapes of market demand and supply curves completely determine tax incidence.

Without taxes, there would be no difference between the price paid by the consumer and the price received and kept by the seller. Taxes drive a wedge between these two prices. For each unit purchased, the consumer pays a price that includes the tax, whereas the seller receives a price that does not. To understand tax incidence it is essential to understand that the consumer price (P_C) is distinct from the producer price (P_P). Letting t represent the tax rate for a per-unit tax and v represent the tax rate (expressed as a decimal) for an ad valorem tax, two simple identities relate these prices:

$$P_P + t = P_C$$
$$P_P \times (1 + v) = P_C$$

When consumers decide upon a quantity to purchase, they care about their out-of-pocket costs, including the tax. They generally do not care what percentage of that price is kept by the seller and what percentage is turned over to the government. Thus, the shape and location of the demand curve logically depend only on P_C. Placing a tax on a good does not affect the location of the demand curve. This is not to say that consumers are unaffected by a tax: the tax will generally change the equilibrium price consumers will pay and so affects the quantity they wish to buy. However, a demand curve that shows how consumers adjust their planned purchases when the consumer price changes is all we need to calculate the effects of taxes on equilibrium. Taxes may move us along this demand curve to a new equilibrium.

When producers decide on a quantity to offer for sale, they care only about the per-unit revenues they can keep. They do not care what the consumer is paying or what the government is getting except insofar as these factors affect the equilibrium producer price they will receive. Therefore, the tax does not change the location or shape of the supply curve, which shows how producers adjust their planned sales when the producer price changes.

As before, equilibrium prices and quantity are determined by the appropriate intersection of supply and demand curves. However, we cannot directly put the supply and demand curves on the same graph, for one is a function of P_P and the other is a function of P_C. Even if we did put them on the same graph, there would be ambiguity as to which of the two equilibrium prices was illustrated by the intersection. The answer to both questions is given by the following trick: we can translate either price scale into the other by using either $P_P + t = P_C$ or $P_P \times (1 + v) = P_C$, as appropriate for the type of tax in question. To translate the supply curve into a statement about willingness to sell at each *consumer price*, we simply add the tax to the respective producer prices, which has the effect of shifting the supply curve up by the amount of the tax.

Figure 8.1A illustrates how this would work. A tax of $2 per unit would create the impression that the supply curve had shifted, in parallel fashion, upward by $2 (from position S_1 to position S_2) when viewed from the perspective of the consumer. To see this, look in detail at a few points on the old supply curve. At a producer price of $10, this supply curve indicates that producers are willing to sell 100 units of the product. Before the tax is instituted, the producer will receive this price when the consumer pays $10; after the tax, the consumer price will need to be $12 in order for the producer price to be $10 and hence induce producers to supply 100 units. In turn, the supply curve indicates that prior to the tax, producers will offer 120 units for sale at a producer (and hence consumer) price of $12. Following institution of the tax, consumers will have to pay $14 to induce the offering of 120 units by producers. When we repeat this process for additional points, it rapidly

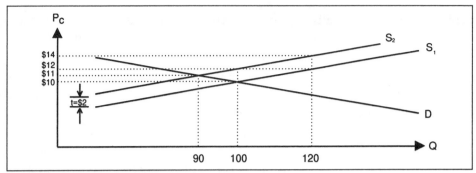

Figure 8.1A Incidence of Tax on Sales: Supply Function Shifts

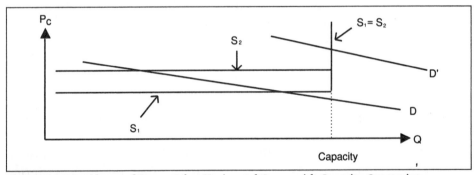

Figure 8.1B Incidence of Tax on Sales: Horizontal Supply Curve

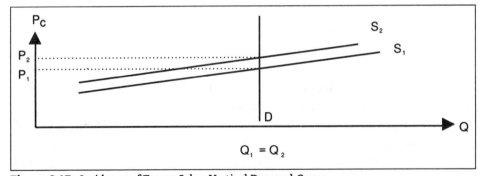

Figure 8.1C Incidence of Tax on Sales: Horizontal Curve with Capacity Constraint

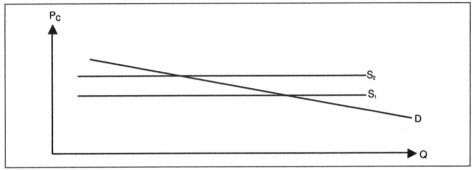

Figure 8.1D Incidence of Tax on Sales: Vertical Demand Curve

becomes clear that a per-unit tax shifts the supply curve upward (when viewed from the consumer price perspective) by the amount of the tax per unit.

Although the supply curve moves upward by the full amount of the tax in Figure 8.1A, the intersection between supply and demand moves up by somewhat less: as was illustrated, the equilibrium consumer price rises by $1. Why is this? The graph indicates that if the entire burden is passed on to consumers (that is, if the consumer price rises by the full $2), 20 more units will be offered for sale than are desired for purchase. Recognizing this potential for excess supply, producers are forced to swallow a portion of the tax so that the post-tax market can clear. In this case, the equilibrium producer price falls by $1. Why? Because if the consumer price rises by $1 and the producer price is the consumer price minus the tax ($2), then the producer price must fall by $1. Since we translated everything into consumer prices to draw the graph, we have to translate back, using either $P_P = P_C - t$ or $P_P = P_C/(1 + v)$ to ascertain the impact on equilibrium producer price. Regardless of statutory incidence, the slopes of the supply and demand curves determine that the economic incidence of a tax in this market is split 50-50 between suppliers and consumers.

Figures 8.1B, 8.1C, and 8.1D illustrate how the burden would be split for markets with differently sloped supply and demand curves. In Figure 8.1B, we consider an industry with a horizontal supply curve. Such industries are rare in the short run but, as we saw in Chapter 7, quite common in the long run with free entry. When we shift this curve upward by the amount of the tax, the intersection rises by the same amount, so that 100 percent of the burden of the tax is borne by consumers. Thus, while tax officials may label this a tax on suppliers and hold them responsible for collecting the tax and turning it over to the government, the real economic incidence of this tax rests entirely on consumers. Why? Producers in an industry with a horizontal supply curve are making a statement: Cut the price I receive by one cent and I will leave this market. If any of the burden is absorbed by producers, they will have negative profits and will eventually exit, causing a shortage that bids up the consumer price.

In Figure 8.1C, we consider a per-unit tax on tickets to an opera performance at a house with a strict capacity constraint: no matter what the price is, the fire code will not allow the company to sell more tickets than there are seats in the house. Here, tax incidence depends on the location of the demand curve in an interesting way: if the show sells out, the entire tax burden is borne by the producers; otherwise, the entire burden is borne by consumers. (Note that when we shift a vertical section of a supply curve upward, it overlaps itself, so that S_2 overlaps S_1 for the vertical portion of the curve.) Demand curves D and D' represent two distinct possibilities for the location of demand (unrelated to imposition of the tax). When the show does not sell out (a situation represented by demand curve D), we are on the horizontal portion of the supply curve, and we know from the previous example why this leads to 100 percent incidence on consumers. When the show does sell out (a situation represented by demand curve D'), we are on the vertical section of the supply curve. Here, suppliers will continue to offer enough tickets to fill the house to capacity even if they have to swallow the entire tax. Indeed, fussy consumers would reduce their ticket purchases if any portion of the tax were passed on, creating an excess supply. Thus, producers are forced by market circumstances to swallow the entire tax.

Figure 8.1D illustrates the case of a vertical demand curve, where the quantity demanded does not change as the price changes. Here, 100 percent of the burden falls on consumers, who, by their readiness to pay higher prices without reducing purchases, become the sole victims of market forces. Nonprofit hospitals likely face vertical demand curves over a range of prices in their markets for highly essential services with no available substitutes, such as kidney dialysis or organ transplants. An excise tax on these services would not hurt the hospitals, nor would it reduce the equilibrium quantity of care provided. However, it would raise the price paid by the patient (or the patient's insurer). Another example is a nonprofit organization that purchases some services, such as heating for its offices, without regard to price. A tax on this kind of input would fall entirely on the purchasing organization unless the utility was prohibited by regulatory authorities from passing on its costs.

A per-unit subsidy is just a negative excise tax. For example, the government of India, in order to help combat overpopulation there, pays clinicians a bonus for each voluntary sterilization they perform. Like taxes, the incidence of a per-unit subsidy will vary with the slopes of the supply and demand curves in the subsidized industry. Clinicians could use the entire subsidy to supplement their per-patient fees, or they could pass on all or part of the subsidy by reducing the fees charged. To see which occurs, we simply shift the supply curve downward by the amount of the subsidy per unit and examine the effect on the new intersection of supply and demand. Reading the panels of Figure 8.1 in reverse allows us to see the incidence of the subsidy: for markets such as the one represented in Figure 8.1A, the incidence is split 50-50; for markets such as the one represented in Figure 8.1B, consumers gain the full benefit of the subsidy; and for markets such as the one represented in Figure 8.1C, producers gain the full subsidy if the show sells out, whereas consumers gain the full subsidy if it does not. Consumers also gain the full subsidy in markets such as the one represented in Figure 8.1D. Some other examples of per-unit subsidies (or their logical equivalent) include vouchers for day-care service, scholarships for higher education, Medicaid reimbursements for health-care services, and food stamps for purchase of essential food.

ANALYZING INPUT MARKETS SUCH AS LABOR

As labor-intensive, service-producing organizations, nonprofits have a special interest in the operations of labor markets. Before analyzing these markets, however, we must understand the special nature of labor demand and supply functions. In a sense, labor markets are mirror images of ordinary markets for goods and services. In the latter, services or goods are ordinarily supplied by organizations and consumed by individuals. In labor markets, the reverse is true. Individuals supply labor and organizations consume labor. Nonetheless, once we understand how demand and supply work in this case, we can analyze labor markets in much the same way as other markets for goods and services. We focus here on paid labor but will comment on the market for volunteer labor after analyzing paid work.

The Supply of Labor

The supply function for labor relates the quantity of hours that people offer for work to the (after-tax) wage rate paid for that work. Different supply functions would, of course, apply to different types of labor: nurses, social workers, legal-aid lawyers, and managers of arts organizations would probably offer different numbers of hours of work at any given wage. Labor-supply functions are often upward-sloping, indicating that people offer to work more hours when the wage rate goes up. However, in many occupations, empirical studies suggest that for males in their prime working years labor supply tilts backward—that is, at some level, higher wages lead to fewer hours worked. Perhaps this is because a higher wage rate allows one to work fewer hours to reach a target income level (e.g., enough to pay the monthly bills). Figure 8.2A illustrates a typical upward-sloping labor-supply curve, and the dotted-line extension of this curve illustrates the backward-bending possibility.

The Demand for Labor

The demand for paid labor is what economists call a *derived demand*. That is, the demand for labor is based on the value of that labor's contribution to the output of an organization. Recall from Chapter 5 that we applied the principle of analysis at the margin to determine how much of a given input to use in the production of an output good or service. In the case of labor, we apply the following logic:

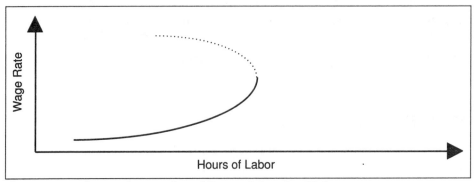

Figure 8.2A Labor Market Supply and Demand: Supply of Labor

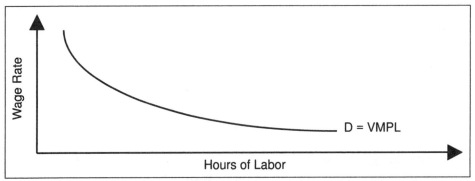

Figure 8.2B Labor Market Supply and Demand: (Derived) Demand for Labor

- The marginal product of labor (*MPL*) is the additional output that could be produced as a result of employing an additional hour of labor, holding all other inputs constant.
- The value of the marginal product of labor (*VMPL*) is simply *MPL* multiplied by *MR*—the value of additional revenues and other (noncash) benefits obtained per unit of additional output. Recall that, in general, *MR* is lower than the price at which the product sells, but in the special case of perfect competition *MR* is identical with price. Thus, in general,

$$VMPL = MPL \times MR$$

and for perfectly competitive output markets,

$$VMPL = MPL \times P$$

Nonprofit managers may view taking care of their employees as part of their mission. This would be especially so in sheltered workshops for the physically or mentally challenged. In many if not most cases, however, workers are viewed by management as a means to an end. In such

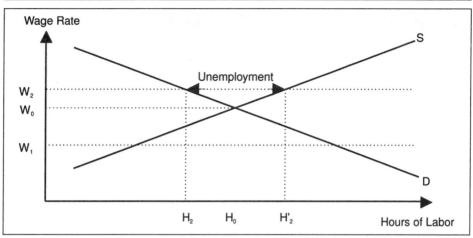

Figure 8.3 Labor Market Equilibrium

cases, management wants a minimum-cost/maximum-productivity labor force, and the rule for selection of a profit-maximizing work force is appropriate:

> **Given the prevailing market wage w and the MR available from producing output, a profit-maximizing organization should employ the number of worker hours that makes VMPL equal w.**

This rule follows directly from the logic of analysis at the margin. Any worker whose *VMPL* exceeds the *w* should be hired, because doing so will add more to organizational revenues than to costs, supplementing the profits earned from earlier hires. As more and more workers are hired, *VMPL* eventually will decline, because a fixed facility size results in crowding and diminished marginal productivity and because added production drives down *MR*. The firm should stop hiring when *VMPL* declines enough to equal *w*.

Repeated use of this rule for alternative values of *w* yields points on the organization's demand for labor curve. Thus, organizational demand is the *VMPL* curve. In turn, the market demand for labor is the horizontal sum of organizational demand curves (the sum of workers desired by each organization at each given wage). If the wage is high, employment of a few workers will bring equality between *VMPL* and *w*; if the wage is low, more workers are needed to attain this equality. Thus, the demand for labor is downward-sloping, as illustrated in Figure 8.2B.

Labor Market Equilibrium

Figure 8.3 pictures the demand and supply for (paid) labor on the same graph. Following our usual market analysis, we can determine that, left to its own devices, this labor market will equilibrate at a market-clearing wage of W_0 with H_0 hours worked. This assumes that the input market is competitive, with many employers and workers, so that no individual organization employs so many workers that it has significant market power (i.e., there is no monopsony) and so that there are no labor unions with sufficient strength to enhance the market power of workers (i.e., there is no monopoly).

Government interferes with this equilibrating process in low-wage markets by setting a legal minimum wage. The U.S. Fair Labor Standards Act, as revised, sets a legal minimum wage for paid employees in most organizations but, interestingly enough, does not prohibit the employment of volunteers. Because for-profit firms infrequently employ volunteers, the law effectively sets a minimum for for-profits while establishing a prohibited range for nonprofits. (That is, people can work above the minimum or at a wage of zero, but not in between.) This suggests that the minimum wage will have differing impacts on the two sectors (see Steinberg and Smith, 1990).

In Figure 8.3, a minimum wage appears as a horizontal line at the minimum required wage rate, for this requirement is independent of the aggregate number of hours worked. From the diagram, we can see that such a law either will have no effect or will prevent the market from reaching a market-clearing equilibrium. If the minimum wage is set at level W_1 in the diagram, the law will have no effect. Wages will rise to level W_0 in order for demand and supply to equilibrate. On the other hand, if the minimum wage is set at W_2, the hours worked will be reduced to H_2. Those who work will receive the higher wage W_2, but there will be unemployment relative to how many would like to work at the wage W_2. This unemployment is represented by H_2-H_2' in the figure.

Labor unions can also affect equilibrium. If the union negotiates a wage rate (W_2) higher than the free-market equilibrium (W_0), the wage will have the same effect as a minimum wage: those lucky enough to keep their jobs will receive a higher wage, while others will be laid off. However, unions also have other instruments available to achieve their goals. For example, if the union can cooperate with the organization in promoting its product (think of the "Buy the union label" and "Buy American" campaigns), this will shift the MR schedule (and hence $VMPL$ and labor demand) upward, increasing both wages and employment without causing layoffs.

Volunteer Labor

By definition, volunteer labor manifests no conventional supply and demand functions because no explicit money wage or price is paid for it.

However, we can analyze volunteer labor in much the same way as paid labor because:

- Organizations do pay a price for volunteer labor. This price consists of the costs incurred for supervision and for benefits provided to volunteers such as awards, training opportunities, and the like. Moreover, volunteers contribute to the organization's production of services in much the same way that paid workers do. Thus, the demand for volunteer labor will be determined by the value of the marginal product of that labor and will decline with hours worked in much the same way as that for paid labor. The function of Figure 8.2B (on page 144) may also be a reasonable representation of the demand for volunteer labor, with an appropriate modification of the scale on the vertical axis to reflect the effective unit costs of volunteer administration and rewards.
- Volunteers do receive benefits or rewards for volunteering. Much of this compensation is intangible and nonmonetary in nature. But some of it, in the form of training and benefits, rewards, and opportunities to socialize with other volunteers or to enjoy the services of the organization, is tangible. As these benefits are increased by the organization, people will generally increase the number of hours they offer to volunteer.

The analogy is not exact, and we will speak here somewhat metaphorically, but market analysis does provide insights into volunteering and volunteer utilization. The costs and benefits to the organization of using volunteers implicitly determine a demand curve for volunteers. The costs and benefits to individuals of volunteering implicitly determine a supply curve for volunteers. The interaction of these curves helps determine the number of volunteers used, equilibrium expenditures on maintaining a volunteer force, and equilibrium benefits received by volunteers. The usual tools of comparative statics can be applied to this equilibrium. Thus, for example, if the after-tax wage rate received by workers in their paid employment elsewhere rises, the opportunity cost of volunteering is increased and the volunteer supply curve will move to the left, all else held constant. Assuming that the volunteer supply curve is upward-sloping, the equilibrium number of volunteers used will fall; organizations will devote more resources per volunteer to recruiting, training, and volunteer perquisites; and, on average, volunteers will receive greater benefits from their volunteering experience.

Without a better empirical understanding of these phenomena we cannot be very confident of our conclusions. In particular, when the after-tax wage rate goes up, the income of potential volunteers will go up (unless the paid-labor supply curve is significantly backward bending), and this too will affect their willingness to volunteer. The available evidence suggests that, at least for some forms of volunteering, higher-income people are more likely to volunteer and to volunteer more hours. This "income effect" pushes the supply curve for volunteers to the right, ameliorating or even reversing the leftward shift in volunteer supply due to the increased opportunity cost of volunteering. Unfortunately, we do not yet have sufficient evidence of the relative sizes of these opposing effects to produce firm qualitative conclusions about the impact of increased wages on volunteering.

Interactions Between the Paid and Volunteer Labor Markets

We have already indicated that the minimum wage creates some interactions between a nonprofit organization's use of paid and volunteer labor by prohibiting a range of intermediate wage rates. There are much simpler interactions as well. If we neglect the possibility that the same person could work as either a paid or a volunteer worker, then we can regard paid and volunteer labor as two distinct inputs to the nonprofit production process. The general analysis of multiple inputs is quite developed in for-profit economics, which distinguishes complementary inputs (inputs that are more effective when used together, such as carpenters and sanding machines) from substitutable inputs (inputs that can be replaced, at minimal cost, with an equally effective alternative, such as, for most tasks, male workers and female workers). When the equilibrium price for one input goes up, the demand for the other input will shift to the left for complements and to the right for substitutes. This analysis probably applies equally well to nonprofit organizations, but we have little evidence on whether particular types of nonprofits regard volunteers as a substitute or a complement for particular types of paid labor. One interesting study by Duncombe and Brudney (1992) estimates some of the parameters needed to characterize the optimal mixture of paid and volunteer workers in fire-fighting companies. Their study found that the costs of training, recruiting, and retaining volunteers must be balanced against the wage rate to determine the best proportions of these inputs.

INTRODUCTION TO NONPROFIT PRICING

In previous chapters, we have considered two archetypal market situations involving the setting of the price of a single output: perfectly competitive markets, where price is determined by the intersection of market supply and demand curves, and monopoly, where the determination of price is made by a monopoly supplier in order to maximize profit or attain some other objective. Later in this chapter we will consider a number of more complex pricing issues involving different prices in related markets as well as a number of pricing nuances and strategies of special relevance to the practices of nonprofit organizations. To facilitate that discussion, we first need to develop an important additional analytical concept: *elasticity*.

Elasticity

Economists use the concept of elasticity to measure how sensitive one (dependent) variable is to a change in another (independent) variable. A variety of elasticity measures are of interest to us here, including:

> *price elasticity of demand,* which measures the response of consumers' desired purchases to price changes;
> *income elasticity of demand,* which measures the response of consumers' desired purchases to changes in their income;
> *cross-price elasticity of demand*, which measures the response of consumers of one product to a change in the price of a different product;
> *price elasticity of supply,* which measures the response of producers' desired sales quantity to changes in price; and
> *income elasticity of supply,* which measures the response of producers' desired sales quantity to a change in owner income.

Elasticity measures are functions, not constant numbers. For instance, the price elasticity of demand depends on the price level before any change: consumers may respond one way to a price increase when the price is high and quite another way when the price is low. Similar arguments apply to our other elasticity measures. Each elasticity measure is also a function of the other determinants of demand or supply, which we hold constant. For example, in computing the price elasticity of demand, we measure consumer responsiveness to price changes while holding constant at particular levels income, prices of other products, and other independent variables. Suppose, for example, income is initially held constant at level Y_1 in order to compute price elasticity of demand. If income rises or falls to some other level, say Y_2, the price elasticity of demand will also change.

In order to provide economic insights, measures of elasticity are designed to gauge responsiveness in proportional terms (that is, by looking at percentage changes instead of absolute numerical changes). Clearly, a one-penny increase in the price of chewing gum is different from a one-penny increase in the price of Rolls Royce automobiles, and measuring in percentage terms captures the essence of this difference. Measuring in percentage terms is also convenient in that we need not worry about the units of measurement. Whether we measure the price in pennies, dollars, rubles, or yen, and whether we measure quantities in gallons, pounds, liters, or six-packs, a 10 percent change means the same thing.

Price Elasticity of Demand

Specified formally, *price elasticity of demand* is the ratio of the percentage change in the quantity demanded of a given good or service to the percentage change in the price of that good or service. Around a given point (P,Q) on the demand curve, price elasticity of demand is computed as

$$e_p^D = \textit{(\% change in Q)/(\% change in P)}$$

To measure percentage changes, we choose two points on the demand curve closely surrounding our point of interest P,Q (and equally distant from this point), measure the difference between the quantities at these surrounding points (symbolized as ΔQ), measure the difference between the prices at these surrounding points (symbolized as ΔP), and compute:

$$e_p^D = \textit{($\Delta Q/Q$)/($\Delta P/P$)}$$

A little thought will reveal that since the demand curve is always downward sloping, the price elasticity of demand must always be a negative number. If ΔP is positive (a price increase), then ΔQ must be negative (the quantity demanded decreases); since Q and P are also positive, the formula indicates that elasticity must be negative for a price increase. We reach the same conclusion for a price decrease, for if ΔP is negative, ΔQ will be positive. The real question is, How negative is e_p^D? The *absolute magnitude* of elasticity is what really counts, because the bigger this magnitude, the larger the demand response to a price change. If, for example, elasticity were −3, a 1 percent increase in the price from its current level would result in a 3 percent decrease in the quantity demanded; if the elasticity were −0.5, a 1 percent decrease in price from its current level would yield a 0.5 percent increase in the quantity demanded.

We will find it useful to distinguish between five ranges for the value of elasticity:

If e_p^D = negative infinity, we say that demand is *perfectly elastic* with respect to price;

If $e_p^D < -1$, we say that demand is *elastic* with respect to price;

If $e_p^D = -1$, we say that demand is *unit elastic* with respect to price;

If $e_p^D > -1$, we say that demand is *inelastic* with respect to price; and

If $e_p^D = 0$, we say that demand is *perfectly inelastic* with respect to price.

If demand is elastic with respect to price, then a price change will lead to a more than proportional, oppositely directed change in quantity demanded. If demand is inelastic, then a price change will lead to a less than proportional and oppositely directed change in quantity demanded. Figure 8.4 illustrates a range of possibilities.

First, look at the straight-line downward-sloping demand curve in Figure 8.4C. Although this appears to be the simplest case, note that the elasticity is different at every point along this curve. If we look at the elasticity formula we can understand why. This formula can be rearranged as follows:

$$e_p^D = (\Delta Q/\Delta P)(P/Q)$$

The first factor is simply the reciprocal of the slope of the demand curve (e.g., if the slope is 2/3, then the reciprocal slope is 3/2). Like the slope, the reciprocal of the slope is constant between any two points on a straight line. However, the second factor, the ratio of price to quantity, varies from infinity (at the vertical intercept of demand, where we are dividing by zero) down to zero (at the horizontal intercept of demand, where price itself is zero). As we move down the demand curve, the absolute value of the price elasticity of demand falls smoothly from infinity to one (at the midpoint) to zero.

Figures 8.4A and 8.4B illustrate exceptions, where the elasticity is constant even though the demand curve is a straight line. In the first of these extreme cases, as the demand curve approaches being exactly horizontal, the elasticity approaches infinity along the entire curve: this is a perfectly elastic demand curve. Elasticity approaches infinity because a horizontal curve has a slope of zero; thus, the inverse slope factor in the elasticity formula (see above) approaches infinity. In the second of these extreme cases, a vertical demand curve is perfectly inelastic along its entire length because the inverse slope of a vertical line is zero.

Although horizontal market demand curves are quite rare, we have already seen how an individual perfectly competitive organization would perceive that the market price is independent of quantity produced. Thus, demand appears to the organization to be perfectly elastic. Demand might

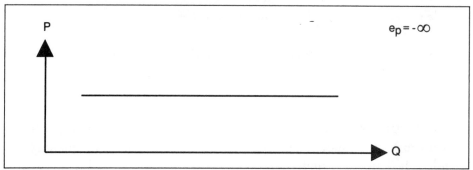

Figure 8.4A Elasticity of Demand with Respect to Price: Perfectly Elastic

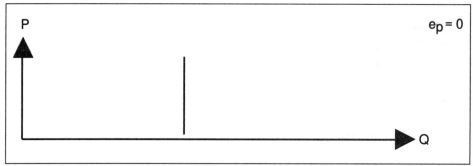

Figure 8.4B Elasticity of Demand with Respect to Price: Perfectly Inelastic

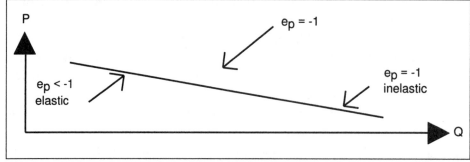

Figure 8.4C Elasticity of Demand with Respect to Price: General Case: Elasticity Varies Along Demand Curve

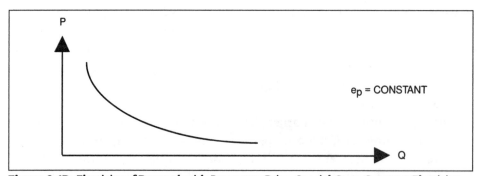

Figure 8.4D Elasticity of Demand with Respect to Price: Special Case: Constant Elasticity

also be horizontal if the price is fixed by contractual agreement (as in group-home services reimbursed by the government at a fixed per-diem rate, or in the Meals on Wheels example in Chapter 4). In this case, the quantity bought would drop to zero if the price were raised above the contractual limit. Vertical demand curves are more common, at least for some range of prices.

When insured patients decide upon the quantity of medical care they need and there is no deductible or co-payment, the price charged their insurer is unlikely to enter their decision making. It is also possible to draw demand curves that have constant elasticity but are neither vertical nor horizontal. Such a curve is illustrated in Figure 8.4D. This curve has the formula

$$ln(Q) = a + b \times ln(P)$$

where *ln* is the natural logarithm function. Anywhere along this demand curve, the price elasticity of demand has the constant value b. Notice how this can happen. In the upper left-hand region the ratio of P to Q is high while the curve is steeply negative, and so the inverse slope is very small in absolute value. On the other hand, in the lower right-hand region, the ratio of P to Q is low but the curve is flat, so that the inverse slope is very large in absolute value. In between, both the ratio of P to Q and the slope of the curve are moderate. In all instances, the ratio of the slope to the fraction P/Q (i.e., the price elasticity of demand) stays the same.

When two demand curves with differing slopes intersect, we can quickly compare their relative elasticities—but only at the point of intersection. Because P/Q is the same at this point, the comparison hinges only on the relative (inverse) slopes, so that the steeper the demand curve, the smaller the elasticity (in absolute value).

Factors that Influence Price Elasticity of Demand We have already considered several factors that affect the price elasticity of demand:

Availability of substitutes. When close substitutes become available, demand becomes more price elastic, for then even a moderate price increase will induce many to switch their purchases to the substitute good or service. For example, the demand for orchestra performances may be elastic, because people can attend other kinds of concerts or buy compact-disk recordings. On the other hand, certain services such as organ transplants and disaster-relief services have few good substitutes and are highly necessary. The demand for such services would be highly price inelastic, as consumers would not substantially reduce their purchases in response to a price increase.

Time frame. When consumers are given a longer time to adjust to a price change, their demand becomes more price elastic. This phenomenon is directly related to the availability of substitutes. What may be a unique service in the short run may allow the cultivation of alternatives in the long run. For example, in the short run one may be highly dependent on the services of a public police force or a private security agency for protection from crime. In the longer run, one can install an electronic security system or move to a safer neighborhood. Likewise, the demand for acute medical care may be more elastic in the long run than the short run because preventive alternatives can be developed to ameliorate the need for acute care.

Importance of the good in the consumer budget. If the price of bubble gum were to increase 50 percent, consumers would not drastically cut back their purchases of this product. They can afford to ignore the price of bubble gum in their decision making because it is a trivial portion of their total expenditures. On the other hand, a modest increase in the price of subsidized rental housing for the indigent would likely provoke a large decrease in applications for this housing. A small increase in the rent would have major budgetary implications for the indigent, requiring them to spend less on other necessities or find alternative places to live. Thus, demand would likely be elastic. In general, demand for a good or service is more elastic when total expenditure on the product (price times quantity) is a large fraction of available resources.

Why Price Elasticity of Demand Is Important The price elasticity of demand is a very useful tool for setting prices. In general, an increase in price will decrease the volume of sales, but the revenue collected on each sale will go up. A decrease in price will increase the volume of sales but reduce revenue per item sold. In particular, reduced revenue will be collected from those consumers who were willing to pay the higher initial price. With these opposing forces at work, the question then becomes, Can we raise more revenue by increasing or by decreasing price? The answer depends on the numerical value of the price elasticity of demand at the current price:

> **When demand is price elastic, an increase in price will decrease total revenue and a decrease in price will increase total revenue.**

When demand is inelastic, an increase in price will increase total revenue and a decrease in price will reduce total revenue.

When demand is unit elastic, neither an increase nor a decrease in price will change total revenue.

Although this result can be proven mathematically, it is not simply a mathematical artifact but, rather, quite an intuitive result. For if demand is price elastic, then a price decrease will result in a proportionally greater increase in quantity sold, more than offsetting the loss of revenue from the price decline. Conversely, if demand is price inelastic, the increase in quantity sold will be proportionally less than the price decrease and will not make up for the revenue loss of the price reduction. These results are illustrated in Figure 8.5A, which shows the effect of a price reduction when demand is elastic. Note that the slender rectangle representing the lost revenue com-

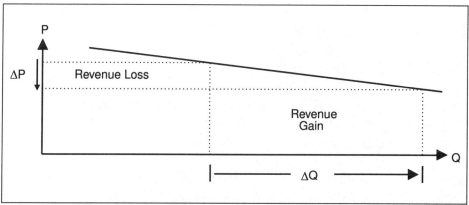

Figure 8.5A Effect of Price Changes on Revenue: If demand is elastic, a decrease in price will increase revenue (MR>0)

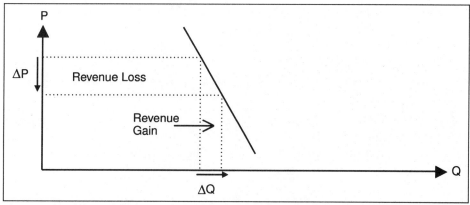

Figure 8.5B Effect of Price Changes on Revenue: If demand is inelastic, a decrease in price will decrease revenue (MR<0)

ponent from the lower price is small, while the rectangle representing the revenue gain from additional sales is large. Figure 8.5B shows the case of inelastic demand. Here, the rectangle representing the loss from the price decrease is larger than the rectangle representing the revenue increase from additional sales.

In short, in situations of price-elastic demand, more revenue can be generated by lowering price and selling more. Where demand is price inelastic, revenue can be enhanced by increasing the price and selling less. Since elasticity varies with both the type of good or service at issue and the particular point on the demand function, it is up to the manager to collect information on elasticity around the point of current operation in order to assess the effects of a price change on revenues. Unfortunately, in the accompanying cartoon, Calvin has it wrong. But he's a smart kid and will eventually figure out that the demand for cold lemonade in winter, if it exists at all, is elastic.

Other Kinds of Elasticity

Each of the other kinds of elasticity is also a ratio of percentage changes:

Income elasticity of demand:
$e_Y^D = (\Delta Q^D/Q^D)/(\Delta Y^D/Y^D)$, where Y^D is consumer income and Q^D is the quantity demanded.

Cross-price elasticity of demand:
$e_{ab}^D = (\Delta Q_a^D/Q_a^D)/(\Delta P_b/P_b)$, where a and b are any two goods or services.

Price elasticity of supply:
$e_p^S = (\Delta Q^S/Q^S)/(\Delta P/P)$, where Q^S is the quantity supplied.

Income elasticity of supply:
$e_Y^S = (\Delta Q^S/Q^S)/(\Delta Y^S/Y^S)$, where Y^S is owner (supplier) income.

Income elasticity of demand measures the impact of changes in income on desired purchases at a given price. For example, if the income elasticity were 0.7, then a 10 percent increase in income would result in a 7 percent increase in the quantity desired for purchase (the price remaining constant). Unlike the price elasticity of demand, the income elasticity is usually (but not always) positive. A positive income elasticity indicates that the good is "normal"—that is, people want more of it when their income rises. A negative income elasticity indicates that the good is "inferior"—that is, people want less of it when their income rises. Public transit may be an inferior good within a certain range of income; when people's income rises, they often buy cars and abandon the transit system. If income elasticity exceeds unity, a percentage increase in income causes a more than proportionate percentage increase in demand, providing a numerical test for labeling goods as "luxuries." In contrast, a normal good whose income elasticity is less than unity could be classed as a "necessity." Jewelry and food are classic examples of luxury and necessity goods, respectively. So may be arts performances and health care in the nonprofit sector.

The cross-price elasticity of demand measures the relationships between two products. Some pairs of goods or services, such as care in a nursing facility and domiciliary nursing care, are regarded by consumers as substitutes. If the price of one of these services—say, facility care—goes up, some consumers will switch and the demand for the other service, domiciliary care, will also go up. Because the percentage changes in the price of one product and the quantity demanded of the other move in the same direction, the cross-price elasticity is positive for substitutes. In the nonprofit arena, examples of pairs of substitutes are dance and opera, direct mail and media advertising in fund raising, and various charities available to donors in a given area. (In the last case, the "price" of a charity may be perceived as related to the proportion of the marginal charitable dollar going to administrative services. See the discussion of fund raising in Chapter 5.) The extent of substitutability revealed by the cross-price elasticity of demand can be important information for the manager contemplating a price change. In particular, the presence of a substitute offered by a competitor will affect the revenues received by the organization. Or, if the substitute service is provided by another division of the same organization, there will be interdivisional budgetary implications involving a loss of revenues for one division and a gain for another.

Other pairs of goods, like symphony tickets and beverages sold during intermissions, are regarded as complements, since they are consumed together. If the price of symphony tickets were to rise enough to reduce the number of tickets sold, then the demand for beverages sold during intermission would fall. Thus, the cross-price elasticity is negative for complements.

In the nonprofit sector, preventive health care and social-work counseling services, or music education and music performances, are probably complements. Nonprofit managers would also like to know about the extent of complementarity revealed by the cross-price elasticity of demand, because when an organization raises the price of one of its products, it will reduce sales not only of that product but also of any complementary products it markets. Even if demand is price inelastic, so that the increase in price adds to the total revenue from sales of the first product, the total revenue from both products will go down if the cross-price elasticity is sufficiently negative.

Finally, a relationship of independence characterizes most pairs of goods and services—say, charitable donations and pencils, cheese and trips to Tahiti, Beatles posters and health-care services. The cross-price elasticity of demand is zero for these pairs of goods. It is harder to guess what the relationship between other products of interest to nonprofit managers is, and so empirical study is needed. For example, it is still an open question whether volunteering and giving to charity are complements, substitutes, or independent activities. There is some evidence that the two are complements, so that the easier one makes it for people to volunteer (the lower the price of volunteering), the more they will give to charity (see *Giving and Volunteering 1992*). Similarly, if the government were to raise the after-tax price of gifts of money (as it did in the 1986 Tax Reform Act by cutting marginal tax rates and eliminating the charitable deduction for non-itemizers), this would reduce not only gifts of money but also gifts of time, if the two are indeed complements. Obviously, this is a matter of importance to nonprofits and one where improved information may be quite helpful.

The price elasticity of supply is generally positive. Again, we can distinguish between elastic and inelastic cases:

If $e_p^S < 1$, then supply is price inelastic.
If $e_p^S > 1$, then supply is price elastic.

Figure 8.6 illustrates three supply functions with different elasticity characteristics. Again, these are special cases where the price elasticity of supply is the same at all points on the curve. In general, however, as with price elasticity of demand, elasticity will vary along the supply function. The horizontal function S_1 in Figure 8.6 illustrates the case of a perfectly price-elastic supply curve. We can imagine this function rising to the right, but ever so slowly. Thus, any increase in price (P) will lead to a very large increase in the quantity supplied (Q^S). The polar opposite case is S_3, where supply is perfectly price inelastic. Here we can imagine the curve leaning ever so

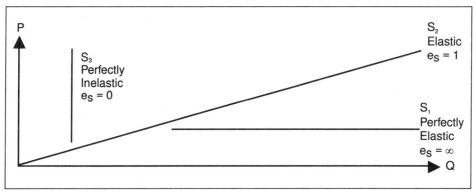

Figure 8.6 Elasticity of Supply

slightly to the right as it rises. Thus, an increase in price will lead to only a minuscule increase in the quantity supplied. Finally, the line S_2 represents unitary price elasticity of supply. Since S_2 is a straight line through the origin $(0,0)$, any change in price will be met with a proportional change in quantity supplied. In fact, any supply function that is a straight line through the origin will have an elasticity value of 1, no matter how steep or shallow it is. And, as with the intersection of two demand curves, if two supply curves intersect at any point other than the origin, we can conclude that the flatter curve will be the more elastic of the two at the point of intersection.

As with demand elasticity, the *time frame* is an important factor that influences the price elasticity of supply. If an industry depends on certain resources that are difficult to adjust quickly, such as large physical plants, highly sophisticated equipment, or a highly trained labor force, then it will have difficulty responding vigorously to price changes in the short run. However, in the longer term, if the price change is maintained, the industry will be able to adjust by investing (or disinvesting) in plant and equipment, or training (or phasing out) sophisticated workers. In general, therefore, supply tends to be more inelastic in the short run and more elastic in the long run. If the industry faces an absolute constraint on expansion (due to a strictly limited supply of some resource needed in production), even the long-run supply curve will be inelastic.

In the nonprofit sector, the supply of services such as heart surgery, graduate-level higher education, or top-quality orchestral performances is constrained by the available supply of appropriately trained professional people and the capacity of appropriate physical plants. Therefore, in the short run—say, one year—the supply of such services may be inelastic. In the long run—say, 10 years—these resources can be expanded and supply may be characterized as elastic.

In economics for the business sector, we rarely use the concept of income elasticity of supply, since the stockholders who own a for-profit firm would seek a profit-maximizing level of production regardless of their personal income. Privately held corporations, partnerships, and proprietorships constitute a possible exception, since the small number of owners in these forms of for-profit organizations may allow the organization to pursue goals other than profit maximization. However, in the nonprofit world, the nondistribution constraint clearly reduces the incentive to pursue profits, and so it is likely that in some cases the income of the organization will affect its supply decisions. For example, when a symphony orchestra has low income, it might need to perform mostly familiar works by Beethoven and Mozart. If that same symphony were to get a grant, it might decide to supply more contemporary and experimental programs at any given ticket price. Thus, familiar works would be "inferior goods," having a negative income elasticity of supply, and contemporary works would be "normal," having a positive income elasticity of supply.

One minor detail is worth commenting upon. The income elasticity of supply is defined in terms of "owner" income. Although the board of directors of a nonprofit organization is the legal owner, it does not have full ownership rights to the income of the organization. Full ownership allows owners to direct the use of the resources owned, receive any profits generated by those resources, and transfer ownership to others who are willing and able to pay for it. The nondistribution constraint disallows distribution of profits and transfer of ownership for profit. Thus, the concept of ownership of nonprofit firms is a muted one. In this situation, it is best to think of owner income as the income the controllers of the organization have the right to direct. Hence, any income received by the organization counts in this category.

ADVANCED ISSUES IN NONPROFIT PRICING

In this section, we consider five advanced issues in nonprofit pricing. First, since nonprofit organizations derive income from different sources, we consider interactions between sales and other sources of revenues (chiefly donations). Second, since organizations often market several products, we explore the scope for cross-subsidizing one output using profits from another. Third, since organizations may charge different prices to different customers (price discrimination), we investigate how nonprofit organizations with different objectives should design their pricing policies. Fourth, we consider "niche behavior," where an organization chooses its quality, ideological bent, and product line with a strategic eye toward pricing implications. Finally, we observe that price plays multiple roles. While the price determines who will buy and how much revenue the organization will collect, it may also have direct effects on organizational mission attainment.

Interactions Between Sales and Other Revenues

In earlier chapters, we noted that the principal source of revenue in the nonprofit sector is sales of goods or services, including sales of items directly related to the organizational mission, sales of items to generate revenue in support of the organizational mission, and contracts to provide goods and services for governments. However, donations—including time, money, in-kind gifts, dues, bequests, and foundation, corporate, and government grants—are important supplements to sales for most nonprofits and the principal source of support for some of these organizations. To this point, we have examined nonprofit pricing in isolation. Now we will consider the possibility that the volume and mixture of sales activities can affect the volume and mixture of donations, and we will see how pricing rules must be altered when these interactions are important.

Sales of any sort may crowd out donations. Donors may feel that there is less need for their donations when an organization markets at least some of its goods and services, or that commercial activity is crass and undermines the organizational mission. On the other hand, some foundations think of themselves as providing seed money, and unless nonprofit organizations can prove that they can diversify their revenue sources, foundations may withhold their grant dollars. Donor perceptions are likely to be affected by many factors: whether the commercial activity is related or unrelated to the organizational mission; whether markets are segmented (so that donors are geographically removed from purchasers and therefore unlikely to perceive a connection, or the commercial venture is spun off in a manner that makes donors unlikely to perceive a connection); whether the product is unique and reminds donors of the organizational mission (as in sales of art posters by museums); whether donors are motivated mostly by altruism or by a desire for personal gain (e.g., the chance to receive a sweepstakes or raffle ticket); whether other charities are engaged in similar commercial activities; and whether the product is of high quality and sold at a fair price. Different donors may respond to nonprofit commercial activities in different ways, and the pattern of responses may be sensitive to historical and cultural factors. Careful empirical studies to determine the signs and magnitudes of these interactions are rare, so nonprofit managers will have to rely on their experience and intuition in applying the following analysis.

Commercial activity may have both fixed and marginal effects on donations. The mere fact that the organization is engaging in unrelated business activity at any scale may cause donations to fall by a substantial amount. Suppose that there are positive net donations (donations minus fund-raising costs) before the commercial activity begins, and that net donations fall by $K if the organization engages in commercial activity. This changes the shutdown rule to the following:

A perfectly competitive nonprofit organization should cease its unrelated business activity whenever $P < AVC + K/Q$.

A monopoly nonprofit organization should cease its unrelated business activity whenever $MR < AVC + K/Q$.

We need only add a term to our earlier shutdown rule to account for the loss in donations per unit of output due to commercial activities. If the market price (or marginal revenue) is too low, the addition to resources resulting from sales activity is smaller than the reduction in resources from donations.

Unrelated business income is, presumably, a means to an end. Profits from unrelated businesses can be used to foster the organization's primary goals. The shutdown rule could be different for "related" business because this form of commerce directly fosters the organizational mission in addition to providing revenues. A hospital would not want to stop providing medical care simply because the incremental profits from medical care are smaller than the incremental decrease in donations resulting from the sale of medical services. However, if the goal of the organization were to provide free medical care to the indigent, and if fee-for-service care were a source of revenue and not otherwise of value to the organization, then the shutdown rule above would apply. Although the rule is stated in terms of the legal distinction between "related" and "unrelated," it is not the legal standards that govern here. Rather, the rule applies to any income source that does not directly contribute to the organization's central mission; it does not apply to income generated from activities that foster that mission directly.

Given that the organization decides to keep its unrelated business open, should it adjust its production level and pricing to account for the interaction with donations? The answer depends on what aspect of the commercial activity concerns the donors—is it the quantity sold, the price charged, or the profits generated from sales? To analyze these possibilities, we first need to decompose the marginal cost (MC) of producing an unrelated good or service into two components—marginal production cost (MPC) and marginal donation cost (MDC). MPC is the ordinary marginal cost of providing another unit of the unrelated good or service. MDC is the incremental loss in donations incurred by producing an additional unit of unrelated output. Overall marginal cost (MC) is the sum of MPC and MDC.

If donors react to quantity, we have the following result (see Figure 8.7):

When donors reduce their donations in response to an increase in the quantity sold, production and pricing decisions use the same rules as always. To calculate prices and quantities, set *P* equal to *MC* or *MR* equal to *MC*, depending on market structure, where *MC* is the full marginal cost (*MPC* + *MDC*).

In particular, if donors react negatively to marginal production (Figure 8.7A), nonprofit organizations should incrementally reduce their production or unrelated output (from Q' to Q_E). In this case, the donative interaction amounts to an increase in marginal cost (*MDC* is positive), which, as we have seen in the previous chapter, leads to a decrease in production and an increase in price. However, it is also possible that donors (especially foundations) will react positively to production so that *MDC* is negative (Figure 8.7B). In this case, the organization should "overexpand"—that is, expand production

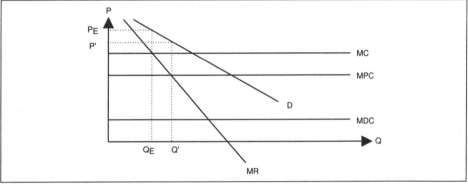

Figure 8.7A Monopoly Equilibrium When Donors React to Sales: Donors Dislike Sales

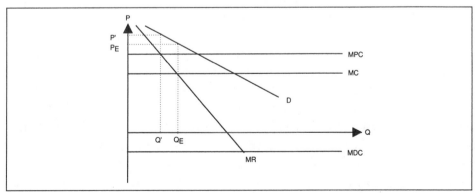

Figure 8.7B Monopoly Equilibrium When Donors React to Sales: Donors Like Sales or Price Reduction from Increased Sales. *(Note: Q_E and P_E are the equilibrium quantity and price respectively; Q' and P' are the equilibrium quantity and price if the impact of sales on donations is ignored.)*

from Q' to Q_E where profits from sales are negative in order to obtain a bigger gain from donations. The only published study to estimate this effect found that donations rise by approximately 7 percent of any increase in sales (Schiff and Weisbrod, 1991), but more empirical work clearly is needed here.

The rule is similar, but more complex, when donors react to the price charged by the nonprofit organization rather than to the quantity. If the organization is a price taker in a perfectly competitive market, then quantity increases will have no effect on price and hence no effect on donations. However, if the organization is a monopoly, any increase in production will drive down the price and will offset donations. If aggregate donations per unit of unrelated output increase by less than $1 in response to a $1 decrease in price, then the organization should select a price and quantity combination according to the rule directly above. Here, the decrease in price increases production. Thus, if donors dislike higher prices, they will like increased production and MDC will be negative. In this case, full marginal cost (MC) will be lower than marginal production cost (MPC), with correspondingly higher output.

Sometimes, however, the organization (even in a perfectly competitive market) should charge a price that is below the demand curve and does not clear the market—that is, a price lower than the highest one it could charge for the quantity produced. This is because the increase in donations resulting from the lower price could exceed the loss in per-unit revenues from sales. Hence, the price should be dropped until these opposing effects cancel each other out at the margin. If, when the price approaches zero, donations continue to fall rapidly, the good or service should be offered for free. In other words, it is possible for sales to be so harmful to donations that sales should cease. Note that whenever price is below the demand curve, as in these circumstances, there is "excess demand" and the organization must be prepared to ration its services on some appropriate basis other than price.

What if donors react to profits from sales per se, rather than to the quantity or price of sales? If this reaction is small, the nonprofit's decisions should be unaffected by the donative interaction. If, starting at maximal profits from sales, a $1 decrease in profits from sales would increase donations by less than $1, then there would be no reason for the organization to adjust its price and output levels away from those generating maximum profit. On the other hand, if, starting from the same initial point, a $1 decrease in profits from sales would increase donations by more than $1, it would be in the organization's interest to somehow reduce its profits from sales. There are many ways to do this—overexpanding, reducing output and raising prices, or choosing a price-quantity combination below the demand curve coupled with rationing. Whatever strategy is chosen, marginal analysis applies. Operating changes to reduce profit should continue until incremental gains from donations are just offset by incremental losses of profit from sales.

The interaction between sales and donations is just one factor that will determine the best mixture of revenue sources for a nonprofit organization. In general, the combination of revenues chosen depends on two factors: the profits from investing in different types of revenue generation and the riskiness of alternative revenue sources. The profits or net returns are the difference between gross revenues and the costs of producing those revenues: donations less fund-raising costs, grants less grant solicitation and administration costs, sales revenues less production costs, and so on. The costs of each revenue source should include the *transaction costs* (discussed in greater detail in Chapter 9) associated with the administration of those sources. Grants, in particular, are accompanied by an array of reporting and accountability requirements that can absorb most of the revenues available from this source (Grønbjerg, 1993).

Finally, some sources of revenue are riskier than others. Riskiness depends on the predictability of a revenue source and also its relationship to other funding sources (i.e., the possibility that one revenue source "crowds out" another). For example, sales revenues are risky not only because the market for sales may be volatile but also because they may negatively affect donations. While the interactions among different types of revenue may inhibit diversification of revenue sources, reducing dependence on any one source can also help an organization protect itself against risk. While we cannot pursue this subject in depth here, the tools of portfolio diversification developed for stock-market investing can be applied to the nonprofit revenue mix decision (see Kingma, 1993).

Multiple Outputs

Many nonprofits market multiple services. Nonprofit hospitals sell parking services, hotel services, flowers, research, and medical services. Nonprofit theaters, dance companies, and symphony orchestras sell refreshments, souvenirs, and educational materials as well as performances. Nonprofit universities sell undergraduate education, graduate education, adult non-degree education, research services, housing services, medical services, recreational privileges, and parking. Religious organizations sell dining and other social experiences as well as books and videotapes, and they rent their facilities for use by nonmembers. Some of these multiple outputs are mission related (undergraduate and graduate education; appendectomies and brain surgery), and some may be unrelated commercial ventures (parking, dormitories).

There are important interactions to consider when an organization markets several outputs. First, there may be *cost complementarities* that make production of multiple products within one organization more efficient than production of each product by separate organizations. Second, there may be *demand complementarities* that make consumption of multiple products from one organization more efficient than consumption of those same products produced in separate organizations. These two kinds of complementarity are referred to collectively as *economies of scope* and are an important reason why multiple outputs are marketed by an organization. The detailed effects of economies of scope on pricing and output decisions are complicated and best left to advanced texts (Sharkey, 1982). However, with some simplifying assumptions, we can develop an essential understanding of the rules for pricing of nonprofit services in this situation.

Suppose that economies of scope affect only fixed costs, so that there are no interactions among the marginal costs or among prices for the variety of products produced. With no such interactions, the multiproduct nonprofit is free to use the appropriate pricing and output rules for each product separately. If the market for computers is competitive, then the university bookstore should sell computers at the going market rate and choose a quantity to offer for sale that makes marginal cost equal to this price. If the market for hospital parking services is monopolized, the hospital should determine the number of spaces that makes marginal cost equal to marginal revenue and should charge the maximum price consistent with filling the lot (assuming the hospital cares only about the revenues generated and not the well-being of parkers).

Similarly, pricing for mission-related activities will follow the organizational objective, rather than profit maximization, as discussed earlier. This case is analyzed by James (1983), who considers three kinds of nonprofit output services: favored, neutral, and disfavored. *Favored outputs* are mission related and *neutral outputs* are unrelated to mission. To this list, James adds *disfavored outputs*, which either actively impair attainment of the organizational mission or are otherwise distasteful to those in control of the organization. For example, the management of a nonprofit art museum may positively dislike special exhibitions that attract vandalism-prone crowds and the poor-quality reproductions sold in the museum's gift shop. Nonetheless, the museum uses both outputs to generate revenues that help maintain its core collection.

In general, neutral outputs will be produced whenever they generate profits, whereas disfavored outputs will be marketed only if they generate sufficiently large profits. Profits from both these outputs can then be dedicated to financing incremental output of the favored good or service, allowing that product to be marketed for a loss or even given away. This practice of transferring profits from one output to support another is known as *cross-subsidization* and is quite common. James cites evidence that universities profit from the sale of education to undergraduates and use this revenue to cross-subsidize graduate education. She also cites evidence that nonprofit hospitals use profits from appendectomies and other routine treatments to cross-subsidize research and prestige-generating but underutilized facilities such as open-heart surgery units.

As we noted earlier, the income elasticity of supply is generally zero for for-profit firms. However, an increase in the fixed revenues received by a nonprofit firm will affect nonprofit supply. The income elasticity of supply is positive for favored outputs, zero for neutral outputs, and negative for disfavored outputs. Consider, then, the effect of a major donation. Such a gift would allow the organization to reduce distasteful but profitable activity and encourage further production of favored (mission-related) outputs.

What about the elasticity of supply with respect to the price of the disfavored outputs? Suppose the price of a disfavored output goes up. This means that a given quantity of the disfavored output will generate more profits, so that clearly the supply of the favored output will increase. However, we cannot say with any certainty whether the quantity supplied of the disfavored output will go up or down. This ambiguity occurs because of two opposing forces. On the one hand, the higher price enables the organization to obtain a given cross-subsidy while selling less of the disfavored output. On the other hand, the higher price implies that each unit of the disfavored output will support a larger number of units of the favored output. This increase in the efficiency of the cross-subsidy may encourage the organization to increase its disfavored activity. The sign of the price elasticity of supply for the disfavored output depends on which of these two opposing forces is larger for the particular organization we are considering. If the first effect dominates, the price elasticity will be negative; if the second effect dominates, the price elasticity will be positive.

Interpreting unrelated business income as a disfavored output, Schiff and Weisbrod (1991) apply the James model to the controversy over "unfair competition" between for-profit and nonprofit organizations. They find that the tax advantages of nonprofits allow them to cross-subsidize and hence to better accomplish their missions, although this may not be the most efficient method of helping nonprofits. They also find that nonprofit organizations may respond to price changes in their commercial markets in the perverse manner explained above, decreasing the quantity they supply when the price goes up or costs go down.

Price Discrimination

There are two types of price discrimination. One practice is to charge the same customer different per-unit prices depending upon the quantity bought (e.g., provide quantity discounts). The other type of price discrimination involves charging different prices to different customers (through devices such as sliding-scale fees, discounts for senior citizens, and tuition breaks for promising low-income college students). It is the second type of price discrimination that is of special interest to nonprofits.

In order to consider price discrimination by nonprofit organizations, we need to understand two underlying factors. First, price discrimination is not always technically feasible. Second, even where this practice is technically feasible, for-profit firms face important informational and incentive limitations in their ability to price discriminate. In particular, we will see how the profit imperative creates distrust among consumers and how a nonprofit organization can overcome this distrust to accomplish two goals: income redistribution and provision of services that have high fixed-cost.

First, the reader should realize that price discrimination is possible only for organizations with some degree of market power. In a perfectly competitive environment, organizations are price takers and cannot set different prices for different customers. Within this context, price discrimination is feasible only for goods and services that are not resellable. It would be difficult, for example, for a street vendor of hot dogs to offer a substantially lower price to indigent customers, because hot dogs can be resold. Indigent customers might buy extra hot dogs and resell them at a price higher than what they paid but still lower than that charged by the vendor. Soon the vendor would sell no hot dogs at the higher price. This process is known as *arbitrage*, and it applies to any resellable good where transactions occur often enough to make it worthwhile for intermediaries to enter the market.

Arbitrage cannot occur for goods or services where the act of consumption is inextricably intertwined with the supply of the good to the consumer. An appendectomy is not resellable. Job-training programs are another example. Here, the recipient, having gained the skills needed for employment, may subsequently decide to teach those skills to others by working as a job counselor, but this "resale" does not use up the training he or she has received. In these cases, price discrimination is feasible.

Arbitrage possibilities should be carefully considered in charity ventures. For example, the distribution of free food to third-world governments may not end up helping needy individuals, for the food can be resold for cash. Distribution of free cheese to homeless alcoholics may not improve their nutrition either, for recipients can sell the cheese to finance additional purchases of alcohol. Provision of owner-occupied housing units at a subsidized price will certainly help those lucky enough to occupy the units first, but often the original occupants will resell their units to the highest bidders, presumably at the going market rate for real estate of this type. While the indigents receive higher income as a result, these units will not remain dedicated to the poor, and even the initial occupants may not end up in better housing units than they occupied prior to joining the program.

Finally, resellability may itself be under the control of the original vendor. In the housing example, we could continue to dedicate housing units to the poor by renting units only to those certified as eligible and prohibiting leasers from subletting their apartments. Concert tickets provide another example. If tickets are sold in advance (with no limits on individual purchases or legal restrictions on scalping), price discrimination in ticket prices is clearly impossible. However, if tickets are sold only at the door and proof of eligibility is required for anyone seeking the lower price, it is possible to price discriminate.

Price discrimination is also impossible if competitors don't follow a compatible pattern of prices. A day-care center that charges a higher-than-cost price to well-off families in order to subsidize lower-than-cost prices for others will not be able to maintain this pricing pattern if competitors of equal quality offer their services to well-off families at a price equal to cost. There are other complications here as well: for example, some of the well-off might be willing to pay extra to place their children in a center with a more diverse clientele. This issue has not yet been fully studied, but the essential point remains that in choosing a pattern of prices, an organization must consider the pricing practices of its competitors, current and potential. This is one reason why we discuss only price-discriminating monopolies below, leaving the complexities of imperfectly competitive situations for future research.

Let us first consider price discrimination by for-profit monopolies. Profit-maximizing monopolies would like to price according to the following rule, which describes a practice called *perfect price discrimination*:

Charge each customer his or her maximum willingness to pay for each unit purchased. Produce a quantity that makes the price charged the last customer equal to marginal cost.

This rule is clearly anti-consumer, since under this pricing pattern all the gains from trade accrue to the seller. Each buyer is asked to pay a price equal to what the product is worth to him or her. Thus, buyers barely "break even" and sellers receive maximal benefit. Nonetheless, this rule does have some social virtue. Perfectly price-discriminating monopolies do not limit

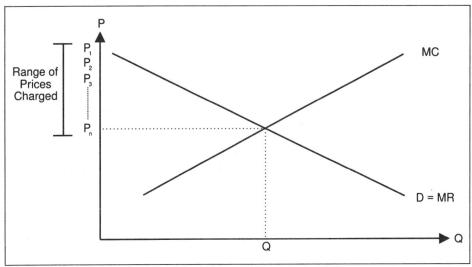

Figure 8.8 Production by a Profit-Maximizing Price-Discriminating Monopolist

production to a level less than that which is socially efficient, as single-price monopolies do. (Recall the discussion in Chapter 5.) This is because the marginal revenue function for a discriminating monopolist traces the demand curve. In order to maximize profit, the discriminating monopolist will move down the demand curve, charging each successive customer less and less, until the level of price becomes equal to marginal cost. At this level the output Q is the same as it would be if the firm were a single-price monopolist whose objective was to maximize social benefit (by setting P equal to MC). This is illustrated in Figure 8.8, in which different prices are charged to each customer, with the last customer charged a price P_n just equal to marginal cost MC.

In addition to producing at socially efficient levels, perfectly price-discriminating monopolies may also find it financially feasible to produce socially valuable goods that have high fixed costs and low marginal costs and that would be unprofitable if a single price were charged. This is made possible by the collection of all the extra revenue engendered by charging each customer as much as he or she is willing to pay.

Realistically, for-profit monopolies never have enough information to price-discriminate perfectly. At best, they may be able to distinguish customers on the basis of credit history, age, ethnicity, gender, zip code, and the like in order to guess which customers, on average, are willing to pay more than others. Discriminating on the basis of these imperfect indicators is sometimes illegal (as in the case of ethnicity or gender); in any case, these indicators are not accurate enough to allow perfect price discrimination. Furthermore, if the monopoly tries to refine its estimates by *asking* individuals how much they would be willing to pay, consumers will have a strong incentive to lie. Anyone who truthfully reported a high willingness to pay would be rewarded with a correspondingly high price. Likewise, a consumer who lied would probably be charged a low price, for it is unlikely that any one consumer's payment will make the difference between providing the good and shutting down production. Understanding these incentives, monopolies do not bother to ask and so do not obtain anything close to the revenues potentially available through perfect price discrimination.

However, if consumers believe they are purchasing from an organization that has no wish to exploit them, they may be more willing to reveal their true preferences. Nonprofit organizations may be perceived as trustworthy in this way. This idea led Hansmann (1981) to suggest that performing arts organizations are nonprofit because they need price discrimination to survive. The performing arts typically have very high fixed costs (rehearsal, set design and construction, etc.), and low marginal costs (an extra performance costs much less than the set-up costs). When a perfectly price-discriminating monopolist can cover fixed costs but a single-price monopolist cannot, we can conclude two things: First, it is socially desirable for the show to go on because, in the aggregate, consumers are willing to pay more than the show costs to produce. Second, the show cannot go on without price discrimination or some other source of supplementary financial support.

Consumers will not trust for-profit performing arts organizations in this context, but they are willing to volunteer information about their willingness to pay by donating to nonprofit organizations. Thus, Hansmann views donations to arts organizations as a form of "voluntary price-discrimination." The implication for nonprofit pricing is that organizations can charge a lower than break-even ticket price with the expectation that donors will step in and allow the organization to survive.

Ben-Ner (1986) observes another way in which nonprofit price discrimination can be helpful. If the organizational mission is to subsidize services for the poor, and if fixed revenues are insufficient to accomplish this mission, price discrimination can help fill the gap. Such price discrimination can take the form of "overcharging" the better-off customers or asking them for a donation as well as a payment. In either case, patrons need assurance that the overpayment will be dedicated to subsidizing the poor rather than enriching those who control the organization—hence the advantage of the nonprofit form in implementing this practice.

In some circumstances, however, nonprofit organizations are not perceived as trustworthy, and their ability to price discriminate is correspondingly impaired. This is particularly true for products that are unrelated to the organization's mission. Purchasers of these unrelated products (e.g., raffle tickets) may have no interest in helping the nonprofit's target beneficiaries. Alternatively, donors may feel that these services are unseemly and may decrease their donations. There can be merit in these complaints, since nonprofit organizations have as much incentive as for-profit monopolies to price discriminate perfectly in unrelated markets, even if the proceeds are dedicated to a nobler purpose.

As noted above, one common practice of price discrimination is to charge a high price to the better-off customers in order to give free service to the deserving poor. Another pattern is to charge even the deserving poor some nominal fee. How should a nonprofit organization choose between these options? Social services and health-care agencies face these issues regularly. If a fee is charged to all consumers, the extra revenue allows the organization to serve more customers. Hence, there is a difficult value trade-off to be made here: Is it better to provide a lower level of assistance to the neediest in order to help an additional person who is a bit less needy? Each organization must decide for itself how it values overall quantity of service in relation to the level of assistance it provides to particular individuals. But framing the question in the foregoing terms—pitting the value of serving one more client against the marginal loss of help to an existing client—again demonstrates how "thinking at the margin" can facilitate determination of the best policy in any given instance.

Finding the Right Niche

Perfectly competitive firms, in the long run and with free entry, do not generate any surpluses from sales, whether they are for-profit or nonprofit. Nonprofit managers must therefore plan to avoid this fate for unrelated businesses designed to support the organization's primary mission. Unrelated business can generate a short-run profit, but if there are no barriers to entry it may not be worthwhile for the nonprofit to enter the market. Profits will be short-lived and the present value of profits may not exceed the set-up costs. In addition to foreseeing the costs of entry, nonprofit managers should anticipate that exit from the market may be costly and should figure this cost into their present value calculations. Staff members hired for their ability to produce and market the unrelated good or service will need to be transferred into the mission-related part of the organization's operation (where they may have less ability) or released (with consequent severance and placement costs and lowered morale among remaining workers). Nonprofit ventures in competitive industries are worthwhile only if short-run profits are sufficiently high, entry by others is expected to be slow, and the costs of one's own entry and exit are sufficiently small.

Product differentiation is a common strategy that for-profit firms pursue to maintain profits in the face of competition. By developing a product with unique quality or stylistic characteristics and protecting this version through patents, reputation, and trademarks, an organization in effect becomes a monopolist in producing its version of the product. However, because there is competition from other versions of the product, the cross-price elasticity among versions will be high and the monopoly profit potential from any one version will be low. If other organizations enter the market by designing their own special versions of the product, profits per supplier can be driven to zero even though each organization has some control over the price it charges. This is the market structure of monopolistic competition described in Chapter 7.

Nonprofit organizations can adopt the same sort of strategy, with the same sorts of long-run considerations. The present value of the costs of developing a unique product, entering into production of this product, and eventually exiting production must be smaller than the present value of net revenues generated from the sale of the product. Entry into a monopolistically competitive market is more likely to be a worthwhile nonprofit strategy because entry of competitors is, arguably, slower in this sector. Moreover, since many nonprofits are unique institutions in themselves, they have great potential for creating special products. A sweatshirt from Yale is different from a sweatshirt from Stanford. A calendar from the Cleveland Museum of Art distinguishes itself from one from the Museum of Modern Art in New York. (And what about the coffee mug sold in the gift shop of the Cleveland Clinic, famous for heart surgery, which reads, "I've been by-passed in Cleveland"?) Nonetheless, nonprofit commercial ventures should be undertaken with an eye to the future and a careful analysis of the long-run competition.

Pricing and the Organization's Mission

The price of a product determines how much the consumer will pay and how much the producer will receive, but the transfer of revenues is not the only function prices play. We have already discussed two aspects of how pricing is related to mission: price discrimination in order to finance a good with high fixed costs and price discrimination to support redistribution through subsidized prices for those deemed worthy. There are several other mission-related facets of nonprofit pricing to consider. Prices also affect attainment of output, the effectiveness of educational and advocacy missions, and client effort, and they can serve as a screening device among different groups of consumers.

Suppose the nonprofit mission requires an increase in the consumption of some service beyond its market equilibrium level. For example, a community health organization may subsidize health care because it believes consumers place too low a value on their own health and do not consider the external effects of contagious illnesses when they decide how much health care to purchase. A nonprofit university may subsidize adult learning, believing that this is something adults undervalue until they experience it. A symphony orchestra may subsidize concerts for elementary school students in the hope that many of them will develop a lifelong taste for live classical music.

In all these cases, the market demand curve, which represents the marginal valuations consumers place on the service, lies below the marginal valuation the organization places on the service in question. We can think of the latter curve as a *beneficial demand curve* because it represents the organization's desired purchases on behalf of consumers at each possible price. As Figure 8.9 illustrates, consumers are willing to purchase only a fraction of beneficial demand at the market price. Hence, the organization must somehow reduce this price. In Figure 8.9A, the nonprofit reduces its price from P_1 to P_2 in order to achieve a level of consumption Q_2, in excess of market demand Q_1, that corresponds to beneficial demand at the original price P_1. In some cases, that price may even need to be negative (Figure 8.9B)—that is, consumers may need to be paid in order to consume sufficiently. For example, schools may have to reward recalcitrant students with valuable gifts in order to increase attendance, or parents in some communities may have to be induced with payments before they have their children vaccinated. The nonprofit organization finances its price reduction using fixed revenues (donations, grants, asset income, etc.), but it may or may not have sufficient fixed revenues to fully accomplish its goal. Whether the goal is fully realizable depends upon the amount of fixed revenue, the price elasticity of demand (which tells the organization how much it must reduce the price to obtain the desired increment in consumption), and the magnitude of the difference between market and beneficial demand.

When consumption of a good or service has beneficial side-effects contributing to the organizational mission, the analysis is identical. Two categories of side-effects are important here: public education and advocacy effects. If, say, a cancer society sells Frisbees imprinted with the seven deadly warning signs of cancer, consumers learn something while playing, which contributes to achieving the educational mission of the organization. Bumper stickers and buttons with slogans highlighting particular beliefs and social causes also foster the advocacy missions of various organizations. In these cases, the market demand curve represents consumer valuations that are lower than the value the organization places on the consumption of the good. Thus, nonprofits want to sell these items below their market value.

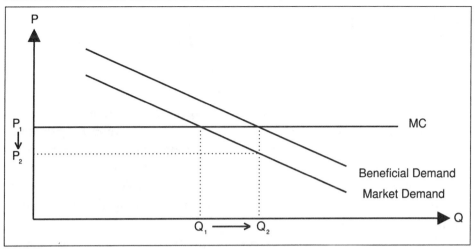

Figure 8.9A Pricing a Mission-Related Service: General Case

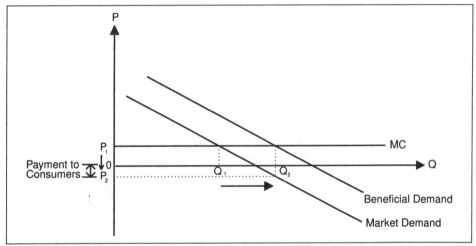

Figure 8.9B Pricing a Mission-Related Service: Circumstance Where Price Should Be Negative

In many cases, an organization may require the active effort of consumers to attain its goals, and the price may affect the client's level of effort. Such an argument has long been championed by psychotherapists to justify their fees and has recently been applied by Habitat for Humanity to housing programs. The Habitat case highlights the fact that the required payment need not be in the form of cash; Habitat requires recipients of housing assistance to provide "sweat equity" by working to build their houses. Twelve-step recovery programs also require noncash payments, as those who are sufficiently recovered pledge to bring the message of hope to those still in need.

Requiring payments may lead a client to work harder toward recovery, but they can induce participation in a very different way as well. Those who would feel sufficiently stigmatized if they were to accept free care may be quite happy to accept aid if they are required to pay a "fair share" of the costs consistent with their ability to pay. Sweat equity has an advantage here over monetary payment, for although individuals are endowed with varying amounts of money, we are all endowed with the same amount of time (even if that time has differing economic value). In addition, payment through sweat equity, like payment of cash, helps finance care for others.

The incentive effects of required payments must be weighed against the value trade-offs considered earlier. Organizations may want to charge a bit more than the price that would induce a desired level of effort because the added revenues allow them to help a few more relatively needy people. Or they may prefer to provide aid, at a lower but positive price, to a smaller number of the neediest.

Finally, price can serve a screening function, restricting the class of customers to those who are willing to pay. This effect can either promote or hinder organizational objectives. A social club that wishes to restrict its membership to the wealthy without being too blatant can simply charge enormous membership fees. University tuition and financial aid serve some screening functions as well. It is difficult for an admissions officer to determine on the basis of high school grades and standardized test scores alone which applicants are truly talented and motivated, but the applicants have some idea where they stand in these areas. To oversimplify for the purpose of illustration: A university that wishes to reserve its spaces for talented and dedicated students might offer student loans instead of grants-in-aid. Applicants who know their grades are inflated and those who do not intend to study hard may not wish to take loans if they calculate that their level of success in college is unlikely to lead them to sufficiently lucrative jobs upon graduation to pay those loans.

In summary, there are a number of social issues that may require nonprofit organizations to adjust their prices beyond what market conditions would dictate. Nonprofits may decide that consumers on their own will not demand as much of a given service as they should, or that the service is associated with educational and advocacy benefits that justify lowering the price. Prices may be seen to have a positive motivational effect on client effort, or they may be used as a signal to attract certain customers and not others. These nuances make the pricing of nonprofit services an important and challenging exercise.

SUMMARY

Market prices and output levels determined by the equilibration of supply and demand may shift for a number of reasons, including increases in the costs of production, changes in technology, the changing tastes or preferences of consumers, changing income levels, and changes in public policy. These changes affect the positions of the supply and demand functions, thus leading to new equilibria. The effects of changes in government policy are of special interest, particularly the impact of taxes and subsidies on consumers and producers. The elasticities of supply and demand determine whether consumers or producers benefit from or bear the burdens of such changes.

Labor markets can be analyzed in much the same way as the markets for output goods and services. Labor markets differ from output markets, however, in that the suppliers of labor are individuals and the utilizers of labor are organizations. The market for volunteer labor can be analyzed in much the same way as that for paid labor, although measures of supply and demand are more difficult to operationalize. The interactions between the paid and volunteer labor markets have important implications for the combinations of volunteer and paid labor that nonprofits choose to employ.

The pricing of output services of nonprofit organizations involves a variety of market and nonmarket considerations and potential strategies. Whether changes in the prices of services result in increased or decreased revenue depends on the elasticity of demand. Elasticity is also a useful concept for describing how demand and supply are affected by other factors such as consumer income or the prices of complementary or substitute goods and services. The pricing of nonprofit services is also seen to interact with other sources of nonprofit revenue, including donations. If sales revenues are found to crowd out donations, then nonprofits need to adjust their prices so that the combination of sales and donated revenues is enhanced.

Nonprofit organizations can also take advantage of a number of sophisticated pricing strategies, including price discrimination among different classes of consumers, product differentiation, cross-subsidy of one service by another, and adjustment of market prices to account for social benefits and motivational effect on client effort. The basic analysis of competitive and monopolistic markets serves as the foundation for analyzing these various possibilities.

REFERENCES

Apgar, William C., and H. James Brown. *Microeconomics and Public Policy.* Glenview, Ill.: Scott, Foresman, 1987.

Ben-Ner, Avner. "Nonprofit Organizations: Why Do They Exist in Market Economies?" Chapter 5 in Susan Rose-Ackerman (ed.), *The Economics of Nonprofit Institutions: Studies in Structure and Policy.* New York: Oxford University Press, 1986.

Brudney, Jeffrey L. *Fostering Volunteer Programs in the Public Sector.* San Francisco: Jossey-Bass, 1990.

Duncombe, William D., and Jeffrey L. Brudney. "Volunteer Demand, Factor Substitution, and the Optimal Mix of Volunteer and Paid Staff in Local Governments, with an Application to Municipal Fire Departments." Paper presented at the annual conference of the Association for Research on Nonprofit Organizations and Voluntary Action, New Haven, Conn., 1992.

Giving and Volunteering 1992. Washington, D.C.: INDEPENDENT SECTOR, 1992.

Grønbjerg, Kirsten. *Understanding Nonprofit Funding*. San Francisco: Jossey-Bass, 1993.

Hansmann, Henry. "Nonprofit Enterprise in the Performing Arts." *Bell Journal of Economics*, 12, 1981, pp. 341-361.

James, Estelle. "How Nonprofits Grow: A Model." *Journal of Policy Analysis and Management*, 2, 1983, pp. 350-365.

Kingma, Bruce R. "Portfolio Theory and Nonprofit Financial Stability." *Nonprofit and Voluntary Sector Quarterly*, 22:2, 1993, pp. 105-120.

Rosen, Harvey S. *Public Finance* (3rd ed.). Homewood, Ill.: Irwin, 1992.

Schiff, Jerry, and Burton Weisbrod. "Competition Between For-Profit and Nonprofit Organizations in Commercial Markets." *Annals of Public and Cooperative Economics*, 62: 4, 1991, pp. 619-640.

Sharkey, William. *The Theory of Natural Monopoly*. Cambridge: Cambridge University Press, 1982.

Steinberg, Richard, and William T. Smith II. "The Minimum Wage and Volunteering." February 1990, 26 pages.

EXERCISES

1. Analyze the incidence of a hotel tax that is designed to raise revenues for local arts organizations by taxing city visitors who stay in downtown hotels. Draw diagrams showing how you expect the demand and supply functions for hotel rooms to look in the short run and in the long run, with and without the tax. What factors will determine how much revenue arts organizations receive from the tax?

2. For each of the following nonprofit services, discuss whether demand is likely to be elastic or inelastic at various levels of output:

    a. shelter care for the homeless

    b. emergency medical clinics

    c. Girl Scout cookies

    d. opera performances

    e. tours to exotic places by environmental groups

How would your assessments in each case influence how the producing nonprofit should price these services?

3. Suppose a nonprofit art museum opens a gift shop and sells commercial art supplies that it claims will encourage amateur artists. How do you think sales will be affected if the government decides these sales constitute "unrelated income" and collects unrelated business income tax on the profits?

4. A community health clinic operates in a heterogeneous neighborhood populated by families with a wide range of incomes. It offers a variety of services, from urgent care to elective cosmetic procedures. If the clinic depends mostly on fees and wishes to ensure that all community residents are well served, how can a strategy of price discrimination be designed to foster this objective? How can the strategy of cross-subsidization also be usefully employed in this case?

5. Suppose a nonprofit nursing home depends on private donations for a major portion of its revenues but is considering various ways of increasing earned income to strengthen its financial base. Which of the following possibilities are likely to have a significant effect on donations and which ones are not? Explain your reasoning and characterize donor revenue in relation to sales of services as elastic or inelastic in each of the following cases:
   a. charging extra for meals and snacks;
   b. putting in a cappuccino bar and selling gourmet coffee to residents;
   c. selling crafts made by elderly residents;
   d. developing and marketing a new line of sports clothing for senior citizens; and
   e. raising prices for basic residential care.

CHAPTER **9**

Market Failure

I n Chapter 7, we analyzed how markets work to bring demand and supply into balance by establishing market-clearing prices at which goods and services can be exchanged without leaving consumers wanting more or producers having more to sell than consumers will buy. This is how markets help to put economic resources to their best uses—that is, to allocate resources efficiently according to the Pareto criterion discussed in Chapter 1. In essence, this is the "invisible hand" that Adam Smith describes when he argues that maximum efficiency is achieved when consumers and producers interact in the marketplace, each individually pursuing his or her self-interest.

But markets do not always work perfectly. Under some conditions, which we call *market failure*, markets do not allocate resources efficiently. We have already seen examples of this. In Chapter 3, we cited conditions of *informational asymmetry* under which the utilization of nonprofit organizations may be a more efficient means of service provision than commercial markets. And in Chapters 5, 6, and 8 we noted that market transactions may ignore certain social benefits and costs that do not directly affect those who make (private) supply and demand decisions.

It is important for us to understand those conditions for a number of reasons. First, market failure is often the basis on which governments intervene in markets by imposing regulations, taxes, or subsidies to ameliorate unintended social costs or benefits. Second, market failure helps explain why we choose, in some circumstances, to utilize institutions other than for-profit businesses operating through markets to allocate resources. In particular, market failure helps explain why nonprofit organizations are used for certain roles in society.

Third, we will find that some concepts of market failure are usefully applied within the *internal* context of managing organizations. Indeed, we can even help explain why organizations exist by referring to situations of market failure where it is more efficient to allocate resources within the rules and confines of an organization than through open-market exchange. However, replacing markets with organizations does not eliminate market-failure conditions; these conditions merely become management problems (see Williamson, 1975).

There is an additional complication when private nonprofit organizations address market failures. Organizational objectives vary and may or may not coincide with broader notions of social efficiency. Thus, in Chapter 8, we spoke of pricing using *beneficial demand* to correct market failures as seen by a particular nonprofit organization with particular objectives, rather than using a *marginal social benefit curve* (discussed later in this chapter) to represent social benefits more generally.

In this chapter, we explore the sources of market failure in more detail and then illustrate how nonprofit organizations have addressed these problems in the markets for day care, blood, and the performing arts. We then illustrate the power of market-failure analysis to provide insights into more general nonprofit management issues: fund raising; volunteers; choosing between contracting and internal production; pricing; and joining trade associations.

CIRCUMSTANCES THAT LEAD TO MARKET FAILURE

The invisible-hand theorem essentially states that equilibrium is efficient when all goods, bads, and services are traded in perfectly competitive markets. If we lived in such a world, there would be no efficiency rationale for either a government or a nonprofit sector. However, many goods are not traded at all or are traded in imperfectly competitive markets, and these market failures lead to inefficiency. In some circumstances, governments, nonprofit organizations, or both can ameliorate these inefficiencies, but in order to understand how this happens, we need to know more about the sources of market failure.

We have already seen how for-profit monopolies control prices, which results in market failure when all customers are charged the same price, and possible inequity when price discrimination is employed. We have also seen how nonprofit monopolies may use one market failure (monopoly) to finance market corrections for some other market; thus, the efficiency consequences of nonprofit monopolies can be ambiguous. Governments can correct market failures by enforcing antitrust regulations, nationalizing the monopolized industry, or regulating the affected firm. Note that we say governments *can* correct the failures, not that they necessarily do so. Limitations on government stem from political considerations and transaction costs within this form of organization; however, we leave the subject of government failure to other texts (see Douglas, 1983).

In this chapter, we focus on four interrelated sources of market failure: transaction costs, nonappropriability, externality, and informational asymmetry. Like monopoly, these sources of market failure undermine the efficiency of market provision. Sometimes they may even preclude the existence of markets for certain goods and services.

Cost of Transactions

In order for markets to work well, it must be relatively inexpensive to arrange contracts and to buy and sell goods and services. Transactions may be costly for a variety of reasons. Goods and services themselves may be complex, hard to measure, or variable in their quality and cost, and thus difficult to specify in contracts. The market for medical care, for example, suffers from these complications. Transaction costs may be high because of various physical, cultural, or institutional barriers to trade—for example, currency or language problems, long distances between consumers and suppliers, or government-imposed tariffs and regulations. Or transaction costs may be high because markets are inherently difficult to police. For example, the market for hunting on private land is made costly by the difficulty of preventing poaching. Markets work most efficiently when transaction problems are minimal. Sometimes the nonprofit institutional form allows for lower transaction costs (as we show later in this chapter); this provides one important role for the nonprofit sector.

Appropriability of Goods or Services

In order for markets to work, consumers must be able to appropriate the benefits of the good or service to themselves, and suppliers must be able to exclude would-be consumers who fail to pay. Lack of appropriability may be associated with the character of a particular good or service itself (e.g., fresh air cannot normally be captured for sale to consumers in heavily polluted regions), or with the failure of government to define and enforce property rights (e.g., if the ownership of mineral rights associated with real estate is left unclear in the law). Thus, an aspect of the appropriability condition is that a governmental framework of laws and contract enforcement is necessary for the operation of efficient markets.

Externality

Sometimes people are forced to consume items they do not want. No such problem applies when a neighbor buys ugly interior furnishings, since no one else need see those furnishings. However, when a home-owner lets his or her house exterior and lawn deteriorate, neighbors are forced to view the unsightly mess. This is an example of a *negative externality*. Sometimes people can consume items that they need not purchase. If one charitable soul encourages a street beggar to adopt a more lucrative and less obtrusive profession, others in the neighborhood enjoy a benefit they did not purchase (either a feeling of gratitude that the beggar was helped or relief that they will not have to encounter unpleasantness). This is an example of a *positive externality*. Finally, an externality is reciprocal if someone in a group purchases a good and the entire group benefits from that purchase (no matter who the purchaser is). This special kind of externality is called a *public good*.

Externalities cause market failure for either or both of two reasons: First, the external cost or benefit may not be appropriable. There may be no way for consumers of external benefits to garner the level of service they desire, and there may be no way for producers to exclude those who do not pay for external benefits (or to include those who would pay to reduce external costs). Second, even if a (secondary) market can be established for the external effect, this market may be quite "thin"—that is, it may have few buyers or sellers, so that monopolistic or monopsonistic conditions result. For these reasons, organizing a market for helping street beggars would be quite difficult. Nonprofit organizations sometimes address this kind of market failure.

Informational Asymmetry

Markets fail where information is costly or lacking. In Chapter 3, we discussed the condition of informational asymmetry under which consumers are disadvantaged relative to producers and thus are led to prefer nonprofit organizations over for-profit providers. The markets for child day care and nursing home services for the elderly provide examples where informational asymmetry is a condition leading to market failure. Informational asymmetry combines elements of appropriability (there may be no way for someone to secure truthful information from a nursing home operator about hidden aspects of the quality of care) with elements of market power (informational markets may be too thin for perfect competition to prevail).

Information creation as well as dissemination may suffer from market failure. Research and the development of innovations sometimes create nonappropriable external benefits, so market failure occurs here as well. Nonprofit organizations may address both problems. However, before we can turn to the applications of market failure to nonprofits, we need to say more about externalities and public goods.

EXTERNALITIES

We use the following as our working definition of an externality:

An externality is a benefit or a cost, not directly accounted for in the market price, that is imposed on a third party as a result of a market-related transaction.

The following are some examples of externality-creating market activities:

Innoculations for communicable diseases. When an individual receives an innoculation, that individual benefits from the protection, but society at large (third parties) also benefits from the reduced risk of the spread of disease. This is a positive externality.

Musical performances. An accomplished musician who practices Beethoven near an open window benefits not only himself but others (third parties) within earshot. (Punk rockers and disco fans may regard this as a negative externality, but others will regard it as an external benefit.)

Traffic congestion. When people drive on crowded roadways, they impose additional delays on other (third-party) drivers; this is a negative externality.

Smoking. When people decide to smoke, they may not take into account the health costs or unpleasantness imposed on (third-party) nonsmokers by secondary inhalation.

Pollution. When people buy non-biodegradable products, or when manufacturers pollute the air or water, they impose environmental costs on citizens (third parties) not accounted for in their decisions.

Recall that the height of the demand curve for a good or service represents purchasers' marginal willingness to pay for, or the value placed on the opportunity to consume, an additional unit. When there are no externalities, only the purchasers are affected by consumption, so that the demand curve fully captures the marginal social benefits (*MSB*) of a good. Externalities create a gap between the marginal benefits to the purchaser—that is, demand—and the marginal social benefit functions. The difference in the height of these two curves represents the marginal value placed on the externality-generating activity by the affected third parties. Letting *MPB* (marginal private benefits) denote the marginal value to the purchaser and *MEB* (marginal external benefits) denote the total value placed by third parties on a one-unit increase in production by the externality-generating party, we arrive at the following identity:

$$MSB(Q) = MPB(Q) + MEB(Q)$$

Each of the marginal benefit components depends on the level of production. *MPB* is the demand curve and is a downward-sloping function of output *Q*. If *MEB* is positive, it reflects a positive externality (external benefit), and if it is negative, it reflects a negative externality (external cost). *MEB* can take any shape, but for simplicity we assume it is a constant with the same value for every level of production. Thus, *MSB* will be parallel to and above the demand curve (*D*) for positive externalities, and parallel and below demand for negative externalities, as illustrated in Figures 9.1A and 9.1B.

If individuals care only about themselves, their private benefits will govern their purchasing decisions, and they will neglect any external benefits or costs imposed as a result of their purchases. If individuals care about others, the idea of externality becomes more difficult to define, for then any activity affecting third parties also indirectly affects the purchaser. Often, self-regarding behavior predominates, and so, for simplicity, we will ignore the subtleties stemming from altruism in much of the discussion that follows.

With this simplification, equilibrium is basically unaffected by the presence of externalities. Perfectly competitive equilibrium occurs where supply (*S*) intersects demand (*D*), as illustrated by the points P_E, Q_E in Figures 9.1A and 9.1B. These equilibria are socially inefficient. In Figure 9.1A, marginal social benefits exceed marginal costs at the competitive equilibrium. This means that society places greater value on a one-unit increase in production of the good (*MSB*) than it does on the value of what must be sacrificed to obtain this increase in production (*MC*), so that we would be better off increasing the level of exchange. As long as *MSB* is greater than *MC*, we can continue to add net social value by expanding production until we reach the intersection of *MSB* and *MC*, where the optimal quantity Q^* is produced.

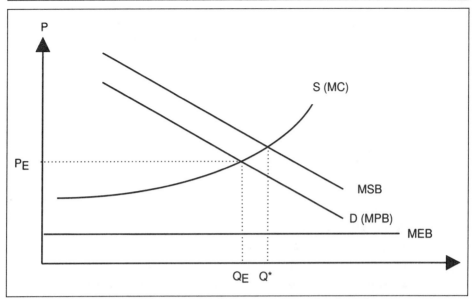

Figure 9.1A How Externalities Create Inefficiency: Underproduction When Externalities Are Positive

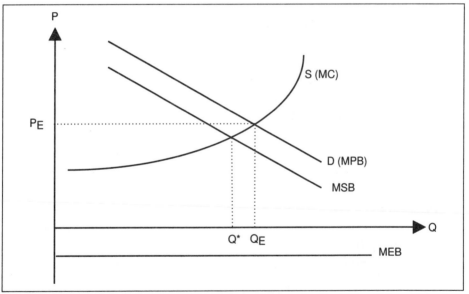

Figure 9.1B How Externalities Create Inefficiency: Overproduction When Externalities Are Negative

In Figure 9.1B, marginal social benefits are less than marginal costs at the competitive equilibrium. In this case, the combined losses to purchasers and third parties when we reduce production by one unit (*MSB*) would be less than the gain from saving the cost to produce that last unit (*MC*). Here, society as a whole benefits if we cut back to the optimal quantity Q^*, where *MSB* equals *MC*. Thus, we conclude:

Competitive markets overproduce goods that create external costs and underproduce goods that create external benefits.

There are many possible solutions to market failures resulting from positive externalities:

Mandates. Government can mandate provision or consumption at a certain level. We do not allow children and adolescents (or their parents) to decide for themselves whether to attend school; we substitute compulsory attendance laws for consumer choice. This prevents the potential underprovision of elementary and secondary education in a free market that would ignore external benefits.

Subsidies. Subsidies can be offered to induce higher levels of production and consumption. Subsidized student loans and work-study programs tied to the recipient's good academic standing at an accredited university provide an example of the subsidy approach.

Education. Information can be offered, through promotional advertising, to increase demand by making the externality-producing good seem more attractive to consumers. A "Go Back to School" campaign is an illustration of this.

Taxation. Alternatives to the desired behavior can be taxed. For example, recreational activities available during school hours can be made more expensive so that youth find it less desirable to cut classes. If movies are a relevant substitute for schooling (with a positive cross-price elasticity), then a tax on movies shown during school hours would help correct the market failure.

Prizes. Prizes can provide tangible rewards to those who most successfully increase their consumption of the desired good. Thus, students can be given awards for exceptional attendance or educational achievement.

Similar kinds of remedies are available to address negative externalities:

Mandates. Government can set limits or impose restrictions on behavior. For example, smoking can be prohibited in public places, and pollution standards can be set and enforced.

Taxes. Taxes can be imposed to discourage externality-producing behavior. For example, cigarettes, gasoline, and even effluents (tail-pipe emissions) themselves can be taxed.

Education. Information campaigns, such as "Quit smoking" and "Take public transportation" advertising, can be mounted to get people to reduce their externality-producing behavior.

Prizes. Sanctions, such as publicly citing the worst industrial polluters, can be applied. Alternatively, a prize or public commendation can be offered to the firm that reduces its pollution the most.

Subsidies. Subsidies can be provided to encourage people to use substitutes for the externality-producing activity. For example, public transit and biodegradable packaging can be subsidized.

Tradeable Permits. A limited number of permits can be issued, and those without permits can be prohibited from engaging in the externality-generating activity. Permits can be bought and sold, so that those who would find it costliest to reduce the externality-generating activity will buy permits from those who find it somewhat easier to reduce that activity.

Note that the various remedies for negative and positive externalities are basically the same and fall into three categories: (1) educating people and hoping that they will change their behavior voluntarily; (2) policing behavior through direct rules and regulations; and (3) providing incentives so that costs and benefits faced by individuals conform more closely with the social costs and benefits implied by their actions.

The last approach is, in principle, the one usually favored by economists, because it does not try to change people's preferences or values or impose uniform standards on everyone. What economists try to do in cases of externalities is find ways of "internalizing the externalities" by bringing the social benefits into the decision-making process of individual consumers or producers in the marketplace through taxes and subsidies. Examples of policies that internalize externalities are:

- taxes based on the carbon content of fossil fuels designed to reduce global warming due to the greenhouse effect;
- tradeable permits allowing the emission of sulfur oxides by fossil-fuel power plants;
- gasoline taxes that reflect the pollution and congestion costs imposed on others by driving;
- highway tolls during peak hours that reflect the congestion costs imposed by automobile commuters;
- tuition scholarships that reflect the benefits to society of undertaking further education; and

- cigarette taxes that reflect health costs imposed on others by smoking.

Each of these solutions has unique advantages and disadvantages. For example, a tax on gasoline would reduce the number of miles driven and hence automobile pollution, but perhaps a more efficient way to reduce automobile pollution would be to improve catalytic converters. A tax based on tailpipe emissions would allow each driver to find the most efficient way to control pollution and thereby reduce the effect of the tax. However, it would also create much larger transaction costs than a tax on gasoline, since installing equipment to measure tailpipe emissions on each car would be very expensive. (For more details of the policy trade-offs involved in choosing an externality solution see Rosen, 1992, or Downing, 1984.)

As we noted in Chapters 4 and 8, nonprofit organizations may depart from competitive or monopoly equilibria to promote their own missions. In so doing, they equate beneficial demand (rather than price or marginal revenue) with marginal cost. Does this promote social efficiency? Possibly. If there is a positive externality, using market demand to determine output creates a market failure. Loosely speaking, if the nonprofit's beneficial demand curve lies above the market demand curve but below the marginal social benefit curve, nonprofit production will enhance social efficiency by moving production closer to the optimum. If beneficial demand coincides with *MSB*, nonprofit production will entirely correct the market failure. However, a nonprofit organization could make things worse. Suppose, for example, that the Corvette Society believed that Corvettes were an underappreciated good (like opera) and subsidized rides in Corvettes to young children in the hopes that someday they would become Corvette afficionados. This organization's beneficial demand would be higher than the market demand, whereas the pollution produced by these cars suggests that marginal social benefits are below market demand. The Corvette Society would worsen economic efficiency by moving production of Corvettes away from the social optimum.

In summary, externalities are a form of market failure in which the costs or benefits of an activity are not fully taken into account by private decision making as reflected in unfettered markets. Economists' approach to externalities involves policies that attempt to internalize externalities through subsidies, taxes, and other means so that both private and social benefits and costs are taken into account by consumers and producers, leading to more efficient resource allocation decisions. The concept of externality is an important one for nonprofit managers and policy makers, for various reasons. First, nonprofits are often involved in addressing social problems and issues involving important externalities—both positive and negative—such as environmental issues, health issues, education, and the like. Second, nonprofit managers may themselves be involved in producing or reducing important externalities. If they are truly to operate in the public interest, they must be aware of, and attend to, these externalities.

PUBLIC GOODS

A *pure public good* is a good or service that has two essential characteristics—*nonexcludability* and *nonrivalry*.

- A good is said to be *nonexcludable* if, once it is produced, consumers cannot be prevented from using or benefiting from it except at great cost.
- A good is said to be *nonrival* if one person's use of it does not reduce the amount available for use by others.

Examples of pure public goods are national defense, public art, lighthouses, and clean air. Chernobyl's radiation leak provided a "pure public bad" (the opposite of a public good). In each case, once the good is produced, it is difficult or impossible to prevent anyone from using it, whether or not they pay for it; moreover, one person's use does not detract from another's use (Lucy's complaint in the cartoon below notwithstanding!).

Notice that our definition of a public good is specific and technical and differs from the common usage of the term in English. A public good, by this definition, may or may not be a governmentally provided good. Sometimes governments provide goods with no externalities, and sometimes the private sector provides public goods.

From a market-failure point of view, of course, if goods can be enjoyed without one's having to pay for them, then the benefits are nonappropriable and for-profit firms will not be able to sell them. Any payment for such goods

PEANUTS® reprinted by permission of UFS, Inc.

would be entirely voluntary, essentially equivalent to a donation. However, consumers would not trust for-profit firms to devote their donations to increments in the level of the public good because of contract failure. That is, consumers could not tell which part of the public good was being financed with their donation and which part was being financed with someone else's donation, so incremental donations could be diverted to dividend payments to stockholders, with donors none the wiser.

Presumably, nonprofit organizations can do better here because they don't have stockholders who would benefit from donors being tricked out of their funds. However, the externality problem remains. Because any one donor's contribution in support of a pure public good benefits all other potential donors, donations have external benefits and therefore will be underprovided in equilibrium. This is the famous *free-rider problem*: All donors hope that some other donor will supply the necessary funds and allow them to enjoy the good for free. As a result, aggregate donations will be inadequate to support an efficient level of public goods.

In reality, many goods and services have some but not all of the characteristics associated with public goods. The taxonomy in Table 9.1 maps the variety of goods and services that have both, one, or neither of the characteristics of pure public goods.

An excludable and rival good that generates no externalities is called a *pure private good*. Private goods are optimally provided by competitive markets, for all the relevant social costs and benefits are taken into account by buyers and sellers.

A *common-pool good,* or *congestion good,* is rival but not excludable. The fish contained in a public pond constitute a common good because two consumers cannot catch and eat the same fish, but anyone is welcome to try.

TABLE 9.1
Varieties of Public and Private Goods

	EXCLUDABLE	NONEXCLUDABLE
	Pure Private Goods	**Common-Pool Goods (Congestion Goods)**
RIVAL	clothing	urban freeways
	food	underground oil
	Excludable Public Goods (Toll Goods)	**Pure Public Goods**
NONRIVAL	symphonies	defense
	open highways	lighthouses
	museums	public art

If any fisher catches a fish, it becomes harder for the others to secure their own catches, so there is a reciprocal negative externality. As with other negative externalities, we expect and see overfishing if the market is unregulated. Similarly, each car that enters a congested freeway adds to the traffic and so makes the going slower for other motorists.

An *excludable public good* (also known as a *toll good*) is excludable but not rival. An uncrowded museum gallery is an excludable public good because an admission fee can be charged, but visitors do not deplete the display or significantly reduce the viewing pleasure of other visitors. An uncrowded highway is also an excludable public good, where tolls serve as the excluding device.

Because at least some of the benefits of consumption of excludable public goods can be appropriated by the supplier, these goods will be supplied by for-profit firms. However, there are two problems with for-profit supply. First, the amount of the good supplied will be less than optimal. This is because nonrival goods produce beneficial externalities. Second, there will be overexclusion unless the for-profit firm can perfectly price discriminate. At any single price, there will be some consumers who would benefit from entering the facility and are willing to pay something to do so but are not willing to pay the going price. For-profit suppliers would not admit these customers because they wish to keep their price, hence profits, high. This exclusion is socially inefficient because there are no social opportunity costs involved in letting additional customers enjoy an excludable public good.

A perfectly price-discriminating for-profit monopoly would provide an excludable public good optimally and would exclude nobody. Those willing to pay any price would be let in at a price equal to their maximum willingness to pay, because the firm values their revenue and suffers no added cost from letting additional customers in. However, in Chapter 8 we argued that perfect price discrimination is not feasible because the firm would need information from consumers to adopt its price structure and consumers would not trust a for-profit firm with the necessary information. This is why, according to Ben-Ner (1986), some nonprofit firms come into existence. Consumers are more willing to trust a nonprofit firm with the information it needs to price discriminate in order to optimally supply an excludable public good.

MORE ON FREE RIDING

A simple thought experiment that is easy to conduct in a classroom setting makes the nature of free riding much clearer. Suppose that four students are given $10 apiece and told that they can either keep the money or invest any part of it in a group investment fund. Everyone shares in the proceeds from this group fund: if any student contributes $1, the fund grows in value by $2, so that each student receives an additional $0.50. What would you do in such a circumstance? If you are selfish, the answer is clear: you would contribute nothing. Although group wealth grows by $2 when you donate $1 to the fund, your personal wealth shrinks by $0.50 because your proportionate share of the investment return is smaller than your investment. If everyone else in the group is also selfish, each will walk out with the same $10 they started with. However, if each group member could somehow be convinced to donate his or her entire $10 to the group fund, the investment return would be $80 and each group member would receive a proportionate share equal to $20.

What does this have to do with free riding? The investment pool is like a pure public good in that if anybody invests, benefits are provided for the entire group. An investment in the fund is like a donation in support of a public good, since the investor loses some purchasing power while everyone else benefits from the investment. The equilibrium massively underprovides this public good, as selfish individuals would free ride and donate nothing in a situation where it would be socially optimal (and to each person's advantage) if each donated his or her entire allotment of funds. Less extreme examples, where selfish people would donate something in their individual interest, can easily be constructed (Isaac and Walker, 1992), but it is always the case that selfish individuals contribute less than the optimal amount for a public good.

For public goods, the collective interest is at odds with individual interests. A group of altruists would be more generous than a group of self-regarding individuals, but altruism alone will not completely solve the free-riding problem. The following are some solutions to these problems (see Olson, 1965):

> *Social pressure.* Social pressure can be used to enhance voluntary provision. This approach is used by nonprofit organizations to raise funds through campaigns that utilize personal networks or take place within small institutions such as religious congregations where everyone knows one another, shares common values, and expects to continue to interact with the same group. In this setting, it is easier to achieve group goals, and free riding may not be in anyone's long-term interest.
>
> *Premiums.* Selective incentives and rewards may be used to tie contributions to private, excludable benefits. This is a mar-

ketlike solution used, for example, by nonprofit organizations (such as public radio stations and environmental organizations) that provide certain unique gifts (private goods such as tote bags with insignias) to recognize charitable contributions.

State support. Coercion can be used to require contributions for the support of public goods. This is essentially what happens when provision (financing) is taken over by government, which then uses the police power of the state to tax the citizenry in support of government-financed public goods.

In the balance of this chapter, we discuss applications of market failure to nonprofit policy and management issues.

POLICY APPLICATION: DAY CARE FOR YOUNG CHILDREN

Day care for young children, which involves consumers who cannot fend for themselves, suffers from two sources of market failure (Young and Nelson, 1973):

Asymmetric information. Parents may have a difficult time assessing the quality of care delivered to their children, particularly those intangible aspects of caregiving that are more difficult to observe than the condition of physical facilities or the availability of toys and other equipment. Since young children cannot report on these intangible aspects to their parents very well, and parents frequently have little time for direct observation, parents suffer an informational disadvantage relative to those who supply the day-care services. For-profit suppliers might take advantage of consumer ignorance by shortchanging on the promised quality level, training, and supervision of staff.

Externalities. The benefits of day care accrue to children, but the purchasing decision is made by parents. High-quality day care provides lifelong benefits for some children. If nutrition and health checkups are offered, children may grow up to be healthier and more productive. If educational programs are included, children may learn more effectively as they grow up, becoming more productive citizens. Although parents are not generally self-regarding in these decisions and try to do what is right for the child, they may not always fully appreciate these benefits or be able to afford them and may thus purchase a lower quality or quantity of care on their own than may be efficient from the perspective of society.

What solutions are available to remedy these market failure problems? Two remedies have been widely discussed and applied.

Nonprofit Supply

Nonprofit suppliers are less likely to take advantage of their superior information, because the nondistribution constraint reduces their incentive to do so. In addition, it is easier to maintain consumer control over a nonprofit organization than over a for-profit organization facing the constant threat of a takeover bid. Nonprofit day-care facilities often place parents on the board of directors and encourage parents to visit the facility more often, thus reducing the information gap (see Ben-Ner and Van Hoomissen, 1993). Finally, nonprofit day-care facilities are often established and run by close-knit groups of consumers who interact repeatedly in other settings and so must maintain an atmosphere of mutual trust. Facilities operated by employers and places of worship gain trust through this mechanism.

Public Subsidy and Regulation

If the quality or quantity of day-care supply is less than it should be because a center fails to account for positive externalities to society at large, this can be remedied by providing public subsidies to effectively increase the demand for quality care. Subsidies can be made available for day-care services meeting certain standards of quality and perhaps targeted to lower income groups for which the externalities are greatest.

Regulation by government can help ensure that suppliers providing subsidized day-care services do indeed offer the standard of care required by public policy. Restricting the subsidy to nonprofit suppliers may be helpful in ensuring the desired quality level, since these suppliers are less compelled to achieve profits at the expense of quality. However, such a restriction may also create inefficiencies if nonprofit organizations, because of their blunted profit incentives, are slow to expand to meet the increased demand for services that may be stimulated by a subsidy.

POLICY APPLICATION: SELLING BLOOD

Several aspects of market failure are associated with a free market in the supply of transfused blood (see Arrow, 1975).

Asymmetric information. People who know that their blood is contaminated by serum hepatitis, the AIDS virus, or some other
pathogen may conceal this fact in order to receive money for
their blood donation.

Externalities. The transmission of infection from donors to recipients of blood is a market transaction with no externalities if
the recipient is symmetrically informed about blood quality.
However, an uninformed blood recipient may receive pathogens as an unintended side effect of the purchase, and this
external cost can be transmitted to others with whom the
recipient interacts.

Transaction costs. "Bad blood" can often be detected prior to
transfusion through the use of biochemical tests, but these
tests are expensive and not completely reliable. The lack of
reliability is a sad fact of life but causes no market failure in
itself because we lack the capability to do better with our
current technology. Testing is a required transaction cost in
the market for blood, not a source of market failure per se.
However, if asymmetric information and externalities are
present, costlier and more intensive testing may be needed,
and this additional transaction cost does reflect market
failure.

What remedies can be employed to address these market-failure
issues? In this case, the key is to analyze the motivations of donors under
different circumstances. While most potential donors may be motivated
by the desire to help others, others may be primarily motivated by the
prospect of payment. It is unlikely that altruistic (potential) donors would
try to conceal knowledge that their own blood was bad. Their aim is to
help, not to harm, the recipients of their donation. However, donors who
are in it for the money would be less concerned with harming others, and
those among them with bad blood would be less likely to withhold the
sale of their bodily fluids. If donors are paid for their blood, blood will be
supplied by untainted altruists and by both tainted and untainted money
seekers. If, instead, blood must be truly donated (that is, payments for
blood are outlawed), then, in theory, only untainted altruists will contribute and the average quality of blood supplies will improve. This is the
solution proposed by Richard Titmuss (1971).

The limitation of the voluntary system is, of course, the free-rider
problem. Despite the fact that blood donations create a public good (i.e., an
inventory of untainted blood available in an emergency for whomever may

require it), individuals will not voluntarily contribute to this good at the level that would be efficient for society as a whole. Thus, by solving the market-failure problems through voluntary donation, we introduce additional problems of allocation that require further attention. How can the free-rider problem be addressed in the case of blood supply? Several alternatives suggest themselves.

Supplementary Profit-Making Supply

With intensive (costly) testing, a parallel system of paying for blood donations may be permitted to operate in order to ensure that an adequate supply is forthcoming. This may create a problem if those who might otherwise volunteer then seek to be paid. However, assuming that altruistic donors find this alternative unappealing, the parallel systems can work in tandem.

Selective Incentives

Voluntary donors can be rewarded with public recognition and tokens of appreciation, increasing the likelihood that they will continue to give and will encourage others to give. However, if the reward is sufficiently attractive, it may risk bringing donors with selfish motives into the system.

A particularly interesting selective incentive is to test each donor's blood for the presence of pathogens. For example, suppose a free test for AIDS is provided to blood donors. Individuals who suspect they have AIDS may decide to give blood in order to take advantage of this test. This will have the beneficial effect of detecting HIV but will draw more high-risk individuals into the donor pool. The HIV test is not perfect, and it is possible that this sort of test will be counterproductive if a large number of HIV-positive individuals are brought into the system and only some of them are identified through testing. In addition, those at high risk for AIDS are also at high risk for other diseases (such as non-type-A, non-type-B hepatitis) for which no blood tests are currently available.

Thus, free AIDS testing is probably not the best incentive to offer donors. If such tests are to be offered for free, they should be offered independently of blood donation in order to eliminate these perverse effects (Thompson, 1990).

Social Pressure

Campaigns to increase social awareness of the need for blood donations and mobilization of smaller work and social groups through events to encourage donations constitute additional strategies to overcome the free-rider problem in this case.

Coercion

The government could by law require healthy individuals to give a certain amount of blood each year. This solution to the free-rider problem would be unsatisfactory for several reasons, not the least of which would be the problem of certifying exemptions for health reasons. Obtaining exemption from giving would require costly medical certification. Thus, some people might decide to give blood even if they were unhealthy. Alternatively, the government could pay for such certification, but that would add another high transaction cost to the arrangement. Another problem is that many would regard control of their own blood as an inviolable right. Those who are already stuck for taxes would object to this additional needling by the government.

POLICY APPLICATION: THE FINE AND PERFORMING ARTS

Museums, symphony orchestras, opera, theater, and ballet companies often operate outside the pure market system because they involve various manifestations of market failure that require alternative solutions (see Baumol and Bowen, 1966).

Externalities. The appreciation of art is one means through which citizens become educated about their culture, learn to be creative, and gain peace of mind. Healthier, more educated, and more creative citizens may contribute to society at large, not just earn higher salaries for themselves. Thus, there are positive external benefits from consumption of the arts. In addition, children who are encouraged at an early age to appreciate the arts may find functional outlets for their creative drives, thereby reducing the quantity (or at least enhancing the quality) of graffiti and similar means of self-expression and hence reducing the negative externalities accompanying these activities.

Public goods. Public art beautifies a city. Art promotes free expression and may cultivate democratic values. Promotion of quality in art symbolizes a society's values of achievement and excellence. Preserving great works of art maintains a society's cultural heritage. These are all goods that can be consumed jointly (i.e., they are nonrival) and without exclusion.

Toll goods. Symphony concerts, theater performances, and museums are toll goods. Once admitted to a museum or theater, individuals enjoy the same paintings or performances without imposing additional costs on or detracting from the enjoyment of others. Although for-profit firms may provide toll goods, they exclude nonpayers, which is inefficient (Feldstein, 1991).

What are the remedies for these various manifestations of market failure in the arts?

Public Subsidy

If performing arts are underprovided due to market neglect of external benefits, then public subsidy can help. Subsidies targeted at children and other key populations may be especially efficient here. Subsidies devoted to particular forms of artistic creation that may ultimately have commercial application may also be helpful if these innovations cannot be copyrighted or patented.

Public subsidies in support of toll goods can be markedly helpful. Because museums, symphony orchestras, and other such toll goods have high fixed costs and low variable costs, average costs fall and marginal costs remain very low over a wide range of output. (See Figure 9.2.) This makes it impossible for any supplier, for-profit or nonprofit, to provide the socially efficient quantity (where price equals marginal cost), charge a single price, and at least break even (see the loss rectangle in Figure 9.2). A price greater than or equal to average cost at the optimal quantity is necessary to avoid bankruptcy, but this would exclude those consumers who are willing to pay more than it costs to increase production from Q_1 to Q_2.

This problem could be solved using either a per-unit or a lump-sum subsidy. Viewed from the perspective of producer price, a per-unit subsidy of the right size would raise demand to D_2, allowing efficient provision to proceed. Alternatively, the organization could be provided with a lump-sum subsidy equal to the area of the loss rectangle on the condition that it provide the optimal quantity and charge consumers a price equal to marginal cost at this quantity.

Public Provision

Pure public goods (e.g., publicly displayed sculptures or commercial-free classical music performances on radio and television) would not be provided at all by for-profit firms. Transaction costs may be lower if, instead of inducing private providers to enter and then subsidizing them (as was done in the early years of National Public Radio), government produces the goods. The British Broadcasting Company (BBC) provides an example of this approach.

Voluntary Provision

Given the limits to government and for-profit provision of the fine and performing arts, another approach is to support public goods and external benefits of the arts through voluntary contributions (Hansmann, 1981;

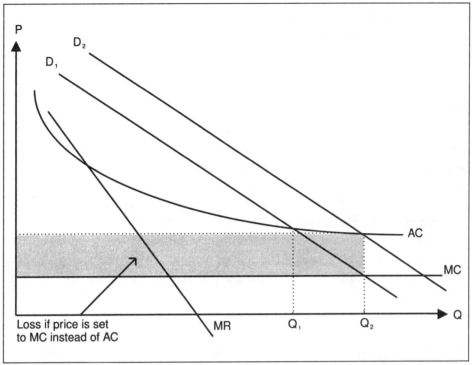

Figure 9.2 Circumstance Where Subsidy Is Required to Break Even and Maximize Social Benefit

Ben-Ner, 1986). Since it is unlikely that such voluntary support would be offered to for-profit providers or even governmental institutions, this solution implies organizing artistic institutions as nonprofit organizations. The reason for this is that donors are concerned that their donations actually go toward support of the programs they want to help. They fear that if they give to for-profits, contributions will simply enrich the owners of the business. If they give to government, they may fear that contributions will simply replace tax dollars that might otherwise have been allocated to the service. If they give to nonprofits, these reservations are reduced or eliminated.

However, nonprofit provision and voluntary support again raise the problem of free riders. Here, exploiting social mechanisms such as peer pressure among board members of a prestigious cultural institution or using selective incentives, such as recognition of contributors through token gifts or listing donors in programs handed out at performances, are means to help overcome free-rider problems.

MANAGEMENT APPLICATIONS

A variety of concerns facing nonprofit managers may be usefully analyzed within the framework of market failure. Here, we consider fund raising, volunteer recruitment, teamwork, contracting out for services, pricing of services, and deciding whether or not to join a trade association.

Fund Raising

The task of inducing donors to contribute funds to support a nonprofit organization requires overcoming the free-rider problem. As we suggested earlier, this task may be addressed through approaches that employ social pressure (in small groups such as boards, work groups, or small associations), or through selective incentives (e.g., prizes awarded for membership support of a public radio station). Alternatively, nonprofits may turn to the marketplace, undertaking profit-making enterprises in market niches where they may enjoy some advantage over their competitors. For example, a nonprofit may have some monopoly power (e.g., the use of its logo on clothing), or a special location (e.g., a bookstore on a university campus). By entering into such monopolistically competitive industries, the organization can subsidize its public goals.

Recruiting Volunteers

This is another area of management that suffers from free riders. Volunteering has both private and external benefits. There is no market failure with respect to the private benefits: someone seeking training, companionship, or volunteer amenities need not be subsidized to contribute. However, there is no assurance that private benefits will suffice to overcome the free-rider problem associated with the public-good benefits of volunteering. Again, the social-pressure strategy can be utilized. Personalized solicitation, friend to friend, is thought to be the most effective means of getting people to volunteer or give money (*Giving and Volunteering 1992*). Thus, the nonprofit organization can tweak the social conscience of its volunteers. It can also provide more private benefits to these individuals in the form of training, volunteer recognition awards, free family use of its facilities, and the like. When social pressure is properly utilized, the external benefits of recruiting additional volunteers can outweigh the added costs of mobilizing social pressure and providing private rewards.

Teamwork

Many kinds of organizational work, such as care for a group of clients or patients requiring custodial care or performances by a musical ensemble, are carried out in teams. The functioning of boards and committees also requires teamwork. In such cases, the output of the team is like a public good. Credit for the output goes to all team members without excluding the slackers. Thus, there is an incentive for team members to free ride on the efforts of their colleagues. This free-rider problem can also be addressed through social pressure: the smaller the team, the more likely it is that other team members will identify the laggards and embarrass or cajole them into better performance. If the group is expected to interact many times in the future, cooperation is even more likely.

One of the problems with teams is that it is difficult to measure the individual contributions to them. One strategy is to divide work in such a way that team members' tasks are more differentiated and hence more easily attributable to specific individuals. This is one reason why musical ensembles are broken into physically separated sections playing different parts. Imagine the first violin's difficulty in leading a violin section scattered at random throughout the orchestra. This strategy of work differentiation is like transforming a public good into a private good so that potential free riders can be identified and individually penalized or excluded.

Subcontracting Versus In-House Work

Brochures can be printed in-house or contracted out. Fund-raising events can be planned, advertised, and managed by staff or by external fund-raising consultants. Lawyers, accountants, conference planners, layout artists, and financial and benefit managers can be employees of nonprofit organizations or can serve the organization on a contract basis. Market-failure analysis provides important insights into this category of choices.

Obviously, the quality and cost of work available in-house and from outside contractors is a prime consideration in this decision. External quality and cost, in turn, depend on whether there is sufficient competition in the market to induce competing suppliers to minimize costs and maintain quality while obtaining modest economic profits. If there is, external quality and cost are likely to be superior to what can be realized in-house. In addition, the organization's own demand for the service will matter. If that demand is large, then the organization can afford to devote specialized resources to it, develop special expertise, and exploit potential economies of scale in order to achieve efficiency. If the internal demand is limited, the organization is unlikely to develop the internal capacity needed to compete well with outside suppliers.

But how is an organization to know whether outside contractors are superior, and how does an organization ensure that a contractor does the job properly? These are even more fundamental questions in the decision to contract out work or undertake an activity internally. In short, the decision to contract out depends on the relative transaction costs of the two alternatives.

In the case of contracting, transaction costs include the cost of obtaining information about prices and quality, the costs of bargaining and negotiating a contract, the costs of monitoring quality as the goods or services are delivered, and the costs of enforcing a contract if something goes wrong. These transaction costs differ for different kinds of goods and services. Contracting for a printed brochure may be relatively simple and inexpensive. One draws up specifications on what is needed and solicits proposals— including prices and proposed designs—from various suppliers. A choice is made based on the proposals, a contract specifies what is to be delivered by a set date and for how much, and contract enforcement is fairly straightforward.

The transaction costs also depend on the type of organization one is contracting with. If the contractee is trustworthy, less effort is needed to write, negotiate, and enforce the contract. (Handshakes are cheaper than lawyers.) Nonprofit contractors and some for-profits are likely to be trustworthy in this fashion. A large for-profit firm providing a fairly standardized product and enjoying substantial brand-name loyalty would have much to lose from an opportunistic reading of contract loopholes; this makes such a firm more trustworthy as well.

The costs associated with this market process can be compared to the in-house capacity (in our example, for printing) and the greater control one may have over an employee's work than over an outside contractor. If the organization has strong in-house capabilities, it may choose to stay in-house. Otherwise, it is likely to go outside.

Organizing a fund-raising event may be different because it is more complex and less easy to monitor than printing procurement. It is difficult to compare the quality and effectiveness of fund-raising consultants on the basis of their success with other clients, since each campaign or event is, to some extent, unique. One never knows the extent to which previous campaign successes are due to a fund-raising consultant's expertise rather than to a favorable fund-raising environment for the particular organization. And once an event is over, one cannot prove the contractee is at fault even if the net returns are disappointing.

Nonetheless, there are advantages to contracting with an external fund-raising consultant. Fund raising has become a highly technical profession, and few nonprofit boards of directors and chief executive officers have sufficient expertise to keep their campaigns at the forefront of fund-raising proficiency. Developing such expertise internally would distract board and executive attention from the charitable mission, which involves the provision of services and not the raising of funds. In addition, because "learning-by-doing" is important in fund raising, an outside fund-raising consultant with experience conducting a variety of campaigns for a variety of organizations is likely to have more success than an in-house campaign conducted by staffers with more limited experience. Finally, there are economies of scale. Outside consultants who work for many charities can spread the organizational overhead (the costs of interviewing and recruiting the best people, and of development and implementation of software, etc.), resulting in lower costs to every client than if the clients conducted separate in-house campaigns.

Pricing

Sometimes the transaction costs of pricing nonprofit outputs can exceed the expected revenue. This is particularly true for toll goods, where in order to collect a fee one has to erect a fence or other structure for keeping out nonpayers. In such a case, it may be better simply to give the good away. More commonly, transaction costs enter into the design of fee structures. If one provides discounts for children and senior citizens (or otherwise differentiates fees by demographic characteristics, ability to pay, and the like), one can serve more customers and collect more revenue. However, it is more complicated and expensive to administer a multipart fee structure, so one might not want to make it available to too many groups.

A sliding-scale fee based on ability to pay has many of the same characteristics as a toll good. In order to fence out those falsely claiming eligibility for low rates, one needs to collect and verify information on the income or wealth of each customer. This cost will be important under three conditions: (1) if there is high turnover of customers/clients, so that a sense of community does not overwhelm incentives for opportunistic behavior; (2) if the organization bears the search costs, as opposed to letting a government agency bear all the costs of verifying eligibility; and (3) if the difference between the highest and lowest price charged is significant, so that the loss incurred from false claims is large.

Joining a Trade Association

Trade associations provide pure public goods for member organizations and others in the same industry. Some lobby their legislatures on matters that affect organizations directly (e.g., tax exemption or eligibility for receipt of deductible donations) or that affect attainment of their mission (e.g., refining spousal abuse statutes to deter domestic violence). Others educate the public about the need for and availability of member-organization services (e.g., by holding a campaign to alert the public to the 10 signs of depression and where to get help). Should an individual organization do its own lobbying and public education? Should it join or organize a trade association? Because nonmembers benefit from these services whether or not they join the trade association, the free-rider problem appears once again. If the industry is small, subtle social pressure may induce industry members to provide support. On the other hand, the advantages of a unified effort may be smaller than the transaction costs (bargaining and maintenance of an organizational infrastructure) associated with establishing a trade association.

Some trade associations solve the free-rider problem by linking private or toll goods to their mix of services. If the trade association obtains supplies for its members through a buying collaborative or organizes professional conferences, it is supplying toll goods. Technical assistance, information services, and training are private goods offered to members at a better price than nonmembers could obtain from alternative suppliers. It then may not be more efficient for a manager to do his or her own lobbying or to free ride on the efforts of others. In any case, the ideas of market failure are helpful in thinking through these kinds of decisions.

SUMMARY

Competitive market outcomes are sometimes inefficient for four reasons: transaction costs, the nonappropriability of costs or benefits, externalities, and informational asymmetries. These problems can be ameliorated by government, the nonprofit sector, or both together. Market failure is a rationale for nonprofit provision in a variety of industries; we have discussed three of these—day care, blood supply, and the arts—in some detail. We have hinted at the many ways that government and nonprofits can seek to correct market failures—social pressure, linking private-good rewards to activities that provide external benefits, education, taxes, subsidies, and mandates—but all these approaches require us to estimate the costs and benefits of nontraded goods. How, precisely, does one locate a marginal social benefit curve in the real world or decide on the proper emission standard? We turn to this question in our next chapter.

REFERENCES

Apgar, William C., and H. James Brown. *Microeconomics and Public Policy.* Glenview, Ill.: Scott, Foresman, 1987.

Arrow, Kenneth J. "Gifts and Exchanges." In Edmund S. Phelps (ed.), *Altruism, Morality, and Economic Theory.* New York: Russell Sage Foundation, 1975.

Baumol, William J., and William G. Bowen. *Performing Arts—The Economic Dilemma.* New York: Basic Books, 1966.

Ben-Ner, Avner. "Why Do Nonprofit Organizations Exist in Market Economies?" In Susan Rose-Ackerman (ed.), *The Economics of Nonprofit Insti-*

tutions: Studies in Structure and Policy. New York: Oxford University Press, 1986.

Ben-Ner, Avner, and Theresa Van Hoomissen. "Nonprofit Organizations in the Mixed Economy." In Avner Ben-Ner and Benedetto Gui, *The Nonprofit Sector in the Mixed Economy*. Ann Arbor: University of Michigan Press, 1993.

Douglas, James. *Why Charity?* Beverly Hills, Calif.: Sage Publications, 1983.

Downing, Paul B. *Environmental Economics and Policy*. Boston: Little, Brown, 1984.

Feldstein, Martin (ed.). *The Economics of Art Museums*. Chicago: University of Chicago Press, 1991.

Giving and Volunteering 1992. Washington, D.C.: INDEPENDENT SECTOR, 1992.

Gramlich, Edward M. *Benefit-Cost Analysis of Government Programs*. Englewood Cliffs, N.J.: Prentice Hall, 1981.

Hansmann, Henry. "Nonprofit Enterprise in the Performing Arts." *Bell Journal of Economics,* 12, 1981, pp. 341-361.

Hart, Oliver. "An Economist's Perspective on the Theory of the Firm." Chapter 7 in Oliver Williamson (ed.), *Organization Theory*. New York: Oxford University Press, 1990.

Isaac, Mark R., and James M. Walker. "Nash as an Organizing Principle in the Voluntary Provision of Public Goods: Experimental Evidence." Working paper, Dept. of Economics, Indiana University–Bloomington, 1992.

Olson, Mancur. *The Logic of Collective Action*. Cambridge, Mass.: Harvard University Press, 1965.

Ostrom, Elinor. *Governing the Commons*. New York: Cambridge University Press, 1990.

Rosen, Harvey S. *Public Finance* (3rd ed.). Homewood, Ill.: Irwin Publishers, 1992.

Smith, Adam. *The Wealth of Nations*. Edited by Andrew Skinner. Baltimore: Penguin, 1970.

Thompson, Amy C. "The Problem of High Risk Individuals Donating Blood." In *Economic Incentives in the Nonprofit Sector: Student Essays*, Mandel Center Discussion Paper. Cleveland: Case Western Reserve University, 1990.

Titmuss, Richard. *The Gift Relationship: From Human Blood to Social Policy*. London: Allyn & Unwin, 1971.

Williamson, Oliver. *Markets and Hierarchies*. New York: Free Press, 1975.

Young, Dennis R., and Richard R. Nelson (eds.). *Public Policy for Day Care of Young Children*. Lexington, Mass.: Heath, 1973.

EXERCISES

1. Identify positive and/or negative externalities associated with the following services that might be provided by a nonprofit organization. In each case, indicate what financing and organizational arrangements you would prescribe to foster efficiency.

    a. libraries

    b. prenatal health care

    c. an early warning system for hurricanes

    d. shelters for the homeless

2. Analyze the following nonprofit management functions in terms of the "free-rider" problem and describe a strategy for dealing with the problem in each case.

    a. organizing a board of trustees for a new organization

    b. carrying out a membership drive for public radio

    c. managing a team project involving staff from different departments of an organization

    d. establishing a "community watch" crime-prevention program in an urban neighborhood

3. Classify the following goods and services as private goods, congestion goods, common-pool goods, toll goods, or pure public goods. In each case, indicate what the classification implies for how the good or service is most efficiently organized or financed. Which goods are best provided by private nonprofit organizations and which ones are not? Why?

    a. bagels

    b. the Internet

    c. major-league baseball

    d. protecting whales

    e. an open-air concert

4. A museum employs an "honor system" to charge visitors. In this system, visitors are asked (by a sign at the door) to put a specific fee into a locked box at the entrance. Use the ideas of transaction costs and free riding to compare the efficiency of such a system to each of the following alternatives:

    a. a conventional system in which payments are enforced through a toll collector or a controlled-access ticket machine

    b. a system that simply asks for donations

5. The board of a small volunteer-based nonprofit environmental advocacy organization is contemplating contracting out for its financial management services rather than hiring a permanent staff member or continuing to rely solely on volunteer effort. Identify and discuss the considerations that members of the board should weigh in this decision.

6. The director of the Association of Stamp-Collecting Clubs would like to induce member clubs to authorize more funding for lobbying against pending legislation that would reduce government support for the Postal Service. The director sees the legislation as a long-term threat to the members of the association. Member clubs agree in principle but seem indifferent to taking action and are more interested in getting the latest information on the new stamps that will be coming out this year. Analyze the director's concerns as a market-failure problem and make a recommendation about how to address the issue.

7. Modern medicine requires the supply of various bodily organs for transplantation. In what ways is the "market" for vital organs similar to the market for blood donations? In what ways is it different? What issues are involved in organizing this market, and what institutional arrangements seem preferable?

8. In what ways are the market-failure issues associated with nursing homes for the elderly similar to those associated with day care for children? How are they different? What policy recommendations would you make in these cases?

CHAPTER **10**

Cost-Benefit Analysis

WHAT IS COST-BENEFIT ANALYSIS?

The concept of market failure, as studied in Chapter 9, lies at the root of the most fundamental problem facing managers and policy makers in nonprofit and public-sector organizations: how to judge the performance of their organizations. In particular, if nonprofits and governmental organizations operate in areas where the market works poorly, then it is inappropriate for leaders of these organizations to use market-based criteria to gauge the success of their operations. If nonprofits and government deal with services characterized by externalities, public goods, informational problems, and the like, then profits will be an inappropriate measure of how well these organizations are performing.

Nonetheless, it is critically important for leaders of any kind of organization to be able to track performance and to have reference to some kind of "bottom line" that tells them how well or poorly, or how much or little good, their programs are doing. The genesis of cost-benefit analysis (CBA) was the quest by government managers to find such a "profit equivalent." Private nonprofit organizations have the same need as government agencies, since they too operate in circumstances characterized by informational asymmetries, externalities, and public goods. While private nonprofits must break even financially, their financial surpluses or profits are not appropriate measures of success. For a commercial business, profits may be seen as the overriding goal, and achievement of service and program goals may be seen as *instrumental* to making profits. For a private nonprofit organization, on the contrary, breaking even or running a modest financial surplus is instrumental to achieving program goals; in other words, breaking even is a necessary financial condition in order for the organization to operate, but it is *not* the bottom line.

With this in mind, we offer the following general definition of cost-benefit analysis:

> **Cost-benefit analysis is a framework for decision making about and evaluation of organizational programs, activities, and initiatives for public-sector and private nonprofit organizations operating in an environment of market failure. It is analogous to the profit criterion used for making decisions and evaluating performance in the commercial business sector, but it is based on social costs and benefits rather than market costs and benefits.**

Cost-benefit analysis integrates virtually all the lessons of economic analysis discussed in earlier chapters. As its definition indicates, CBA is needed to account for the various forms of failure—externalities, public goods, information deficiencies, and the like—in order to estimate the gains and losses that result from decisions in a nonmarket environment. CBA builds on the basic concept of economic efficiency but also attempts to address issues of equity and distribution in order to provide meaningful guidance to nonprofit organization decision makers in a social context. In studying CBA, we will revisit and extend familiar concepts, including opportunity cost, demand and supply functions, the aggregation of costs and benefits over time, marginal analysis, and other useful ideas that help us think through organizational decisions involving the allocation of valuable resources.

In itself, CBA is an imperfect methodology that suffers from a number of conceptual problems and a host of measurement difficulties. Estimating economic values for the arts, criminal justice, or public health is, àt best, an approximate exercise. Nonetheless, resource allocation decisions must be made, and CBA forces one to make explicit the underlying assumptions behind such decisions. This allows decision makers to identify their areas of agreement and disagreement and provides an empirical framework for resolving differences of opinion.

PRINCIPLES UNDERLYING COST-BENEFIT ANALYSIS

Whose values determine the "bottom line"? In the private for-profit sector, stockholder values dictate that the bottom line be profit. However, profit neglects the side effects of market processes (e.g., externalities, public goods) as well as the distribution of net benefits among different affected groups. By contrast, in the government sector, a set of consensus values—overall social costs and benefits affecting the entire citizenry, not just those individuals directly engaged in market transactions—ideally drive decision making. In the private nonprofit sector, values are reflected in organizational missions. A mission may be aligned with the idealized government mission of social consensus, but more commonly nonprofit organizations prefer to advance their own visions of the public good. Thus, CBA can facilitate decision making by organizations as varied as the National Association for the Advancement of Colored People, the Ku Klux Klan, the National Right to Life Organization, and Planned Parenthood. In each case, the organization would want to incorporate its own private notion of social good (beneficial demand) into its decisions rather than pretending to subscribe to a common notion of social costs and benefits. In this chapter, we will use CBA to refer to social goals and PCBA (private cost-benefit analysis) to refer to private notions of the public good.

In its simplest form, CBA implores the public or nonprofit sector decision maker to embrace the following logic:

For each alternative, compute the economic benefits and the economic costs incurred, irrespective of who benefits and who pays, and suitably discount these costs and benefits over time to reflect opportunity values. Subtract costs from benefits for each alternative and choose the alternative yielding the highest net benefits.

Note that we do not say that one should pick the project with the largest ratio of benefits to costs, a common misconception. For example, given the choice between a centralized soup kitchen and a mobile Meals on Wheels program, we might find that the soup kitchen costs $500 and yields $1,000 in benefits. Thus, it yields a net benefit of $500 and a benefit/cost ratio of 2.0. Suppose, now, that the Meals on Wheels program costs $600 and yields $1,150 in benefits. Its net benefit would be $550 but its benefit/cost ratio would be only 1.9. Although the centralized plan has a higher benefit/cost ratio, an organization would obtain greater net benefits from the Meals on Wheels program. This illustrates the general principle that benefit/cost ratios are unreliable guides to decision making.

Note also that the foregoing rule applies only to discrete choices where one alternative is selected from a relatively small set of alternatives. The rule is appropriate when one is deciding, for example, whether or not to build a facility of a specific size; it is inappropriate (indeed, impossible) to use where there is a continuous choice to be made, such as picking the size of a facility from a range of possibilities. For the combined choice of whether to build and, if so, at what size, CBA requires use of the logic for maximizing social benefit developed in Chapter 9:

> **Choose the facility size that equates marginal social benefit (*MSB*) and marginal social cost (*MSC*). If, at this size, the net benefit (benefits minus costs) is greater than the net benefit for the next best option, build the facility at this size. Otherwise, choose the alternative project.**

Finally, note that we have been considering choices from among a set of mutually exclusive alternatives. One cannot build a facility that is more than one size. One can buy either a mobile van or a building for distributing meals. When choosing among mutually exclusive alternatives, therefore, one should pick the alternative with the largest net benefit. If, however, one has the opportunity to choose a variety of projects simultaneously (e.g., a soup kitchen and a child immunization center), one should choose every alternative with positive net benefits. If one must choose from among a set of compatible (non-mutually exclusive) projects because of budgetary limitations, the situation is more complicated. Only in this case does the ratio of benefits to costs help to inform decision making through a more complex set of calculations. (For a more detailed examination of this issue, see Rosen, 1994.)

Like the profit criterion for a business operating in a competitive market environment, the foregoing rules are intended to maximize economic efficiency—that is, to put resources to their most highly valued uses. In principle, this is a desirable thing to do. In practice, however, the implementation of cost-benefit analysis runs up against some knotty problems, including:

- the special concern in the public and nonprofit sectors with the *distribution* of benefits and costs as well as the maximizing of total net benefits; and
- the difficulty of *measuring* benefits and costs in an environment of market failure.

Much of the deliberation over whether and how to apply cost-benefit analysis in the public and nonprofit contexts revolves around the resolution of these two issues.

THE ISSUE OF DISTRIBUTION

Cost-benefit analysis is based directly on the economist's notion of efficiency—putting economic resources to their most highly valued uses. In broadest terms, this notion appears to be uncontroversial. After all, everyone should be concerned about minimizing waste and making the best use of limited resources. However, cost-benefit analysis in its simplest form does not explicitly attend to the question of who gets what—only how much net value is produced altogether. If we are also concerned about questions of equity and fairness, then cost-benefit analysis, narrowly conceived, will not be sufficient for making important social judgments. Thus, economists have worked to incorporate assessments of distributional consequences into their cost-benefit analyses.

Recall that the concept of economic efficiency is based on the Pareto criterion (see Chapter 1). That is, an action is considered to be "Pareto preferred" over others if it makes some people better off (provides them with net benefits) without making anyone else worse off. In its pure form, this means a project or action only can be efficient if those who bear its costs also receive benefits equal to or exceeding those costs, *or if cost bearers are compensated* for any losses they incur. Practically speaking, the Pareto criterion is a very limiting concept, since it is the rare project or program that does not harm anyone economically or compensates all cost bearers completely for their losses. Thus, cost-benefit analysis compromises the pure notion of economic efficiency by employing a "potential Pareto" standard called the Kaldor-Hicks criterion, named after the two economists who formulated it:

A project or program is efficient if it produces benefits in excess of costs and if the beneficiaries could, in principle, compensate the cost bearers and still be better off.

The Kaldor-Hicks criterion is both the concept that makes cost-benefit analysis practical as an analytical tool widely applicable to situations where full compensation of cost bearers is unlikely as well as controversial as an overriding gauge of performance for an organization concerned with social issues. After all, if compensation of cost bearers does not actually take place, who is to say whether society as a whole is better off when some gain and some lose? How do we compare the welfare of one person with that of another? Is society really better off because I gain $20 while you lose only $10? Even in situations where no individual incurs a net loss, application of the cost-benefit principle is somewhat controversial because we may care about improving the lot of the least fortunate in society or making the distribution of society's wealth more equitable. Unadorned, cost-benefit analysis is not geared to take these considerations into account.

Why, then, should the nonprofit manager study cost-benefit analysis, and how can it help in guiding organizational decisions? First, it is important to appreciate that while cost-benefit calculations may not produce sufficient information with which to make socially relevant decisions, they do produce information necessary for gauging the efficiency of resource use. CBA allows one to identify ways of maximizing the size of the economic pie. While this does not guarantee that everyone gets a larger slice, it at least makes it a possibility. Therefore, CBA is a prerequisite to a broader analysis of conditions under which it is possible to redistribute winners' gains so that nobody loses. Combined with information on distributional implications, political considerations, ethical concerns, and other matters, cost-benefit analysis can produce more informed, better-considered decisions.

Second, the cost-benefit framework can be enhanced to highlight the distributional as well as the efficiency consequences of various courses of action. That is, we can calculate and display who gets what in a manner that, while it may not produce a bottom-line answer, at least produces the information we need to contemplate efficiency and equity concerns. In this way, we can accommodate the political and practical realities associated with the realization that benefit sharing does not accompany most social initiatives, and we can insert explicit judgments about distributional justice.

MEASURING COSTS AND BENEFITS

CBA is necessary because market prices fail to reflect social costs and benefits; this is also why CBA is hard to do. It is paradoxical that while many of the problems associated with applying cost-benefit analysis stem from difficulties in measuring benefits and costs in nonmarket situations, we employ CBA precisely because these variables are not easily measured. In a competitive market situation, the prices people pay for what they buy reflect the marginal economic value or benefit they attach to those goods and services, while the prices of inputs used to produce those goods and services are an accurate gauge of their marginal (opportunity) cost. Market equilibrium equates these two marginal values and hence maximizes net benefits. Thus, absent market failure, markets themselves perform the necessary calculations and yield the resulting prices as suitable indices for gauging the marginal values of actions taken. Not so in the situations of market failure in which nonprofits operate, where prices may not exist and those that do cannot necessarily be taken without modification as appropriate indicators of value. It is in these situations that CBA may be called on to do the work of the market by applying the generic definitions of benefit and cost and then searching for relevant data with which to estimate them.

Thus, study of CBA must begin with the basic definitions of benefit and cost, and proceed to ask how we apply these definitions when markets fail. We are already familiar with the definitions from earlier chapters:

The economic cost of a given action is the opportunity value of resources used, measured in terms of the value that could have been produced by employing those resources in their next best uses. This is the familiar concept of opportunity cost. If the resources committed to a given alternative are purchased through competitive markets, then market prices will be accurate estimates of marginal opportunity costs. If not, less direct ways must be found to estimate opportunity costs.

The economic benefit of a given action is the value of resources that people are willing to pay for that action. In a competitive market for private goods, the marginal benefit is represented by the height of the familiar market demand curve, which may be interpreted as consumers' willingness to pay for the next (marginal) unit of service.

In situations of market failure, however, the demand curve, if it can be estimated at all, does not fully capture the value that people assign to additional service; hence, other ways of estimating willingness to pay (WTP) must be employed. There are two general approaches to estimating marginal willingness to pay: *contingent valuation* and *hedonic valuation* (see Downing, 1984). Contingent valuations are derived from surveys in which people are asked to declare what they are willing to pay. Because answers to this hypothetical question may be contaminated by the information presented to the respondent, these values are said to be "contingent." The trick is to structure the survey in a way that minimizes the divergence between the contingent values and the true underlying values. Because survey answers can be used in CBA in the same way that prices observed in markets are used to represent WTP, they are sometimes called "shadow prices."

Shadow prices can also be estimated by hedonic methods. Goods and services that are not bought separately in competitive markets may be bought as part of a package sold competitively. For example, when one buys a house, one is buying not only a residence but also a location. Thus, housing services, local law-enforcement and fire-fighting capabilities, pollution levels in the area, convenience to work, and convenience to shopping are all part of a package purchase. Using statistical methods, one can sort out the portion of the price paid that represents WTP for each attribute related to location. By looking at variations in housing prices across neighborhoods with differing crime rates, one estimates the shadow price for a reduction in crime. Similarly, the variation in housing prices across neighborhoods with differing levels of pollution allows one to estimate the shadow price for environmental improvements. We can appreciate the idea of shadow prices by considering briefly some examples of cost and benefit estimation.

The direct costs of a program for training unemployed teenagers in job skills may include paid staff, supplies, and capital equipment. These resources are usually purchased in competitive markets. Consequently, the prices or wages attached to these resources are usually reliable estimates of their opportunity value. On the other hand, such a program may also utilize donated resources such as in-kind gifts or volunteer labor. Because these resources have no market price, their opportunity value must be estimated indirectly—for instance, by observing the prices of similar resources in related markets. Here, the wage rate for a given type of paid work could serve as an appropriate shadow price for volunteer labor doing the same kind of work. The cost of using donated pens and pencils could be estimated by observing the price of similar pens and pencils in the commercial marketplace. Shadow prices are generally good approximations, but one must be aware of complicating factors. For instance, if a volunteer were unable or unwilling to do similar work for a wage, the wage rate would not represent the opportunity cost of using that volunteer.

Even in the nonprofit setting, most of the costs of projects, programs, and other major initiatives are provided by direct market prices because most of the resources are purchased in competitive markets. Other costs, such as the opportunity cost of using volunteers, are gauged indirectly through market prices. In contrast, because many nonprofit services are not sold in competitive markets, are sold at subsidized prices or given away free, or are associated with external benefits, benefit measurement often requires creative approaches to estimation.

Consider briefly the benefit side of the program for developing job skills for unemployed teenagers. In the course of such a program, the trainees may produce marketable goods and services (e.g., basic automobile repairs or office work) that employers or consumers are willing to purchase at a competitive price. The value of such production can be estimated by market prices. However, the principal benefits of such a program may be the enhanced productivity of the teenagers in future years, perhaps a reduction in crime, and other benefits for which there are no direct markets. We can indirectly measure willingness to pay for their enhanced productivity by estimating the present value of the increase in expected lifetime earnings attributable to their training. Similarly, if we observe reductions in criminal behavior as a result of the program, we can then calculate the value of this effect by multiplying the estimated reduction in participant crimes by the average market value of the damages incurred per crime, approximating the losses avoided as a result of the program. Since avoiding these losses is something that members of society are (or should be) willing to pay for, such a calculation would also serve as an estimate of one component of program benefit.

DISTRIBUTION REVISITED

As we already noted, in its purest form CBA deals only with the aggregation of costs and benefits attributable to a particular activity or initiative. One reason for this is that once we ask who gets what, cost-benefit calculations can become significantly more complex. Nonetheless, the issue of distribution is important, if only because various programs or policies are explicitly designed to address the needs of certain groups, and we want to know whether those groups indeed benefit. Moreover, for political reasons, we are often interested in who bears the costs of programs. Finally, we may be concerned with how well the benefits and costs of a program are distributed according to some concept of fairness.

In the example of a training program for unemployed teenagers, we may be interested not only in the net difference between aggregate benefits and costs but also in how benefits and costs fall differentially on the teenagers who participate, the families of those teenagers, and the taxpayers who support the program. In a program designed to enhance the collection of Asian art in a local museum, we may be interested in the impact on art museum members, taxpayers, the scholarly arts community, the local community as a whole, and perhaps various income groups within the community. The particular subgroups that are important for distributional analysis will vary from case to case, but rarely do programmatic, political, practical, or philosophical considerations not warrant an examination of the distribution of benefits and costs.

The analysis of distributional questions requires the introduction of some additional concepts to describe how benefits and costs are disseminated within a complex economy. These include the concepts of *transfer payments* and *secondary effects*. We also need to discuss the idea of *distributional weights*.

Transfer Payments

Recalling our discussion in Chapter 6, we reintroduce the definition of the first of these terms. Transfer payments are shifts of resources from one group of individuals to another that do not involve a net change in the value of resources available to society as a whole. That is, no resources are used and no new value is created through the payments. Examples of transfer payments include taxes, welfare or income-maintenance payments to dependent families or individuals, unemployment benefits, excess profits, and payments for the use of resources that would otherwise not be utilized. In all these cases, there is a flow of resources (money) from one group to another; except for certain subtle effects, no new value is created and no value is used up. Thus, from the viewpoint of society, transfer payments are irrelevant to the calculation of net benefits and costs.

However, when we introduce distributional considerations, the picture changes significantly because, from the viewpoint of particular groups, transfer payments *do* represent net changes in resources. For example, while taxes may simply move resources from those taxed to those on whom tax revenues are expended, from the viewpoint of taxpayers, taxes represent a real cost, while from the viewpoint of those receiving payments from the public treasury, such payments represent real benefits. Similarly, payment of wages to someone who would otherwise be unemployed is a minimal real cost to society because the opportunity value of that labor is only the leisure value of that time. Nonetheless, from the viewpoint of the employer, this payment represents a substantial real cost, and for the worker it represents a significant real benefit.

In the same way, profits received above the level at which an employer is willing to remain in business represent a transfer payment from consumers to the producer. If greater competition were introduced, some of these profits would be competed away and consumers would recapture some of the surplus for themselves, with no net change in value. Such profits represent benefits to producers, costs to consumers, and transfers (zero net benefit or cost) for society as a whole.

To summarize, in CBA, if we are interested in the effects on subgroups, we need to analyze transfer payments. Two principles apply to the identification and measurement of transfer payments:

1. At the level of particular groups, transfer payments resemble conventional benefits and costs (i.e., resources they are willing to pay to acquire or resources that represent a loss of opportunity value when expended).
2. At the level of society as a whole, the sum of costs and benefits to particular groups attributable to transfer payments must add up to zero. That is, no net value or cost is created by transfer payments, only shifts from one group to another.

Secondary Effects

The next concept we need to understand if distribution is to be taken into account is the idea of secondary effects, which can be defined as follows: Secondary effects are the ripples created in the economy by changes in the prices of resources associated with the primary program activity under evaluation. Since the owners of resources may gain or lose from such ripples, these effects can be important in evaluating distributional consequences in a cost-benefit analysis. However, such effects are merely reflections of the primary benefits and costs to society as a whole. Adding these effects to the primary ones would be double counting.

To illustrate, suppose a university decides to build a new facility at some distant site. The value of that facility would be accounted for by the primary benefits to students and to beneficiaries of the research and other activities that would be carried on via new programs at the facility. Having the facility nearby might also make local businesses, government agencies, or other nonprofits more productive by giving them access to knowledge or information that was not previously accessible. These would all be primary benefits.

At the same time, land prices and wage rates might rise in the vicinity of the new facility because additional businesses would compete for nearby locations, providing gains to local landowners and workers. However, many of these gains might be offset by losses (lower land prices or wage rates) in other locations that experienced a reduction in economic activity as a result of a shift of interest to the new site. Moreover, the gains in land prices and wage rates at the new site would only be reflections or partial captures of the primary benefits by resource owners who capitalized on these gains by charging higher prices to the primary beneficiaries for land or labor. (Indeed, this is why hedonic analysis works.) These secondary benefits to local resource owners at the new site would not add to the primary benefits, just as the losses at other sites would not subtract from those benefits. Nevertheless, as a distributional matter, the secondary effects might be important if we were interested in how benefits and costs of the project affect different groups or communities. For that reason, we may wish to estimate secondary effects in some cases.

Distributional Weights

Distributional concerns can be formally introduced into CBA calculations by assigning distributional weights to benefits and costs to different population groups. Under this regime, one divides the population into a small number of distinct groups, calculates the net benefit enjoyed by each group, and then inflates or deflates this number to reflect the relative weight given to the group according to its social priority. For example, suppose an organization provides job training to teenage children and calculates that such training increases the present value of the lifetime earnings of each trainee by $100,000 more than the per-capita cost of the program. A training program conducted in a wealthy suburban area would presumably provide the same net benefits as a program in the inner city, but the organization would not regard the two programs as equally beneficial. Added earnings for those who would likely earn much on their own may be judged far less important than added earnings for those who are otherwise likely to earn little.

If the organization feels that gains to inner-city teens are twice as important as gains to suburbanites, it can compare per-person *weighted* net benefits of $66,666 for the suburban program (2/3 × $100,000) with *weighted* net benefits of $133,333 for the inner-city program (4/3 × $100,000). The fractions 2/3 and 4/3 are distribution weights that reflect the organization's view of distributional justice. In this example, the inner-city program will be more attractive as long as the inner-city weight is greater than the suburban weight. However, sometimes the precise values of the weights are more consequential. Suppose, instead, that the net benefits are $300,000 per student in the suburbs and only $100,000 per student in the inner city. In that case, the far more "productive" suburban program is rated better using the 2/3 and 4/3 weights ($200,000 vs. $133,333). Alternatively, the inner-city program is superior if the organization believes that benefits to inner-city youth are at least three times more important than benefits to their suburban counterparts.

Weights reflect answers to the ethical question, What net benefit to group A will exactly compensate for a $1 loss in net benefits to group B? Because it is difficult for anyone to answer this question precisely and confidently or to secure consensus on this within an organization, *sensitivity analysis* is needed. That is, the consequences of using various weights should be carefully considered. CBA can be illuminating by revealing the *critical values* for distribution weights that would shift favor from one program to another. Then, if all concerned can agree on how the proper weights are different from the critical values, a decision can be made in favor of one alternative or another.

Extending the above example, if the weight for suburbanites were 1/2 and the weight for inner-city youth were 3/2, then the two programs would be valued equally. If organizational decision makers agreed that inner-city youth benefits were worth at least three times those of suburban youths, then they could comfortably decide in favor of the inner-city program.

MORE ON MEASURING BENEFITS: CONSUMERS' SURPLUS AND PRODUCERS' SURPLUS

For many types of initiatives undertaken by public-sector or private non-profit organizations, a concept called *consumers' surplus* is useful for classifying and measuring benefits. The idea of consumers' surplus follows directly from the construct of the demand function. Recall that the level of the

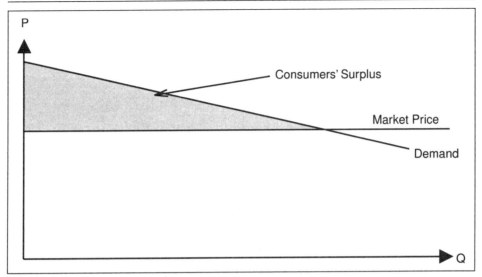

Figure 10.1 Consumers' Surplus

demand function may be interpreted as the amount consumers are willing to pay for the next unit of service. If that level of willingness to pay exceeds the price charged to the consumer, then the consumer experiences a "surplus." In the marketplace for a normal good or service offered at a given price, consumers will continue to purchase additional units as long as their willingness to pay exceeds the price. Thus, they will receive a (diminishing) amount of surplus with each succeeding unit they purchase, until the surplus diminishes to zero for the last purchased unit (see Figure 10.1). Any initiative that lowers the price will increase the consumers' surplus by providing consumers with additional benefits in two ways: by providing more surplus to those who would buy at the original price, and by providing surplus to consumers who purchase additional units because of the lower price.

Consider a project, represented in Figure 10.2, that lowers the cost of providing low-cost group meals for the elderly in a community center by replacing on-site preparation with volume purchase of frozen meals and installation of microwave ovens. In the figure, S_1 represents the supply function for the old technology and S_2 the supply function for the new one. D is the demand for meals, which remains the same assuming the quality of the meals under the two alternatives is equivalent. By introducing the new technology, the community center can offer a given volume of meals at a lower price. As a result, consumers benefit in two ways: (1) Those who would purchase Q_1 meals at the old price P_1 receive those meals at a lower price P_2 and hence experience an increase in surplus equal to rectangle 1 in the figure (Q_1 multiplied by the price reduction); (2) because the price has been reduced, $Q_2 - Q_1$ additional meals are purchased, presumably by new

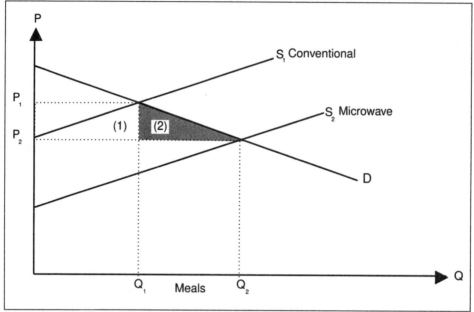

Figure 10.2 Change in Consumers' Surplus

consumers who now enjoy an additional component of consumer surplus (represented by the area of triangle 2 in the figure). The area of this triangle is $Q_2 - Q_1$ multiplied by the average amount $(P_1-P_2)/2$ by which the willingness to pay for the new units exceeds the new price P_2.

In a general sense, the foregoing analysis of consumers' surplus is a nice way of conceptualizing the two kinds of benefits derived from any new project or program that lowers the costs of providing a service and enables additional use. Additional surplus is produced (1) by increasing the margin by which benefits exceed costs for existing use, and (2) by permitting new use from which additional surplus is generated.

A symmetrical concept—*producers' surplus*—is useful when projects increase the demand for services rather than lowering the costs. This concept is illustrated in Figure 10.3. Producers' surplus represents the difference between the minimum amount of money sellers are willing to accept, at the margin, for their product or service (as represented by the supply curve) and the amount they actually receive. This amount is represented by the triangle in Figure 10.3A between the market price and the supply curve; this surplus derives from selling the inframarginal units at a market price higher than the price at which producers would have been willing to sell them. In Figure 10.3B, we see that a program that raises the demand for the good or service will lead to an increase in producers' surplus represented by the shaded strip. As for consumers' surplus, there are two components to this increase: rectangular area 1 represents the increase in producers' surplus resulting

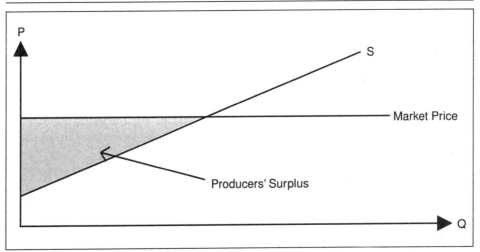

Figure 10.3A Producers' Surplus

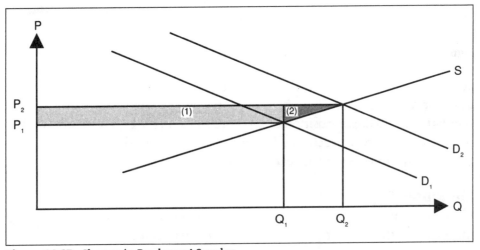

Figure 10.3B Change in Producers' Surplus

from the increased price received for units at the initial level of production, while triangular area 2 represents the additional producers' surplus received on new units sold after demand increases.

For complex projects where changes occur in both consumers' and producers' surpluses, benefits should reflect *total surplus* equal to the sum of both of these components.

CORRECTIONS TO MARKET PRICES

Frequently we observe market prices that appear to reflect the costs or benefits we seek to estimate. However, if such prices are not manifested in unfettered competitive markets, it may be appropriate to make certain

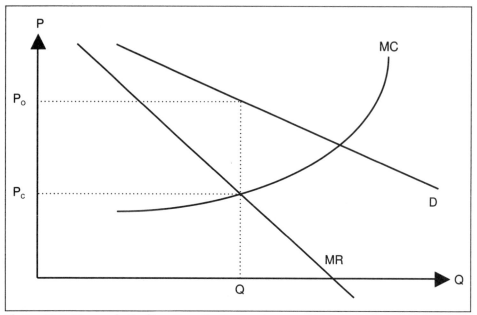

Figure 10.4 Monopoly Profit as Transfer Payment

corrections so that the prices more closely approximate actual opportunity costs or willingness to pay. Monopolistic conditions, externalities, price regulations, and the imposition of taxes are all factors that may distort market prices and require corrections. In particular, these conditions often reflect transfer payments as well as real resource use.

Monopoly Supply

If, as in Figure 10.4, a good or service is provided by a profit-maximizing monopolist, the market price of that service will not accurately reflect its opportunity cost. For example, suppose a nonprofit theater buys its stage lights from the only theater-lighting supplier in its region. The supplier sets the price in this monopolistic market by equating marginal revenue (MR) with marginal cost (MC). The resulting price (P_0) accounts for a substantial element of profit as well as cost. The extra profit is a transfer payment from consumers to producers, not a cost *per se*. The corrected price estimate (P_c), which deflates the price to account for the extra profit margin and reflects the marginal cost at the existing level of purchase (Q), is a more accurate reflection of the opportunity cost of expending the given resource.

Taxes

Often government imposes taxes on the sale of goods and services for general revenue-raising purposes rather than to correct any existing deficiency (externality) in the market price. Such taxes distort the price of the good or

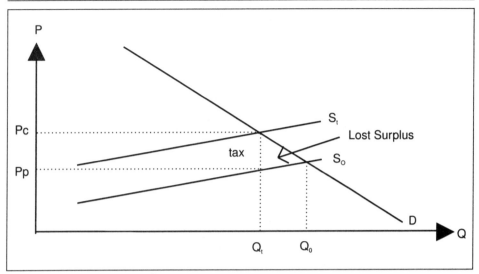

Figure 10.5 Taxes as Transfer Payment

service by making it more expensive than its opportunity cost alone would dictate. Moreover, the tax represents a transfer payment from the consumers and producers of a particular good or service to the government, or to whomever the government spends the money on. This situation is represented in Figure 10.5. Suppose a nonprofit day-care center purchases toys in a competitive market, but state laws do not exempt the organization from paying sales tax on these goods. The effect of the tax is to raise the supply curve for toys from S_0, where it would be without the tax, to S_t with the tax (the new supply curve seen from the viewpoint of consumers). The resulting consumer price P_c reflects both the tax, which is a transfer payment, and the opportunity cost of provision. This price is an accurate reflection of marginal social benefit (MSB) because consumers purchase up to the point where their marginal willingness to pay equals the price (including the tax). However, it is not an accurate reflection of marginal social cost (MSC). The producer price P_p, which subtracts out the tax, accurately reflects the marginal opportunity cost.

Finally, it is worthwhile observing here that the tax illustrated in Figure 10.5 also causes a loss of real economic value by reducing output from Q_0 to Q_t, thus causing a reduction of total (consumers' plus producers') surplus. This loss is represented by the small triangle between Q_0 and Q_t bounded above by the demand curve and below by the untaxed supply curve S_0.

Price Regulation

Sometimes prices in otherwise competitive markets are regulated in some manner by the government. One example of such a policy is the minimum

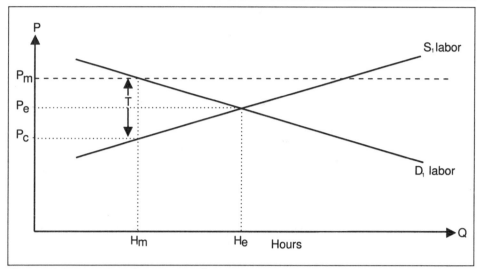

Figure 10.6 Wage Premium as Transfer Payment

wage law, which requires that employers not pay less than the prevailing minimum wage to paid employees. Figure 10.6 depicts the effect of such a law under conditions where the minimum wage is higher than the wage that would prevail under freely competitive conditions. In the figure, P_e is the equilibrium wage that would result if the supply and demand for hourly labor were allowed to equilibrate, while P_m is the minimum wage imposed by government regulation. At this wage, H_m is the hours actually worked, compared to the H_e hours that would be offered for work by employers if the market wage were allowed to find its own level. Note that P_m is not an accurate reflection of the opportunity cost of employing hourly labor. Rather, this wage reflects both a transfer payment T from employers to workers and an actual opportunity cost of labor represented by the corrected wage estimate P_c.

Externalities

Sometimes markets are operative but imperfect because they generate external benefits or costs that are not accounted for in the market price. In such cases, too, prices will not accurately reflect opportunity cost or willingness to pay and may require corrective estimates. For example, suppose a nonprofit organization buys its paper supplies from a profit-making concern that pollutes the air or water without paying for the environmental costs imposed by its activities. This situation is represented in Figure 10.7. The supply curve S_p for the industry fails to reflect the external cost of pollution; hence, the market price P_0 is lower than it would be if that cost were internalized into production decision making. A corrected price P_c would add the cost borne

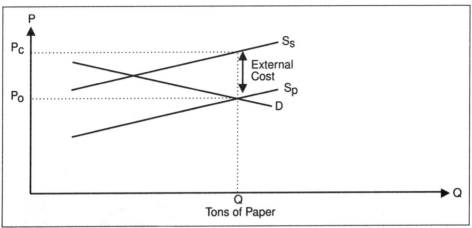

Figure 10.7 External Cost Associated with Pollution

by citizens affected by the degraded environment. This external cost component may be difficult to estimate, but it is a real opportunity cost that, if ignored, leads to inefficient decisions from a social point of view.

AN ACCOUNTING FRAMEWORK

Given the many dimensions and factors involved in a cost-benefit analysis, it is important to work within an organizing framework that incorporates all of those dimensions and factors into a structure useful for decision-making purposes. The basic dimensions we want to include in such an accounting framework are as follows:

Alternatives: What are the different projects or program options to be evaluated?

Costs: What are the different elements of opportunity cost that must be accounted for?

Benefits: What are the different elements of gain that must be considered?

Beneficiaries and cost bearers: Who are the different social groups that receive benefits and/or bear costs?

Transfer payments: What transfers of resources take place between beneficiary and cost-bearing groups?

Timing of costs, benefits, and transfers: What is the pattern of incidence of costs, benefits, and transfer payments over time?

Bottom lines: What is the net present value of benefits and costs to each group, and what is the net difference between benefits and costs for society as a whole as well as for each possible course of action?

We have already discussed most of these items in some detail. One consideration worth special attention is the *timing* of costs, benefits, and transfer payments, which can be very important to the outcome of a cost-benefit analysis. The costs of a new initiative are often concentrated in the near term, while benefits accrue over the long term, so that the choice of an appropriate discount rate may be critical to determining whether an alternative is efficient or not. (The method for adding up costs and benefits over time by calculating present values was discussed in Chapter 6.) Because the choice of discount rate can be critical, it makes sense to recalculate present values using several different discount rates within a reasonable range to see if the assessment of whether benefits exceed costs or vice versa is sensitive to the choice of this rate. This is an application of *sensitivity analysis* similar to our experimenting with different distributional weights on benefits and costs to different groups. More generally, applying sensitivity analysis is a good idea whenever estimates must be made of parameters that can critically affect conclusions based on cost-benefit calculations.

Table 10.1 is an example of a matrix format that brings together the relevant dimensions of CBA. This matrix is similar to that utilized in Long, Mallar, and Thornton's (1981) analysis of the Job Corps program. The important groups on which the program under assessment may have an impact are listed along the horizontal dimension. Along the vertical dimension, the matrix lists each type of benefit, cost, and transfer payment, calculated in present-value terms so that the effects of different patterns of incidence over time are taken into consideration. The bottom row adds together the benefits, costs, and transfers to yield the net effect of the alternative on each relevant group and on society as a whole. Three important attributes of this matrix should be understood:

1. Groups should be defined so that they don't overlap and together they add up to the total part of society affected by the program. For example, in a program aimed at teaching unemployed workers new job skills, the groups could be the workers, their families, and taxpayers (assuming the unemployed and those not in the labor force are unaffected). Where there is overlap among groups—for example, workers' families may include taxpayers—it is important not to double count benefits or costs. Together, the foregoing groups presumably account for all the important benefits, costs, and transfers, and they do not overlap significantly. (For cost-benefit analysis carried out from the narrower "private" perspective of a given organization [PCBA], the groups should add up to that portion of society encompassed by the organization's mission.)

TABLE 10.1
Cost-Benefit Matrix Framework

	Group 1	Group 2	Group 3	All Society
PV of Benefits				
Benefit a	+			+
Benefit b			+	+
Benefit c		+		+
PV of Costs				
Cost d		+		+
Cost e			+	+
Cost f			+	+
PV of Transfers				
Transfer g	+		–	0
Transfer h		–	+	0
PV of Net Benefits				
(a + b + c) – (d + e + f)	+	+ or –?	+ or –?	+ or –?

PV = present value

2. Net transfer payments to any particular group may be positive or negative, but the sum of transfers for society as a whole (i.e., across all the groups) must be zero as shown in the corresponding rows of the matrix.
3. Some benefits, costs, or transfers may be difficult to estimate in quantitative terms. However, they can be identified in the matrix and entered qualitatively by using + and – symbols to indicate the direction of effects. While these items cannot be included in the quantitative summations of the last row, they can be viewed as caveats to the quantitative calculations and as signaling what additional data would be useful for further analysis. (Note that although in Table 10.1 all entries are represented by + or – symbols, most of these would be replaced by quantitative estimates in any actual application.)

AN EXAMPLE OF THE COST-BENEFIT APPROACH

The utility of the accounting framework and the application of the cost-benefit approach are best appreciated through an illustration. Consider the following program undertaken by a hypothetical nonprofit organization:

In a collaborative effort supported by the Music Foundation of America, the Philharmonic Orchestra of Viola, Kansas, works with the Viola School District to identify children with outstanding musical talent who are from underprivileged families. The program offers special musical instruction provided by volunteer orchestra members. Instrument rentals and lessons are provided without charge to selected children. The foundation grant pays for staff support and instrument rentals. The grant also offers modest stipends to participating students and their families to ease the financial pressures they face while participating in the program. The school district makes its facilities available for practices and performances. Several times a year, the participating children give free public concerts. The program is scheduled to continue for a period of three years.

The first question we might ask is, Which groups stand to gain from this program and which groups bear the costs of the program? Consider the following:

- The selected children receive special instruction in music.
- Donors to the Music Foundation pay for staff and instrument costs and receive satisfaction from helping out.
- Orchestra members bear the costs of volunteering and receive the special satisfactions of giving.
- Citizens/taxpayers bear the costs of using the school facility. They also pay the policing and clean-up costs associated with the concerts. On the benefit side, citizens/taxpayers receive free concerts; they are spared antisocial behavior that might have occurred if the participating children were not in the program; and they may receive increased future tax payments from children who go on to pursue productive careers in music.

Thus, it appears sensible in this case to calculate benefits and costs for the following distinct groups:

participating children and families
music foundation donors
orchestra volunteers
citizens/taxpayers

Within reasonable approximations, this set meets the criteria of having groups with few members in common while being inclusive of all relevant beneficiaries and cost bearers. While there may be some overlap between taxpayers and orchestra volunteers, foundation donors, or the families of participating children, for analytical purposes this overlap may be small enough to be ignored. Note that we are also making no distinctions between the local citizens/taxpayers of Viola and citizens/taxpayers elsewhere. It is probably reasonable to assume that most of the citizen/taxpayer benefits and costs associated with the program are confined to Viola. Exceptions will occur when participating children grow up and move away, thereby imposing costs or benefits on other jurisdictions. If such effects are anticipated to be significant, then the analysis can be expanded to include an additional group of "citizen/taxpayers elsewhere."

To fill out the rest of the prototype matrix (see Table 10.1), we need to identify relevant costs, benefits, and transfer payments.

Costs are the most straightforward items to identify. They include:

salaries and benefits for project staff;

supplies and services (including office supplies, computers, photocopying, telephones, postage, etc.) used to carry out the program as well as the cost of providing and maintaining instruments;

facility costs, including maintenance and repair expenses, clean-up after concerts, and forgone benefits from potential alternative uses of the school space during hours when the program is in session;

volunteer time, reflected in the opportunity value of the time donated by orchestra members; and

user costs, including travel costs and the opportunity value of lost time borne by parents who carpool their children to practices and concerts.

Note two key characteristics of these items. First, they all represent real uses of resources, not just financial transactions. Second, the value of many of these items can be estimated by reference to observable market prices that are likely to be documented within printed budget reports. For instance, salaries and benefits, supplies and services, and maintenance and repair costs can be estimated in a straightforward fashion by referring to market prices and departmental budgets.

Estimating the value of other cost items may require greater investigation. For example, the opportunity value of using the facility may be approximated by the rental value of commercial space in the Viola area. However, it may be wise to modify this approach for several reasons:

- If it is known that the space would otherwise go unused, the opportunity value should be estimated as zero.
- If the space is known to have other demands on it and commands a specific use fee, the forgone revenue can be used as an estimate of the opportunity value.
- If the space would have been used for another school program, then the opportunity value should be an estimate of the benefits lost by not allowing the other school use to take place.

Evaluating the cost of time volunteered by orchestra members poses other challenges. It can be estimated as equal to the wage rate of the volunteers, assuming that they would be working for pay elsewhere if they were not volunteering. However, if this is known not to be the case, a lower estimate of the value of this resource would be appropriate.

Estimating user costs also requires some investigation. The out-of-pocket costs of driving children to and from the school or using a school bus for the same purpose may be estimated in a straightforward manner by multiplying distance traveled by appropriate mileage-cost estimates. In addition, parents may incur significant opportunity costs associated with the use of their time, especially if they must take time off from work to carpool their children. (On the other hand, parents might have to take care of their kids at home if they weren't at practice.) In addition, selected children may incur opportunity costs as a result of participating in the program. Specifically, some of these children may have to forgo working at part-time jobs or pass up team sports or other school-related activities in order to participate in the music program. In the former case, the wages they would have earned can be used to estimate the opportunity cost. In the latter case, an estimate of the benefit forgone as a result of not participating in the alternative activity is the appropriate measure.

Note that all of the foregoing costs are incurred on a regular basis over the three years of the program. The present value of these costs can be estimated in the conventional way by discounting over the three-year period.

Benefits are not as easily identified or estimated as costs. In this case, we have the following benefit items:

Direct benefits to participants can be of two kinds. Some of the children may go on to become professional musicians; hence, the program potentially increases their future economic welfare. Many of the children will also be able to enjoy music to a greater degree as a result of the program, whether or not they pursue music as a career.

Benefits of satisfaction accrue to donors and volunteers as a result of their support of the program.

Benefits of enjoyment accrue to the citizens of Viola who take advantage of the free concerts.

Social benefits accrue to citizens insofar as they avoid potential antisocial behavior, since children are engaged in a constructive cultural experience rather than left on their own to get into trouble.

Unlike its costs, most of the program's benefits are difficult to estimate by simply observing salient market prices. Some of its benefits may be not be estimable at all in quantitative terms; in other cases, however, we can obtain approximate estimates by asking the basic question, What should the beneficiaries be willing to pay for these benefits?

In the case of *participant benefits*, we might try to estimate how many of the children will go on to professional music careers and what their earnings will be compared to an estimate of what they would earn otherwise. For example, we might assume the children would earn an average blue-collar salary if they did not become musicians. The present value of future earned income above (or below) what would otherwise be earned would be an estimate of what the participants should be willing to pay to participate in the program. This estimate would be constructed from existing market data on the wages of people in music-related careers compared to the alternative baseline career.

Another participant benefit might be the *consumption value* of enjoying music to a greater degree as a result of taking part in the program. This benefit would be difficult to estimate in quantitative terms but could be identified qualitatively as a benefit of the program. Alternatively, graduates of similar programs could be asked to assign a value to this consumption through a contingent valuation survey.

Benefits to donors and volunteers would also be difficult to estimate quantitatively. Some volunteers might obtain valuable training that would enable them to earn extra income later on as music teachers. Others might derive benefits from social contacts they made in the program. These contacts might have economic value if, at a later date, a volunteer decided to pursue a political career or went into business providing music lessons or selling musical instruments. In such cases, the value of additional future income can serve as a partial estimate of value to volunteers. Because the transactions are voluntary, we know that these benefits exceed the amount donated as well as the value of forgone time. Contingent valuation techniques would also be useful here.

The *benefits to citizens/taxpayers* of free concerts might be estimated by noting the prices of tickets to similar events and assuming that these prices are roughly equivalent to what citizens/taxpayers would be willing to pay for the free concerts, were they so charged.

The *social benefits* of avoiding antisocial behavior might be estimated by determining how many of the participating children would have gotten into various kinds of difficulty (crime, drug abuse, etc.) and the costs or damages associated with such behavior. If pursued in detail, this can be a complex matter involving property damage, personal injury, loss of life, and welfare and criminal justice system costs. In our example, assuming that social benefits are not a major program effect, rough estimates of the costs of crimes or other averted incidents would be sufficient.

Unlike its costs, several of the program's benefits have a pattern of incidence over time that extends well beyond its three-year operational framework. Immediate donor and volunteer satisfactions as well as enjoyment of the free concerts are confined to the three-year period. However, participant benefits such as enhanced future income and increased enjoyment of music, career-related benefits to volunteers, and the social benefits of antisocial behavior averted may extend over long periods of time (the lifetimes of the beneficiaries, in some cases). Clearly, then, the stream of future benefits must be appropriately discounted to estimate present values in order to be comparable with the cost estimates.

Transfer payments are relatively unimportant in this example because virtually all resource transactions (payments) are associated with consumption of real resources or creation of new economic value. There are two exceptions:

- The stipends to participating students and families represent a transfer from the foundation donors to the participants.
- Any incremental income-tax payments resulting from the additional future income earned by program participants represent transfers from participants to citizens/taxpayers.

Like benefits and costs, transfer payments must be discounted over time to estimate present values, in order to ensure comparability. Note that the stipends are paid over the three-year time frame of the program, while the additional income-tax payments would likely take place far (10 or more years) into the future.

The scope of this book does not permit detailed calculations of all estimated items in the cost-benefit matrix. However, Table 10.2 gives an idea of which items may be estimable in quantitative terms, which items can be identified simply in terms of direction and incidence on particular groups, and what the magnitudes of the quantifiable benefits and costs might look like. A few explanatory notes are needed here in order to understand the numbers in the table:

- A nominal discount rate of 5 percent is assumed.
- The costs of salaries, benefits, services, and supplies are assumed to be specified in the project budget at the level of $50,000 per year for salaries and benefits and $10,000 per year for services and supplies. The table shows the present values of these numbers, calculated over the three-year period of the program.
- The facility cost is approximated by the rental value of equivalent space in commercial buildings nearby. This is estimated at $500 per month, or $6,000 per year. The present value given in the table is calculated over the three-year period of the program.
- The cost of orchestra members' volunteer time is estimated by assuming that these individuals would otherwise be giving music lessons at $20 per hour. If five volunteers each work two hours per week over a 40-week period per year, the total annual cost is $8,000. The present value of this figure, calculated over the three years of the program, is shown in the table.
- User costs are estimated by assuming that, in order to transport their children to and from the program, the parents of the 20 participating children drive 10 miles per week at 20 cents per mile over a 40-week period. This totals $1,600 per year. The table shows the discounted present value of this figure over the three-year period of the program.
- The opportunity costs of the time children spend in the program and the time parents spend transporting and assisting their children are shown to be positive but difficult to estimate based on existing data.
- Benefits to participating children are estimated by assuming that five of the 20 participating children go on to music-related careers that they would not have otherwise pursued. (This estimate might come from an initial assessment of the talents and motivations of the participants.) It is further assumed that in such careers these participants will earn approximately $10,000 more per year during their 30-year careers, beginning 10 years after the program starts, then they otherwise would have. The present value of this increment over the lifetimes of the participants is shown in the table.

TABLE 10.2
Benefits and Costs: Viola Music Program
(5% discount rate)

	Participants	Donors	Volunteers	Other Citizens	All Society
Costs					
Salaries and benefits		$136,162			$136,612
Supplies and services		$27,232			$27,232
Facility use				$16,339	$16,339
Volunteer time			$21,786		$21,786
User cost	$4,357				$4,357
Opportunity cost of time	+				+
Benefits					
Participant income	$471,868				$471,868
Concerts				$8,170	$8,170
Social benefit				$153,725	$153,725
Enjoyment	+				+
Satisfaction		+	+		+
Transfers					
Stipends	$10,893	($10,893)			$0
Tax payments	($94,374)			$94,374	$0
Total Benefit	$482,761	$0	$0	$256,269	$633,763
Total Cost	$98,731	$152,501	$21,786	$16,339	$205,876
Net Benefit	$384,030	($152,501)	($21,786)	$239,930	$427,887
Net Qualitative Benefit	+ or –?	+	+		+ or –?

- The benefits to participants of enjoying music to a greater degree as a result of the program are shown to be positive but not quantifiable here.
- The benefits of satisfaction for orchestra volunteers and for foundation donors are also shown to be positive but not quantifiable here.
- The benefits to citizens who enjoy the free concerts are estimated by assuming that there are three concerts per year, each attended by 200 people, and that these attendees would, if necessary, be willing to pay $5 each, the minimum cost of concerts given elsewhere in town. The present value of this total annual benefit of $3,000, discounted over the three years of the program, is shown in the table.

- The social benefits of the program are estimated by assuming (again based on initial assessments of participants) that one child is diverted from a life of crime and drug abuse because of the program. The value of this benefit is estimated by assuming that $10,000 per year is saved in treatment and damage costs over the next 30 years of that child's life. The discounted present value of that figure is shown in the table.

- Stipends to children and their families are assumed to be $200 per family, or $4,000 per year, for the families of the 20 participating children. The present value of this figure over the three-year period of the program is shown in the table as a transfer payment between donors and families.

- Additional tax payments by participants are calculated by assuming that the additional income earned by the five students who go on to music-related careers is taxed at the rate of 20 percent. Thus, a total of $10,000 per year represents transfer payments between participants and the rest of society. The present value of this figure over the 30-year earning period of the participants, beginning 10 years after the program begins, is shown in the table.

Given the foregoing estimates, one can see that on the basis of quantifiable costs and benefits, the program benefits exceed program costs by a margin of more than $400,000 in present-value terms, not counting intangible benefits and costs that have not been quantified. Hence, it seems reasonable to characterize the program as efficient according to the criterion of cost-benefit analysis. In addition to this overall assessment, it may be observed that certain groups, specifically the participants and other citizens, benefit on balance, while other groups, such as the donors and volunteers, bear the principal costs. However, since donations and volunteering are voluntary, it must be true that the (intangible) benefits to these groups exceed the costs they bear.

In addition to our "best-guess" estimate of benefits and costs, it is advisable to carry out sensitivity analyses to assess the dependence of the conclusions on the particular assumptions made in the calculations. In view of the different time streams of benefits and costs, this is especially important with respect to the choice of discount rate. Table 10.3 shows the results of alternative calculations using different discount rates. One can see that the results are somewhat sensitive to the choice of discount rate. At a rate of 10 percent, quantified benefits still exceed quantified costs by more than $95,000, but this represents a fourfold reduction in the net-benefit estimate

TABLE 10.3
Sensitivity of Net Benefits to Discount Rate
(Quantified Benefits less Costs)

	Participants	Donors	Volunteers	Other Citizens	All Society
Discount rate					
5%	$384,030	($152,501)	($21,786)	$239,930	$427,887
10%	$151,347	($139,265)	($19,895)	$123,154	$95,447
15%	$70,400	($127,860)	($18,266)	$75,041	($18,951)

over the calculation at 5 percent because, in general, benefits accrue farther into the future than costs. Note that at a rate of 15 percent, the present value of costs exceeds that of benefits. If we were to neglect intangibles, the project would be considered inefficient if 15 percent were taken as the correct opportunity cost of capital (interest rate) in the economic environment in which the Viola program operates.

It is also interesting to observe the effect of changes in the discount rate on the distribution of benefits and costs. Note that, as the rate rises, the beneficiaries (participants and citizens/taxpayers) are most adversely affected: their benefits shrink dramatically while the costs borne by donors and volunteers do not shrink significantly. In the case of a 15-percent rate, the program might thus be justified in terms of its distributional consequences (taking resources from wealthier donors and volunteers and creating benefits for less wealthy participants and average citizens) but not necessarily in terms of creating net economic value (depending on what one assumes about the non-quantified benefits).

SUMMARY

Cost-benefit analysis brings together a variety of concepts that we have studied in earlier chapters. Analysis of costs is grounded in the idea of lost opportunity value, while benefits reflect the idea of consumers' (beneficiaries') willingness to pay at the margin. While cost-benefit analysis serves to analyze economic efficiency where markets fail, it also depends on our ability to take signals from existing markets and to make corrections for market failures in order to make useful estimates. Since the time sequences of costs and benefits frequently differ from one another, CBA also utilizes the concept of present value in order to allow us to make proper comparisons of benefits and costs incurred at different points in time. In addition, CBA provides clarity on the question of "who gets what" and offers a way to analyze the distributional as well as efficiency consequences of programmatic and policy decisions.

Taken in the context of other information on the political, organizational, and social consequences of decisions, CBA can provide the nonprofit manager with a powerful way of thinking through important decisions that have significant resource consequences. For the nonprofit manager devoted to a social mission, CBA is the rough equivalent of an analysis of returns on investment.

REFERENCES

Apgar, William C., and H. James Brown. *Microeconomics and Public Policy*. Glenview, Ill.: Scott, Foresman, 1987.

Downing, Paul B. *Environmental Economics and Policy*. Boston: Little, Brown, 1984.

Gramlich, Edward M. *Benefit-Cost Analysis of Government Programs*. Englewood Cliffs, N.J.: Prentice Hall, 1981.

Long, David A., Charles D. Mallar, and Craig V. D. Thornton. "Evaluating the Benefits and Costs of the Job Corps." *Journal of Policy Analysis and Management*, 1:1, 1981, pp. 55–76.

Rosen, Harvey S. *Public Finance* (4th ed.). Homewood, Ill.: Irwin Publishers, 1994.

EXERCISES

For each of the two cases presented here, answer the following questions:

- What are the benefits?
- What are the costs?
- How can the benefits and costs be estimated using observable data?
- What is the timing of benefits and costs? How sensitive is the calculation of present values likely to be to the assumed discount rate?
- Who are the affected groups? What benefits and costs accrue to each group?
- What are the important transfers and secondary effects among these groups?

Construct a matrix for adding up the benefits and costs and identifying the distribution of benefits and costs among affected groups.

Case 1: Flu Prevention

A community foundation is considering whether to support an influenza prevention program that would inoculate vulnerable groups (young children, the elderly) in the region against the expected outbreak of the Liechtenstein flu this winter. The program involves publicizing the availability of flu shots and reimbursing doctors and clinics at a fixed price for the flu shots they administer to qualified recipients.

Case 2: Upward Bound Program

The Winding Creek School District is a low-income community concerned with the success of its student population. It is considering undertaking an Upward Bound Program that would send underprivileged high school students to a special college preparatory course in order to increase their chances of getting into, and succeeding in, college. The program would be paid for with tax dollars and a grant from the local community foundation and would be administered by a local private nonprofit school that specializes in compensatory college preparatory work. The program would use volunteer tutors from the community as well as paid staff and teachers.

CHAPTER 11

Concluding Thoughts

The manager of a nonprofit organization is a generalist who must be aware of all the special functions and activities of his or her organization—marketing, finance, human resources, legal issues, and the like. While not an expert in most of these areas, the manager must be sufficiently familiar with them to communicate effectively with experts and specialists, to evaluate what they are saying, and to work productively with them. The nonprofit manager need not, for example, be an accountant in order to deal effectively with the issues of financial development and control, or an attorney in order to deal with statutory requirements or legal challenges. But he or she does need to have a general sense of accounting and legal principles, as well as of how accountants and lawyers think, in order to know when to consult them, and in order to evaluate and act on their advice.

The case for understanding economic principles, as developed in this book, is similar. Our purpose has not been to turn nonprofit managers into economists. That would be impossible and perhaps unfortunate (although economists aren't really such bad folk once you get to know them). As the perceptive reader will have observed, the application of the methods of economic analysis to the problems and issues affecting nonprofit organizations can be complex and highly technical, fraught with nuance, and sometimes require mathematical agility and sophisticated analysis of data. Nonetheless, the ability to speak the economist's language and to frame and articulate issues in economic terms allows the nonprofit manager to understand how and when an economic consultant could help and to place the consultant's advice into proper overall perspective.

Still, this book would be of limited (and self-serving) value if all it did was help nonprofit managers determine when and how to employ the services of economists. The larger contribution it makes (we hope) is to argue that the basic concepts economists use to analyze issues involving the allocation of valuable resources are essentially intuitive and that, with some study, managers who are not economists can use these concepts to think about the problems and decisions they face. If the lay reader comes away from this book with a basic understanding of opportunity costs, how to think at the margin, the nature of demand and supply and how these forces interact within different market contexts, how changes in market parameters such as taxes or subsidies influence the resource decisions of nonprofit organizations, and how cost-benefit analysis can help structure programmatic decisions when market analysis alone is inadequate, then this book will have made a contribution. For, if such is the case, the reader/manager will have considerably enhanced his or her intellectual toolkit for dealing with the many challenges involved in managing nonprofit organizations.

To illustrate this point more dramatically, let us return to the thirteen short vignettes with which we opened in Chapter 1. How can the concepts developed in this book help the managers of these various hypothetical nonprofit organizations structure their thinking so as to effectively address the particular issues they face? This discussion will be suggestive, not definitive, and we hope the reader will be stimulated to elaborate on and extend what we say here.

ANALYZING THE VIGNETTES

A community agency for the elderly runs a day-care program and a Meals on Wheels program. How should it allocate its limited staff and budget between the two programs?

The manager of this organization needs to think at the margin. How many additional meals can be served by shifting a staff position from the day-care program to the Meals on Wheels program, and what will be the loss in terms of output in the day-care program? What values can be attached to these changes in outputs at the margin? Is marginal revenue the appropriate measure of value, or should the changes in outputs be gauged in terms of a more comprehensive measure of social benefits for each service? Thus, the manager must ask what the organization's objectives are before he or she can make the appropriate trade-offs.

Having identified the appropriate measures of value, our manager is left with a classic case of equating the marginal contributions of a given input resource in different uses. Following the principles studied in Chapter 5, the manager should shift staff resources between the two services until the marginal benefits produced in each are equal. The same idea would apply to 'other budgeted input resources, such as supplies or equipment, that may be allocated to one service or the other.

It is also possible that the manager sees the two services as addressing different objectives. Meals on Wheels might be a "cash cow" producing profits that can be used to subsidize the day-care program. The objective of the day-care program might be to expand service as much as possible under the assumption that social benefits, although hard to measure, justify maximum output. In this case, the manager will want to allocate resources to Meals on Wheels to the point that achieves maximum profit (where marginal revenue equals marginal cost). Once the maximum profit is in hand, this surplus may be allocated to day care so that staff and other resources can be deployed to maximize the output of that service. Inputs to day care would again be determined by analysis at the margin: staff and other factors of production should be chosen so that the last dollar spent on each input makes the same contribution to output.

A relief agency receives a grant for planning a program to help refugees. Should it add a staff member or buy a computer with these funds?

The question here is, Which of these inputs will make the larger marginal contribution to the organization's output? If assisting refugees is the output, then the question is, Which input will enable the agency to design and implement a system of assistance in a timelier and more effective way? Adding another staff member might move current planning efforts along faster and allow implementation of refugee services at an earlier date. Adding a computer might delay planning initially as new methods and procedures are learned by existing staff, but in the longer term the computer might allow the staff to design a better system or to run it more efficiently.

These considerations suggest that ideas about evaluating costs and benefits over time, as studied in Chapters 6 and 10, should be brought into play. The time profiles of the benefits and costs of each alternative need to be articulated and compared, and the manager needs to consider the appropriate discount rate (prevailing interest rate) for comparing the value of benefits and costs from one year to the next. With these considerations in mind, the manager can calculate the present value of the benefits and costs of each alternative and thus evaluate whether it is important to get the system up and running sooner or implement a potentially better system later on.

A private college wishes to raise money to build a new wing for its library. Should it undertake a direct-mail campaign, seek funds through personal solicitation, or use some combination of both? How much money should the college invest in these fund-raising efforts?

Fund raising is a component of nonprofit operations that has a profit-making objective. Thus, the college's president and trustees can look at this issue as a traditional business problem. What combination of the alternatives will yield the most net revenue for the college? As we saw in Chapter 5, the issue may be thought of as having two parts. Of the budget allocated to fund raising for the library, how much should be allocated to direct mail and how much to personal solicitation? Here the manager can apply the principle of equating the marginal revenue contributions of the last dollar allocated to each method. Next one can ask, How large should the total fund-raising budget be? If the college seeks a maximum return on its solicitation, then the budget should be expanded until a dollar more yields only a dollar in return.

Fund-raising campaigns have additional nuances that the college may wish to consider. For example, direct mail may yield results faster than personal solicitation, but over time personal solicitation may yield more money. The two methods may also have different donor-retention rates, and these could affect giving for many years to come. Thus, the college leaders must also ask themselves about the appropriate discount rate. If the personal solicitation approach takes too much time, for example, it could jeopardize the financing of the library project. Again, the time streams of all revenues and costs must be understood and properly aggregated according to the present-value principle before an efficient decision can be reached.

A church runs a popular adult-education program that is losing money. Should the church expand or contract that program?

This issue may be addressed at several levels using ideas from Chapters 4 through 8. First, following the thinking laid out in Chapter 7, the program administrator could ask what kind of market the program operates within. If it is perfectly competitive, then the prevailing price will be given and the question will be how much to offer at that price. Alternatively, if the church has been operating below its demand curve, it may be possible to raise prices without losing customers. Finally, if the church has monopoly power, then price and quantity are adjustable and the question becomes what marginal (net) revenue is brought in or lost by expanding or contracting service, compared to the marginal cost of doing so.

Given an understanding of the market environment, one can ask whether the church, within its existing capacity, has simply not offered enough service, or has offered too much. If expanding service contributes more revenue than it costs, then the program should be expanded; if contracting saves more costs than it loses in revenue, then the program should be contracted. This marginal adjustment process can help guide the church administrator in finding the right level in the short run.

However, more may be at stake here than short-run marginal adjustments. The church administrator should take note of the shutdown principle discussed in Chapters 4 and 7. If, after adjusting production to the point where marginal revenue equals marginal cost, the agency is still losing money, the administrator must determine whether it is best to close down entirely. As we have seen, the answer depends on whether maintaining operations will allow the organization to cover variable costs and make some contribution toward fixed costs. In this calculation, one should neglect fixed revenues. However, one must also account for any decrease in donations that would result from cessation of a valued program.

Finally, the foregoing issue should engage the administrator in thinking about both long-run and short-run operations. It may be that the church is operating at an inefficient scale because, in the short run, its facility size is too small or too large. So, too, changes in government policy may affect the demand for adult-education services. Thus, the adminstrator should think about what the long-run equilibrium of the market is likely to be and whether adjustments in reaching the long run promise to make the program solvent.

A museum sells art reproductions in its gift shop. At what quality and price should these items be offered for sale?

The sale of art reproductions by a museum may have dual objectives— to generate profits that can be used to support the operations of the institution and to promote art appreciation through the dissemination of knowledge about cultural treasures. To the extent that the latter is considered an important objective for the art-reproductions program, the museum may face complex trade-offs between the two objectives in choosing the best price/quality combination. For example, assuming the museum has some monopoly power, a profit-maximizing objective would lead to a lower quantity of production (less dissemination) than an objective to maximize output or to maximize the net social benefits of the reproductions. Moreover, the best quality level for maximizing profits may be different from the quality level that best represents the art as a cultural treasure or allows for its wide dissemination.

One way to conceptualize this situation is to assume that the purpose of the reproduction program is essentially to generate profits for the museum and that such profits may then be used to subsidize other aspects of its operations. (Such profits could even be used to provide discounts for purchases of high-quality reproductions!) From this point of view, the museum needs to find the level of quality that maximizes its profits, assuming that it will price the reproductions according to the profit-maximizing rule ($MR = MC$). Each possible level of quality will be associated with a different demand curve, hence a different marginal revenue function, and, of course, a different cost function. In other words, higher quality will increase cost, but it may also increase the level of demand. In addition, if a quality "niche" can be found that increases the museum's monopoly power, that will further enhance the museum's ability to generate profits. Thus, what the museum needs to do is to estimate maximum profit at different quality levels and then choose the most remunerative quality level.

In short, the museum manager should make good use of the market-pricing principles discussed in Chapters 4 and 7 as well as the strategies of niche pricing and cross-subsidization introduced in Chapter 8.

A community foundation receives a major gift from a local benefactor. How should it invest the funds?

The answer to this seemingly simple, straightforward question can be quite complex in practice and often requires consultation of a professional investment manager. If the funds are used for endowment, for example, the foundation manager must assess how much risk he or she is willing to bear and how much growth in purchasing power he or she hopes to achieve over time. This, in turn, depends on the time perspective of the foundation. If it plans to be around for a long time, it can tolerate substantial risk in exchange for greater long-term growth. If its purpose is to address an immediate issue or problem and then go out of business, it may be more interested in putting its funds into investments that minimize the risk of short-term fluctuations. (See Salamon, 1992 and 1993, for a discussion of foundation investment principles and behaviors.)

The analysis of economic decisions under risk and uncertainty is an advanced topic that we have not addressed in this book. However, we have touched on several principles that would help the foundation manager think through his or her choices in this situation. The first question to ask is, For what purpose has the donor given the funds? Ultimately, funds will be spent for a programmatic purpose, so investment of the funds should be contingent on how best to meet those purposes over time. Thus, a useful way to conceptualize the problem is to think of it as an exercise in generating benefits and costs over time, as we did in Chapters 6 and 10.

Consider two extremes: One way to use the funds is to spend them on a program that generates an immediate stream of benefits. But once the funds are used up, the benefits will cease. At the other extreme, suppose all the funds are put into an endowment, a portion of the returns on the endowment is reinvested to maintain the purchasing power of the endowment at a constant level over time, and the rest of the returns are spent on new programs of interest to the donor. This alternative would generate a much lower level of benefits (and costs) in the early years, but net benefits would continue indefinitely over time.

The choice between the two alternatives depends on many factors, not the least of which is the interest rate selected to discount future benefits and costs. But the choice will also depend on the relative impacts of smaller and larger programs. Making a large early investment in certain programs, such as research into a communicable disease, might produce a cure whose benefits endured long after the funds were gone. On the other hand, funding of a program that required continuous renewal—say, maintenance of public recreation facilities—might best be allocated evenly over time, with funds invested in a manner that maintained the capital for such investment.

A small hospital wishes to provide home health-care services. Should it do so on its own or in partnership with other hospitals?

The resolution of this issue depends on the hospital's assessment of the market structure for home health-care services and on its own objective for offering this service.

Suppose the hospital's motivation is to make profits that can help finance the other services it offers. If there are economies of scale (declining long-run marginal costs) in home health-care services over the foreseeable range of demand so that the market could be dominated by a single provider, then the hospital must determine whether it has a chance to become that monopoly provider or run the risk of being crowded out by a more efficient and/or better-positioned provider.

If the latter is likely, then it would be advisable for the hospital to join a partnership arrangement instead, assuming that the partnership would be able to monopolize the market and that the hospital would have a share. This would be especially advisable if there were complementarities between the hospital and its potential partners such that the coalition could provide home health-care service at a lower cost than other providers. If one provider had an especially expert staff and another had state-of-the-art information technology, the combination might be more efficient than either partner acting alone or than any potential competitor. Finally, if the transaction costs associated with negotiating the arrangement were lower than the fixed costs the nonprofit would have to incur in order to enter the market alone, this would also weigh in favor of entering a partnership.

If the market is perfectly competitive, or contestable in the long run, the hospital would want to weigh short-run profits against the costs of setting up shop. In this case, the hospital might decide not to enter the market, or to do so alone if short-run profits were high, or to do so in partnership if a deal could be worked out that allowed the hospital's share of short-run profits to exceed its share of set-up costs.

Suppose, however, that the hospital wants to offer home health-care services as a convenience to its patients and at a reasonable price without necessarily making a profit on those services. If the home health-care market is perfectly competitive, the hospital may just as well leave supply to other providers, since in the long run the cost to patients will be the same whether the hospital provides the services or refers its patients to other providers. However, if the home health-care market is monopolistic, the hospital should consider either providing its own services as a monopoly or becoming part of a monopoly partnership. In this case, the hospital could use some of its monopoly profits to offset the cost of home care and keep prices low for those patients needing it.

A further consideration in this situation is the cost of negotiating a partnership arrangement and participating in its production of services. If transaction costs are high and coordinated production is not as efficient as that of a single monopolist (because of coordination problems or the inability of partners to consolidate operations into a single efficient mode), then the partnership may not win the competition to become a monopoly provider. In this instance, the hospital is better advised to go it alone or to leave the market to another monopolist provider. Alternatively, potential economies of complementarity and the fixed costs of entering the market alone may favor the competitive advantage of a partnership.

Finally, suppose the hospital's competitor is an existing for-profit monopolist provider. What leverage might the hospital have for securing home health care for its patients at the best possible price? If entry barriers are not too high and the hospital can mobilize charitable revenues to subsidize the cost of its services, it might use this leverage to negotiate a good price in lieu of entering the competition. Alternatively, it might actually enter the home health-care market at a price below that which the for-profit could sustain in order to wrest the monopoly from the for-profit provider or induce it to negotiate a partnership arrangement or a lower price for consumers.

ZIGGY © ZIGGY AND FRIENDS, INC. Distributed by Universal Press Syndicate.
Reprinted with permission. All rights reserved.

An orchestra requires major repairs to its concert hall. Should it dip into its endowment to undertake these repairs?

In this situation, much depends on the seriousness of the conditions requiring repair as well as the alternatives for financing the repairs. Suppose the endowment funds are the only available source for financing the repairs. In this case, the orchestra managers must ask, What is the opportunity cost of using these funds, and what benefits are produced by spending the funds on the repairs? The opportunity costs would involve lost investment returns on the endowment funds, a proxy for lost future benefits from the orchestra programs those funds would have supported. The benefits would include savings of future maintenance costs realized by not allowing the hall to deteriorate further, as well as savings of potential losses in revenue that might result if the hall were to reach such a state of disrepair as to require cancellation of events or cause aggravation and discomfort for patrons or performers during events. (Debussy's "Clouds" takes on a whole new meaning if the concert hall's roof leaks!)

A similar analysis applies even if other funds (say, a bank loan) are raised for the repairs and the endowment is left intact. First, one must compare the costs of a loan with the opportunity cost of using endowment funds. Next, one should consider whether a bank loan could be put to better use (e.g., staging more performances, recruiting better musicians) and whether other banks will make loans available for these purposes. In any case, the orchestra manager would do well to employ the concepts outlined in Chapter 6, including opportunity costs and the comparison of those costs over time, in considering his or her decision.

A local united fund wishes to attract a well-known youth agency into its system. What terms should it offer for sharing the proceeds of community fund raising with this new member?

This management challenge may appear to be simpler than it really is, since any move to offer special terms to a new member runs the risk that existing members will ask to renegotiate their terms. Analyzing such a dynamic would take us into the more advanced realm of game theory. However, the principles of basic economic analysis that we have laid out can help the united fund manager approach this issue with new insight. Here, the operative principles are again analysis at the margin and opportunity cost.

Suppose the united fund leadership were to look at this issue simply from the narrow point of view of existing members. In this context, the question would be, How much more in the way of charitable revenues will the united fund attract as a result of having this new member in its constellation? And how much will it cost existing members to share the proceeds with one more recipient organization? If the incremental net revenue (incremental revenue less incremental cost) from adding a new member exceeds the existing average net revenue per member, then it is worthwhile for the united fund to invite the new agency in. (Recall the observation in Chapter 4 that when the marginal value of the next unit exceeds the average value, it brings the average value up. Incremental value—the change in value when a whole organization joins, as opposed to a one-unit increase in some activity—works the same way as marginals: average net revenue increases whenever incremental net revenue is above the average.) This conclusion is predicated on the assumption that the new member receives shares on the same basis as existing members. Alternatively, the new member can be invited in on the condition that it accept a share smaller than an amount that would lower the net receipts of existing members.

A similar analysis could be applied by the manager of the applicant agency. Presumably, if the agency joined the united fund it would be restricted from raising its own funds independently, so as not to compete with the united fund-raising efforts. If the share of united funding exceeded the loss (opportunity cost) associated with forgone independent fund-raising efforts, then it would be worthwhile for the organization to join the fund.

An environmental advocacy group is mounting a campaign to clean up hazardous waste in its community. Should it hire a paid public relations staff or continue to rely exclusively on volunteer efforts?

For this decision, the leaders of the group would be well advised to employ the ideas of opportunity cost and transaction costs, as discussed in Chapters 6 and 9. If the organization hires a paid staff member, it must bear the straightforward costs of that individual's salary and benefits as well as of the supplies and services needed to support his or her work. If volunteers are utilized, the organization must consider the opportunity cost of the volunteer time (in terms of its value in the next best uses), the cost of supplies, and the costs of recruiting, organizing, and supervising volunteers. These transaction costs are likely to be substantial because of the number of individuals needing supervision and the more informal, part-time nature of voluntary employment. Employing a paid staff member would also entail supervisory costs, but these would likely be substantially lower than those associated with managing volunteers.

Note that in calculating the opportunity cost of volunteer time, the manager may wish to include the value of the volunteer's forgone leisure or work and will certainly want to include the opportunity cost to the organization. If volunteers are scarce, a volunteer used in the advocacy campaign is a volunteer who cannot be used elsewhere in the organization. If volunteers can be recruited to fill these other roles, the opportunity cost to the organization of employing an existing volunteer in advocacy is exactly equal to the cost of recruiting someone to fill the other roles. If no additional volunteers can be recruited at a reasonable cost, however, the opportunity cost of using volunteeers in advocacy equals the net value the organization would assign to the volunteer's output if he or she were employed in the highest alternative use within the organization.

The leaders of the environmental group will, naturally, also want to consider possible differences in effectiveness between a paid professional's work and a volunteer's work. If the additional cost of employing a paid professional (above the cost of using volunteers) proves to be smaller than the marginal increase in benefit achieved by this change, then the employment of the paid staff member is justified.

A community theater located in a working-class neighborhood must revise its ticket prices in order to account for increased expenses. How should it design its price schedule in order to stay fiscally healthy while accommodating community members who cannot pay much to attend performances?

Clearly, resolution of this issue would benefit from consideration of the concepts discussed in Chapters 4, 7, and 8. If the theater operates in an environment that is perfectly competitive, there is not much it can do; it must offer its services at the prevailing market price and hope it can earn enough to break even. If it cannot, it must either find ways to reduce its costs without sacrificing quality or go out of business. However, even if the theater can compete at the market price, that price may exclude members of the community who cannot afford to pay it. The theater may try to address this issue by raising charitable funds that it can use to subsidize tickets for lower-income patrons.

More than likely, the theater has some monopoly power within its immediate vicinity. If it does not, it may try to create such power by adjusting its product to create a unique niche, allowing it to move from an environment of perfect competition to one of monopolistic competition. Given some monopoly power (i.e., a downward-sloping demand curve), the theater can consider one of the price-discrimination strategies discussed in Chapter 8 in order to enhance its capacity to help its lower-income consumers. In particular, patrons who can well afford to attend performances could be charged a higher price while those who cannot could be charged a lower price. The theater would, in effect, be tracing the downward-sloping demand curve so as to capture the consumers' surplus. Such a strategy might be implemented by tying ticket prices to proxies such as age that correlate with levels of discretionary income. Or a strategy of voluntary price discrimination might be employed by asking patrons to contribute voluntarily, as donors or members, over and above their subscriptions. The nondistribution constraint helps make this strategy feasible by providing some assurance to wealthier customers that their payments will be used to subsidize ticket prices for lower-income customers rather than to enrich those who run the theater.

A nonprofit mental health agency is considering raising money by offering its services, at a profit, to local businesses as part of their employee-benefit plans. However, it could lose money if donors react adversely or not enough businesses sign up. Should the agency go ahead with this initiative?

In this case, the managers of the mental health agency must think about two sets of issues. First, what is the market for the agency's services in the business sector? Second, what will happen to its contributions base if it engages in extensive profit-making activity?

The first issue involves a relatively straightforward business decision. It is likely in this case that the agency would be entering a competitive marketplace where the price of its services is dictated by market conditions. If the market is perfectly competitive, the agency will be able to sell as much as it wants at that price. The profit-maximizing level of production equates the market price with marginal cost, provided that price exceeds average variable cost. If the organization is already producing these services in its existing (social service) markets, this analysis can be done incrementally. Services could be expanded slowly into the new market and could continue to expand as long as price exceeded the marginal cost. At the same time, the organization should pay special attention to donations. If crowding out occurs, the decision rules discussed in Chapter 8 should be employed to determine an efficient level of output or whether to shut down.

If the organization has monopoly power, then the previous analysis still applies, although the organization should estimate what the demand curve looks like before entering the market. The steeper the slope (i.e., the less elastic demand is), the more likely the organization is to make substantial profits. Again, the organization could proceed incrementally, comparing marginal revenue with marginal cost at each step.

A nonprofit research institute is considering a performance compensation system whereby its staff members would receive salary bonuses tied to the dollar value of the research contracts they bring in. Should the institute go ahead with this proposal?

This proposal addresses the most basic concept of economic analysis—the incentives under which key economic actors operate. A performance contract system presumably would spur staff members to greater levels of productivity in exchange for greater monetary rewards. This is not a given, however. It is possible that self-motivated staff researchers would resist the new system because they preferred to have the freedom to choose interesting projects rather than those that were the most remunerative. It is also possible that the system would induce the most self-motivated staff members to leave and more materialistic but less productive staff members to stay. Thus, the managers of this organization will want to weigh carefully the potential consequences of the proposed incentives (see Nelsen, 1991, and Steinberg, 1990) before they implement the new system.

The new system may also entail additional transaction costs in connection with monitoring performance and administering monetary rewards. Assuming that the increased transaction costs are outweighed by positive productivity gains, the proposal may result in lowering overall costs associated with a given level of output (research contracts) and hence an outward movement (to the right) in the organization's supply curve.

It is also possible that the new system will affect other incentives—for example, the willingness of donors to provide charitable contributions (see Steinberg, 1990). Donors may feel that the performance contract system overemphasizes material rewards, making the organization too much like a profit-making business despite its laudable mission. Thus, any productivity

gains the new system delivers could end up crowding out charitable donations. If that happens, the change will also affect the full marginal revenue
function, moving it downward so that less net revenue is received per dollar
of research contracts received. As a result of the potential changes on both
the supply and demand sides, the organization is likely to reach a new
equilibrium level of output (research contracts) and profits.

Many of the changes that could occur as a result of the new compensation system may be difficult to measure or predict. However, the concepts
of economic incentives, transaction costs, crowding out, and variable demand and supply conditions can help structure the problem in a way that
assists the managers of the organization to think through the probable
implications of the proposed changes.

SUMMARY

These brief analyses of our thirteen vignettes are meant to suggest how
economic analysis can help the nonprofit manager to structure his or her
thinking about a wide variety of management problems and issues. Any one
of these analyses could benefit from a much more detailed and rigorous
study. But the main point is that even a rudimentary application of the basic
concepts of economic analysis can yield substantial insights into the nature
of critical nonprofit management issues and establish the basis for more
informed information gathering and effective decision making. We hope
these insights will aid managers in their own work and in their ability to
assess consultants' work.

Similar comments apply at the policy level. As we have hinted throughout, a variety of issues affecting nonprofit organizations can be understood
in economic terms and usefully analyzed using the concepts explained in this
book. Such issues as taxation of unrelated business income, changes in
deductibility for charitable contributions, changes in minimum-wage laws,
mandates for employee-benefit packages, modifications of antitrust law,
nonprofit exemptions from property and sales taxes, changes in subsidies for
public services delivered by nonprofit organizations, and policies affecting
the terms on which nonprofit organizations contract with government to
deliver services are all subject to evaluation and clarification using the basic
tools of economic analysis. We hope that the reader will now begin to think
about such issues in economic terms so as to engage in and influence public
debate more effectively.

Finally, the observant reader will have noticed allusions throughout the
book to a number of theoretical tools that would allow analysis in greater
depth of some of the issues discussed. Among these tools are *game theory* (used

to analyze oligopolistic markets and united funding arrangements), *decision theory* (used to analyze decision making under uncertainty), and *portfolio theory* (used to analyze investments). Another such tool is *econometrics*, the science of estimating economic functions, such as supply and demand, from observed data. While these subjects tend to be studied at very high levels of abstraction, we do not mean to imply that they are inaccessible to the lay reader. Like the basic concepts of economic analysis presented in this book, the core ideas of these related fields of study can be comprehended by, and be useful to, the practicing manager and policy maker. We hope to incorporate chapters on these topics in future editions of this book. In the meantime, the reader is invited to digest what we have been able to offer in this edition and to provide the authors with any suggestions that will aid the digestion of future readers. That will be our just dessert!

REFERENCES

Nelsen, William C. "Incentive-Based Management for Nonprofit Organizations." *Nonprofit Management and Leadership*, 2:1, Fall 1991, pp. 59-69.

Salamon, Lester M. "Foundations as Investment Managers; Part I: The Process." *Nonprofit Management and Leadership*, 3:2, Winter 1992, pp. 117-137.

Salamon, Lester M. "Foundations as Investment Managers; Part II: The Performance." *Nonprofit Management and Leadership*, 3:3, Spring 1993, pp. 239-253.

Steinberg, Richard. "Profits and Incentive Compensation in Nonprofit Firms." *Nonprofit Management and Leadership*, 1:2, Winter 1990, pp. 137–151.

INDEX